Praise for *In the Shadow of Eagles:*

"In the old movie serials, the hero invariably cheated what looked like certain death only to survive, incredibly, to star in the next palpitating episode. The real-life saga of pioneer Alaska bush pilot Rudy Billberg puts to shame such Hollywood hokum. . . . This book sparkles with reality because these adventures really happened."

—*General Aviation News & Flyer*

"A simply written autobiography full of excitement and descriptions of daring. . . . [Billberg] met local heroes, lived among natives 150 miles from the North Pole, learned to navigate the turbulence of mountain ranges the hard way, and flew by sight—no instruments, no radio— following braided rivers and descriptions of landmarks he had never seen. His loving accounts of antediluvian planes and their characteristics will intrigue the general reader and enthrall aviation buffs."

—*Booklist*

"[Billberg's] account is full of difficult situations, anxious moments, and close calls. . . . Appealing for aviation buffs as well as for dreamers."

—*Library Journal*

"Billberg's skill at managing midair crises makes for dramatic reading. . . . For the reader, it is a pleasure flight through a bygone era."

—*Publisher's Weekly*

"In this likeable autobiography, Billberg teamed with Homer writer Jim Rearden to tell about the adventures that made him love flying. . . . *In the Shadow of Eagles* is a smooth flight for the reader. Billberg is one of those lucky people who loved his job passionately. This enthusiasm keeps his story soaring, and makes this a delightful book."

—*Homer News*

"One of those daring young men in their flying machines who pioneered [aviation] was Rudy Billberg. . . . This book isn't just a book about Billberg's life. It's a book about an exciting occupation that was essential to the growth of 'the great land.' And it is about the fliers who conquered Alaska in airplanes ranging from open-cockpit Swallow biplanes to military transport command C-47s."

—*Bellingham (WA) Herald*

IN THE SHADOW OF EAGLES

From Barnstormer to Alaska Bush Pilot,

A Flyer's Story

RUDY BILLBERG
AS TOLD TO
JIM REARDEN

C A R I B O U   C L A S S I C S

ALASKA NORTHWEST BOOKS™
Anchorage • Seattle • Portland

First edition 1993
Second edition 1998

Library of Congress Cataloging-in-Publication Data
Billberg, Rudy, 1916-
    In the shadow of eagles : from barnstormer to Alaska bush pilot : a flyer's story / Rudy Billberg as told to Jim Rearden.
      p.   cm.
    Includes index.
    ISBN 0-88240-507-1
    1. Billberg, Rudy, 1916-   . 2. Air pilots—United States—Biography. 3. Bush pilots—Alaska—Biography. 4. Aeronautics—Alaska—History. I. Rearden, Jim. II. Title.
TL540.B545A3   1992
629.13'092—dc20
[B]   91-39311
                                       CIP

Edited by Ellen Harkins Wheat
Cover painting by Fred W. Thomas
Cover design by Constance Bollen
Interior design by Alice C. Merrill
Maps by David Berger

Photo credits: All photos courtesy of Rudy Billberg unless otherwise noted. Three chapters in this book were previously published in *Alaska* magazine and were edited for inclusion here: (22) Rescue at Cape Romanzof, (23) Agates of the Nowitna, and the otter drama in (24) Wildlife Dramas.

Cover painting: The Hornet Pilgrim piloted by Rudy Billberg flies through the remote, jagged wilderness of Alaska's Wrangell Mountains. In a land where trails end and humans seldom go, the 575-horsepower engine shatters a million years of silence. Watercolor on paper, 1991.

Alaska Northwest Books™
An imprint of Graphic Arts Center Publishing Company
P.O. Box 10306, Portland, OR 97296-0306
800-452-3032

Printed on recycled paper in the United States of America

To my wife, Bessie, and our children, Cathy and Roy

—Rudy Billberg

Should all things perish,
fleeting as a shooting star,
Oh God, let not the ties break
that bind me to the North.

—*Evening prayer*

✢ Contents ✢

✝ Foreword ✝

Few things get my blood racing like being near a piston-driven airplane, its throbbing engine at idle, waiting to take off for the wild blue yonder. I still remember my dad escorting me at age four to see, hear, and smell the Bergholt monoplane built by Erling Mickalson, assisted by the then-teenage Rudy Billberg and others. In the early 1930s my dad was a mechanic at Brude Motors, the Ford agency at Roseau, Minnesota, where the Bergholt stood, wings off, testing its new modified Model A Ford engine.

In the Shadow of Eagles is essential reading for all interested in old airplanes and their evolution. It's a fascinating series of connected stories by one of the real eagles of the Northland, Rudy Billberg. His experiences are more intriguing than fiction. They will enlighten and entertain those fascinated with the history of aviation in the uncharted North.

Historians and scholars will find the research and anecdotes here useful in following the role of the airplane on our frontiers during the 1920s and '30s, as was the horse during the previous 200 years in our history.

This book is fun reading, and Rudy Billberg, with his modest style, has done us all a great service.

—Bob Bergland

Former senator Bob Bergland, born and raised in Rudy Billberg's hometown of Roseau, Minnesota, represented Minnesota's 7th Congressional District in the U.S. Congress from 1971 to 1977 and served as President Jimmy Carter's secretary of agriculture. Currently he is executive vice president and general manager of the National Rural Electric Cooperative Association in Washington, D.C.

✝ Preface ✝

My nearly 40 years of friendship and association with Jim Rearden and his family have been rich and rewarding. Jim and I agreed long ago that the recording and preservation of aviation's progress during our lifetime could be both important and fascinating. Our many discussions led to the writing of this book.

I pored through my files, and I reviewed hundreds of pages of my diaries. I reminisced by the hour as Jim asked questions and recorded. Jim's wife Audrey transcribed the tapes, and from the typed transcripts of those sessions, we selected and condensed the material. We went through aviation volumes from both of our libraries, to ensure that the book would be as historically accurate as we could make it.

Beyond intending the book to be a contribution to aircraft history, we have tried to share the thrills and adventure of 46 years of flying in Alaska and Minnesota. Perhaps the stories will inspire both young and old to venture to Alaska, where flying continues to provide the major access to distant villages and to the back-of-beyond wilderness that makes up most of our forty-ninth state.

Because one man could never experience it all, I have injected stories of other Alaska pilots I knew. There was not room in this book to mention all of the airmen with whom I flew and all of the memorable incidents we shared. Each and every one of these pilots has led a life that is fully as interesting and exciting as mine. Pilots I was unable to name but with whom I enjoyed a close association during my flying years include:

With Northern Consolidated Airlines: Ray Anderson, Dick Ardaiz, Swede Blanchard, Harold Bogenrife, Ray Christiansen,

Pat Crozier, Bob Desmarais, Jimmy Hoffman, Don Johnson, John Lynn, Ray Petersen, Edward J. Steger, R. J. Stevenson, Rheinhold Thiele, Orville Tosch, Oscar Underhill, Joe Vanderpoole, Oscar Winchell.

With Munz Northern Airline, Nome: Vern Bookwalter, Lloyd Hardy, Sig Krogstad (Alaska Airlines, Unalakleet), Mike Tavis.

With the Bureau of Land Management, Alaska: Paul Hanson, Bob Johnson, Bob Schlaeffle, Ed Thorsrud.

While flying out of Fairbanks: Dick McIntyre.

With Cook Inlet Aviation, Homer: Bob Gruber, Jim Reinhart, Clint Riis.

—Rudy Billberg
Roseau, Minnesota
March 1991

I first met Rudy Billberg in 1951 when he signed up for a wildlife class I taught at the University of Alaska, Fairbanks. He was quiet but friendly. We became friends. His hair was flaxen then, it is silver now. His eyes are the bluest of blue.

It was months before I learned he was a commercial pilot, and it was years before he told me he had once been a barn-stormer. Typical. Rudy is modest. He also has a wonderful sense of humor, and he often laughs at himself.

I know many pilots he flew with: Rheinold Thiele, Ray Christiansen, Dick McIntyre, Bob Gruber, Jim Reinhart, others. They speak of Rudy as a perfectionist in the air. Bush residents he served remember him with fondness.

During the 20 years I was an editor for *Alaska* magazine, I urged Rudy to write of his flying experiences. Instead, he chose to write about wildlife and agates. He was too modest to write of flying. That is, until he learned that a nurse, Betty Shamblin, who had flown with him on a medivac, was seriously ill. Then he penned "Rescue at Cape Romanzof" (Chapter 22). He wanted Betty to receive public credit for volunteering for the hazardous flight.

He finally agreed to write about his life as a pilot if I would work with him. To capture Rudy's fascinating story with authenticity, I have attempted to retain his modesty and straightforward style by preserving his memories in his own words.

Rudy denies being an aviation pioneer. "Got into barnstorming at the very end. Came to Alaska after the real pioneering was done," he says. This led to the title *In the Shadow of Eagles*, which Rudy feels accurately reflects the timing of his flying career: he came along in the wake of the great early flyers—the eagles. His admiration is genuine for those he feels were the true aviation pioneers in Alaska and for the old-time barnstormers he learned from. This led to our including chapters about some of Alaska's early pilots he has known.

Rudy Billberg flew during some of the most interesting years in aviation. He took to the air only three decades after the Wright brothers' first powered flight and he flew into the age of jets. He saw the development of instrument flying and radio navigation. He witnessed the river-bar and baseball-field runways of early Alaska changing into the modern paved strips of today. Along the way, Rudy Billberg enjoyed life.

In the Shadow of Eagles is an attempt to describe personal highlights of over half a century of flying, as seen through the perceptive, honest eyes of Rudy Billberg.

—*Jim Rearden*
Sprucewood
Homer, Alaska
March 1991

✢ Acknowledgments ✢

Thanks to Annette Hermansen of Roseau, Minnesota, who gave much advice and help on the early manuscript for this book. Thanks, too, to Ellen H. Wheat, senior editor, Alaska Northwest Books, who understands the romance of flying. Her editorial advice was invaluable.

I also want to express my appreciation to all the great eagles who taught me enough to stay alive as a pilot.

—*R.B.*

✢ Introduction ✢

No single technological development has had a greater impact on human lives than aviation. In the span of a single lifetime, aviation has evolved from flights in gasoline-powered box kites to spacecraft that televise images of distant planets back to earth. Few would dispute that America has led the world in the development of aviation.

While the exploits of American aviators have been heralded throughout this century, the role of Alaskan pioneer flyers has largely been relegated to folklore and myth. Until very recently Alaska was viewed as a foreign land by most Americans. Consequently, Alaskan aviation usually has been considered a remote regional subject. But the Alaskan aviation saga is a uniquely American story.

Alaska is the last great American wilderness frontier, the end of the line for the North American migration westward that had its origins in the 1500s. As hardy souls pushed north and west into Alaska in search of gold, furs, and adventure, time caught them on the threshhold of the twentieth century with all its gadgets and mechanical innovations. Fortuitously, these technological developments included the airplane, for Alaska, one-fifth the size of mainland United States, was virtually impenetrable, with gigantic mountains, sprawling forests, huge swamps, and endless regions of tundra.

Unmapped and storm-swept, Alaska often proved fatal to early European explorers because of the harsh climate and difficulty in finding food. Travel and settlement was restricted largely to coastal and river waterways. Going any distance from these aquatic thoroughfares was slow and dangerous. The airplane was

Alaska's only hope of traversing "The Great Land" as the Natives called it. The Territory's first pilots—Roy Jones, C. F. LaJotte, A. A. Bennett, the Wien brothers, Joe Crosson, Russell Merrill, Carl Ben Eielson, and a legion of others—made their way to Alaska, climbed into open cockpit biplanes, and flew over the treacherous land. Their amazing feats were accomplished with few aircraft instruments, roughly drawn maps, little communication, no reliable weather forecasts, and few real landing strips.

Many early Alaskan pilots lost their lives. But through courage, resourcefulness, and stamina, they broke trail for an aviation infrastructure that would connect every remote area of the Territory. Living and working in Alaska became a reality for many, as bush pilots were able to reach every corner of the region. Food, supplies, medical care, and transportation could readily be had by any person in the Territory. Air travel facilitated an economic base for Alaska in mining, furs, fishing, and general commerce.

The air pioneers blazed the way in the 1920s, and Alaskan aviators of the 1930s made aviation a common factor in Alaskan lives. Fleets of light aircraft in scores of air service companies jostled for business throughout the Territory. These new flying enterprises still had to contend with primitive conditions, however. Runways were often crude or nonexistent. Waterways, liquid and frozen, served as airports for most towns and villages. Aeronautical radio communication wasn't generally available until late in the 1930s. Great areas of Alaska were still labeled "unsurveyed" on maps. Flying was still largely a seat-of-the-pants skill.

With the advent of World War II, the last great pioneering feats of Alaskan aviation history began to unfold. Government-developed airfields and communication facilities brought a new era of Alaskan aviation. Larger aircraft began to provide service between Alaska (still a Territory) and the States. Alaska became an international air crossroads, with airplanes flying polar routes to Europe via Alaska as well as the Great Circle Route across Alaska to Asia.

Today, in the pressurized comfort of modern airlines, we can travel six miles above the still-rugged climate and land of

Alaska. How many passengers of jet liners over Alaska reflect on the adventures and sacrifices of the early flyers who paved the way far below, fighting weather and flying near the treetops? The conveniences we now know were hard won, and these pilots deserve tribute.

We are fortunate to have a few of these noble pioneers still with us. Author Rudy Billberg can be counted as one of this cadre. His book, *In the Shadow of Eagles,* adds to the record of the great twentieth century aviation pioneers. Man has known heavier-than-air powered flight for about 90 years. Billberg piloted airplanes for fully half of those years. Rudy Billberg's exciting account of his barnstorming years and of his four decades as a bush pilot in the Alaskan skies will be read with pleasure by all who love aviation and adventure. And may it serve as inspiration for the pioneers of the future.

—*Ted M. Spencer*
Director
Alaska Aviation Heritage Museum
Anchorage

The Minnesota Years

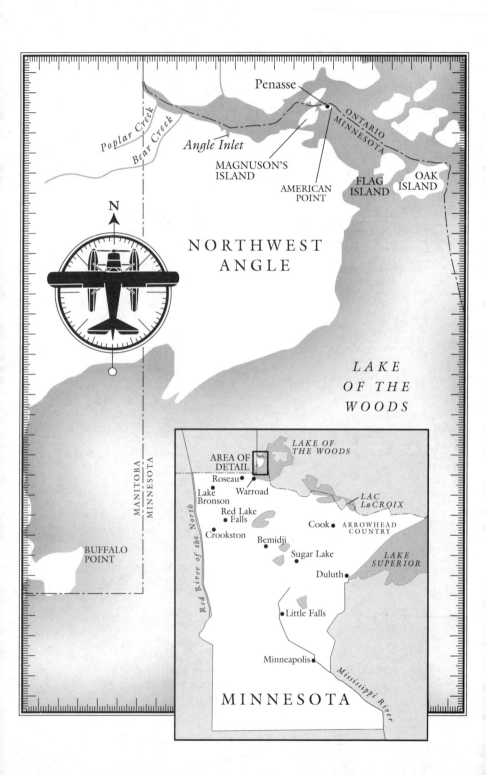

First Flight

IT WAS AN open cockpit Travel Air biplane, powered by a Curtiss OX-5 engine. I wanted to fly in that airplane more than anything I had ever wanted, but most of my family regarded flying as extremely hazardous. My dad understood, bless him, and gave me the $2.50 for the flight. I still had a hard time getting around my mother and my older sister, Inga. But I persisted as only a determined 11-year-old can.

It was July 1927, and my family was attending the county fair at Roseau, Minnesota, where the Travel Air pilot was selling rides. It was my first close encounter with an airplane. I remember the smoothness of the fabric and the penetrating smell of nitrate dope, leather padding, and gasoline. The pilot put me in the front seat and strapped me in with the wide, web safety belt. The heady roar of that OX-5 engine—a sound I was later to know very well—and the sight of the whirling propeller made my heart pound with excitement. I was surprised to feel myself pressed back against the seat as the pilot opened the throttle. I hadn't dreamed that an airplane could have such acceleration.

The "airport" was a farmer's hayfield at the edge of Roseau. The crop had been cut, and the ground was level and firm. As the airplane climbed into the cloudless sky, the country unfolded beneath me. It looked like a checkerboard, just like photos taken from Lindbergh's airplane which I had seen in newspapers and magazines. The land around Roseau is absolutely flat, and until then the highest I had ever been was on a barn roof. To be able to see for miles in all directions from high in the sky was almost more than I could comprehend. I was thrilled with the bird's view. Fencerows and forested areas appeared before my astonished eyes. I spotted the Roseau River, winding away in the distance.

The pilot circled and I peered down at cars on the roads, at the town, at houses, at ant-sized people, and at horses and cattle—all like miniatures. The pilot gave me a long ride because it was his first flight of the day; he wanted to attract passengers by flying around the countryside.

It was over too soon. My family—my mother, father, sisters, Inga and Helen, and brother, John—asked what the flight was like. I was almost tongue-tied. It was such an overwhelming experience that I couldn't describe my feelings.

The $2.50 my father spent—more than a day's wages at the time—was perhaps the best investment he ever made on my behalf. From the moment of that flight I knew that I was going to become a pilot. I didn't think then of making a living as a pilot: I simply wanted to fly. Amelia Earhart once wrote that every pilot at first flies for aesthetic reasons: to climb into the sky and soar like a bird has always been a dream of man. Perhaps that was the dream that pushed me toward flight.

I was born in Roseau in 1916. When I was five, my father, Eddy Billberg, moved us to a farm three-quarters of a mile west of town. My father was elected to the office of county superintendent of schools, a position he held for 20 years. Before that he had been a businessman and a schoolteacher.

The first airplane I remember, in about 1920, flew across the sky with a loud noise. Everyone stopped what they were doing to watch until it was out of sight.

The next airplane of memory I was able to identify as a Standard biplane powered by a Hispano-Suiza engine. I was old enough then to have started to learn something of airplanes. It was flown by a barnstormer selling rides near Roseau. I especially remember the parachute jumper, who called himself Ace Waldron. He jumped from the wing of the Standard wearing three chutes. When the first opened and he was comfortably drifting down, he released himself from the harness to again drop like a rock. He then pulled the rip cord on the second chute. When it opened, he rode it to perhaps a thousand feet, where he cut himself loose and fell again. Near the ground, he pulled the rip cord of the third chute and floated to a safe landing. Late in my flying career I made my only parachute jump, and I realized then the chance that Ace Waldron took.

I was fascinated by both Ace Waldron and the barnstormer. I watched that airplane fly as long as I could, but I didn't get close to it. I was impressed by the water-cooled engine of nearly 200 horsepower. I asked older, knowledgeable friends how an engine small enough to fit on an airplane could have so much power. "It can't be that powerful," one answered. "I bet that two horses could keep that airplane from moving." Misconceptions about airplanes, engines, and horsepower were then common.

As I grew up, aviation was developing too. Transoceanic flights were being attempted. The first one I was aware of was Charles Lindbergh's. My dad was particularly interested because the Lindberghs were from Little Falls, Minnesota. The elder Lindbergh had been a congressman. Dad was also proud that Lindbergh was Swedish, like himself.

In those exciting hours in May 1927 when Charles Lindbergh flew his Ryan monoplane from New York to Paris, we were anxious to know how he was doing. Like most people in

Roseau then, we had no radio. A friend who had one promised to telephone us as reports on Lindbergh's flight were broadcast.

Hours went by and we heard nothing. When the hands of the clock reached the time he should have been approaching Europe, if indeed he had gotten that far, our family sat around the dining room table, reading, playing games, and sewing while we waited for a call. Eyes often strayed to the wooden hand-cranked telephone on the wall. Finally, it let forth with two long rings and Dad picked up the receiver. We could tell from his excitement that Lindbergh had made it.

We were more excited at Lindbergh's success, I think, than we were a scant 42 years later when our astronauts walked on the moon. Lindbergh received a quarter of a million cablegrams and three million letters after his New York–to–Paris flight, an indication of the emotions his achievement stirred.

Today I understand that the methodical and careful Lindbergh chose to use a single-engine airplane for his flight with the great Wright Whirlwind J-5-9 engine because it was probably the most reliable airplane engine in the world at that time. Lindbergh's Whirlwind delivered about 220 horsepower. Because it was air-cooled, it was about 25 percent lighter than the more popular liquid-cooled engines of comparable power. The Whirlwind was also more fuel-efficient. Its design dissipated heat so effectively that the engine could burn a lean mixture of gasoline and air without overheating. Earlier air-cooled engines guzzled a rich but cooling air-fuel mixture, requiring more fuel.

Lindbergh's flight lit a fire that heated all aviation. Quite simply, that renowned aerial feat ushered in the golden age of aviation. Every Roseau schoolboy wanted to become a pilot. My ride in the Travel Air biplane two months after Lindbergh's flight cinched it for me.

In late 1927, there was an explosion of aviation activity. Many pilots sought headlines as they tried for endurance and speed records. There was a frenzy of polar flights, transoceanic flights, around-the-world flights. Special distance races between various points in the United States, Europe, and elsewhere were sponsored by major business firms anxious for publicity.

Americans eagerly read about airplanes and their flights, and many pilots of the day became famous. The names Bernt Balchen, Jimmy Doolittle, Noel Wien, Carl Ben Eielson, Wiley Post, and many others were constantly in print. Barnstorming became more and more popular, and scores of pilots acquired airplanes and flew around the country hauling passengers for hire at country fairs, political picnics, horse races—any public gathering. Many Americans, like me, made their first flight with one of these barnstormers.

After my ride in the sky I read everything I could about airplanes in books and in magazines like *Popular Aviation* and *Aero Digest*. The advertisements, "Let airmail pilots teach you to fly," told of flight schools in the large cities to the south. I wanted desperately to go to one of those schools.

Since I was too young to let an airmail pilot teach me to fly, I did a lot of dreaming. Erling Mickalson, an older friend, sent five dollars to a magazine for plans to build a Bergholt Sport Monoplane, a high-wing, parasol-type, open-cockpit plane that carried only the pilot. I helped build that airplane, which was one of the first built in the Roseau region. I held parts while Erling put them in place. I cleaned the floor and ran errands. From that experience I learned how airplanes worked, why they flew. To me, the homebuilt Bergholt Sport Monoplane was a masterpiece. Nothing in my young life had loomed so large.

The Bergholt was designed to be powered with a relatively light-weight, four-cylinder Model A Ford car engine. Arnold Habstritt, a part owner of the plane, was the son of the local Whippet auto dealer. Erling and Arnold assumed that a Whippet engine would do as well as a Model A engine. For them, the Whippet engine was also cheaper.

The airplane refused to fly with the Whippet engine. Next, they installed a six-cylinder Chevrolet engine. The airplane again refused to fly. Finally, they installed a Model A engine, and the airplane managed to get off the ground. But it didn't fly very well. At the time I had no idea why.

I watched Erling take off one Sunday. A small crowd had gathered. Women gasped as the airplane lifted off. As it did, the left main landing wheel fell off and rolled across country. Several of us waved our shirts to catch Erling's attention as he circled. He saw our signals and decided to land to see what the problem was.

He found out when he touched down. The wheelless axle dug into the ground, and the airplane flipped onto its back. Erling was unhurt, but the airplane had to be rebuilt. Again I helped, eager to participate.

I wasn't there when he flew again, but I heard about it. Erling flew around and around. He climbed the Bergholt up to about 300 feet, the highest altitude it ever attained. Then the engine conked out and the Bergholt Sport Monoplane ended in a peat swamp. It never flew again.

About then I read "Simple Aerodynamics" by Cy Caldwell, an article in *Aero Digest*. I almost memorized it. Even today, more than half a century later, I recall details from that article. I could parrot the words, but I didn't understand "simple aerodynamics." Later, when I started flying, I realized that the Bergholt Sport flew close to a stall all the time. Erling was lucky that the plane didn't spin out. In flying, we used to refer to the stall point as "the burble point of the wing." We kiddingly said that the Bergholt Sport "flew on the third burble point."

For the remainder of the 1920s I was increasingly taken with aviation. The exploits of certain pilots particularly fascinated me. I read every news account when, in 1928, Carl Ben Eielson and Hubert Wilkins made their famed 2,200-mile flight in a Lockheed Vega across the Arctic from Barrow, Alaska, to the island of Spitsbergen. Eielson was from nearby North Dakota, and everyone in our part of the country was proud of his achievements.

Then, in March 1929, headlines splashed details of the plight of the *Elisef*, a trading vessel caught in the ice off North

Cape, Siberia. A cargo of furs worth $600,000 was aboard. Noel Wien, an Alaskan pilot who hailed from Cook, Minnesota, was to fly the 600 miles from Nome to the vessel to retrieve the valuable furs.

Wien's plans fired my imagination. Like most Minnesota farm kids, I trapped mink, muskrat, red fox, and other furbearers each winter. The thought of $600,000 worth of furs was staggering. I followed the news day by day, hour by hour, as Wien waited for good weather. His flight to the *Elisef* in a Wasp-powered Hamilton Metalplane was the first commercial flight from North America to Asia. (In the next decade the Pratt & Whitney Wasp engine and the similar Wright Cyclone deposed the Whirlwind as the finest of contemporary aircraft engines.) After one flight, in which he flew back about a quarter of the furs, the Russian government canceled permission for Wien to fly to the ice-locked ship.

That fall Noel Wien and his wife, Ada, flying in a new airplane, visited Minnesota. I read every news item about how the Wiens were fêted wherever they went. Wien became one of my heroes.

Incredibly, in October of 1929, the *Nanuk*, sister ship to *Elisef*, also became ice-bound off Siberia's North Cape. She carried $1 million worth of furs. With the same Hamilton Metalplane that Wien had flown to the *Elisef*, Ben Eielson flew from Teller, Alaska, to retrieve the furs from the *Nanuk*. He made one successful round trip to the *Nanuk*. On his second attempt, Eielson and his mechanic, Earl Borland, disappeared.

Vivid accounts of the search for his plane made headlines for weeks. I read every word. Alaskan pilots Joe Crosson and Harold Gillam, who eventually found the Eielson plane, became two more of my heroes. At the time, I couldn't have dreamed that one day I would know Joe Crosson, and that I would actually work for both Noel Wien and Harold Gillam. After that I had a special interest in arctic flying.

I completed high school at the age of 17 with an

undistinguished scholastic record, perhaps because I spent much of my time staring out the window dreaming. Being men of the world (high-school graduates), my friend, Robert Story, and I decided to see that world. We had no money, so we decided to ride freight trains and bum our way. We overcame family obstacles, and with five dollars stuffed in each of our belt bands, we boarded a noisy freight train in Roseau and left town sitting atop a boxcar.

In that Great Depression year of 1933, freight trains carried many penniless traveling men and a few women, trying to reach distant relatives or hoping to find a job. Some had small children with them. Others, professional hobos, made bumming a way of life. These men on the move were well organized. In every railroad town there was a hobo jungle or camp where they gathered, slept, and ate.

As we made our way west, the professionals watched us to see if we had any money. I think they'd have tossed us off a moving freight train for fifty cents.

When Robert and I reached Glendive, Montana, each person staying in the local jungle was sent to town to beg for the makings for a stew. One man was to ask for meat scraps, another for vegetables. We were to ask at a bakery for day-old toppings. We didn't know what toppings were, but one of the old hands explained that they were day-old pastry.

We were ashamed to beg. Instead, I asked the baker if we could work to earn some day-old toppings. He put us to scrubbing floors and walls. That darned place must have covered half a block. We scrubbed and scrubbed. Our task took so long that we saw a couple of bums from our jungle looking in the window to see what was delaying us. We finally returned to the hobo jungle carrying two big sacks full of toppings. We arrived about the time everybody was ready for dessert.

Robert and I were away from home for two weeks. Our hobo trip was a great adventure for two innocent farm kids.

In Roseau, I found a job in Sjoberg's hardware store. I

was lucky, for jobs were hard to get that year, especially for an inexperienced kid. Mr. Sjoberg had once been a partner of my father. I lived at home and walked the three-fourths of a mile back and forth to work. I also worked on the family farm.

It was July 29, 1934, according to an old pilot's log which I still have, when, coming home from work I saw an airplane perched in a field next to the road. I walked rather apprehensively toward it. Leaning against the fuselage was the pilot, a man of medium build. He studied me as I approached, and I studied him as well. He wore a felt hat with the brim turned down. His eyes were eagle sharp. He seemed to look right through me. His lips were pursed, his teeth clamped together—an expression I was to see often. His shirt and trousers were immaculate and neatly pressed. He struck me as a man who could make quick decisions with little chance of error.

"Is that an OX-5 Robin?" I asked, pretty sure of the answer. "Yep. Sure is," he responded.

I had seen pictures of the OX-5-powered Curtiss Robin and had actually had a brief ride in one a year earlier. That was an interesting experience. A pilot had landed the Robin in the field in front of our house beside the highway, and had sold rides. I watched longingly as the airplane left the ground and soared overhead. I scraped enough money together for a ride, and afterward continued to watch the pilot and the plane.

The next day, after I had again watched the plane for hours, I was crossing the road to go home. A car drove by and stopped. The driver asked me how long the plane had been there. "It got here yesterday," was all I could say.

"The pilot stole that airplane and we've been trying to catch him for days," the man said. I watched as he intercepted the plane the next time it landed. That ended passenger flying at Roseau for that Curtiss Robin. Strangely, the pilot took off in the Robin, and the man in the car drove off. I assumed they had come to an agreement.

Years later I took a course in air law and learned that in the early years of aviation there was no way of convicting an airplane thief. An aircraft wasn't a car, a boat, a train, or any other mode of transportation identified by statute. That would be rectified, of course, but in those days airplane thieves apparently got away with their crime.

And here, a year later, was another OX-5 Robin, in the same field. I walked around the plane, studying it. The pilot followed. "You should learn to fly. It's a great profession," he said. I forget what else he said, but he was trying to convince me that I should pay him to teach me to fly. He sensed that my interest in airplanes went beyond wanting a ride. He was a great salesman, but his pitch was wasted on me: I was already sold. For $10 an hour, he said, he would give me dual flight instruction in the Robin.

That pilot was Roy Duggan. He was to have more influence on my professional life than any other man, and we were to become lifelong friends.

Solo

I DIDN'T have ten dollars for an hour of instruction in Roy Duggan's Curtiss Robin on that July day. Duggan promised he'd wait, and I ran back to town, waylaid my friend, Seth Abrahamson, and borrowed five dollars. I ran all the way back to where Duggan was waiting and breathlessly bought a half-hour of flight instruction.

The Curtiss Robin, built by Curtiss-Robertson, was a boxy-looking airplane, partly because of the radiator needed for the water-cooled OX-5 engine. But it was quite efficient, and with the OX-5 it cruised about 80 mph. Like all 300 of the OX-5 Curtiss Robins built in 1928, the fuselage exterior was a burnt-orange color, with yellow wings spanning 41 feet, and black trim. A skylight overhead and full-length windows provided good visibility. It had two doors—one in front for the pilot, one in the rear for the two passengers. There was no tail wheel; it had a tail skid. The landing wheels were 30 inches in diameter, with 3.5-inch-wide pneumatic tires that helped absorb the roughness of the airfields commonly used then. The Robin had no brakes.

Duggan walked around the airplane and showed me the elevators, the ailerons, and the rudder. He explained how they controlled flight. This I already basically knew.

He put me in the front seat. I was so excited I hardly noticed the fine upholstery and the shiny nickeled door handles and window lifts. The two seats in the rear had another set of controls. Duggan gave me a lecture on the controls—a stick, two rudder pedals, throttle, and the Lunkenheimer primer. He pointed out a temperature gauge for the water-cooled engine, as well as oil pressure, tachometer, and airspeed gauges. A compass was mounted at the top of the windshield. There were no other flight instruments.

I could hardly hear what Duggan was telling me. I had relived again and again my flight in the Travel Air six years earlier, and I had dreamed so long about flying. Finally, I was actually going to be at the controls of an airplane.

Duggan primed the engine with the Lunkenheimer, a pump that projected from the instrument panel. He set the throttle, and started the engine by standing in front of the airplane and pulling on the eight-and-a-half-foot wooden propeller because there was no self-starter. The engine started with the first pull, and Roy climbed into the back seat. "Hold the stick lightly," he said. "Put your feet on the rudder pedals and follow me through. Don't resist when the controls move. Just follow them. As the controls move, notice what the airplane does."

I put my right hand on the stick and my left hand on the throttle. My feet fit naturally on the rudder pedals. He turned the airplane's tail with a blast from the propeller as the rudder was deflected.

As we started our takeoff run from the edge of the field, Roy ran the engine up to maximum rpms to be sure its single magneto was functioning with the engine working at full power. As we roared into the air, I tried to drink in every movement, every sound, every smell of that airplane. Leaving the ground and climbing into the sky in that wonderful machine was an experience almost beyond mortality. I was literally and figuratively in heaven. I followed the control movements on takeoff and felt the changes as Duggan circled, but I didn't have any idea what was going on.

I was amazed at how little control movement was needed to change the direction of flight. The airplane would turn, climb, or dive without my being aware that the controls had moved. Roy climbed to a safe several thousand feet, leveled off, and let me try flying.

The OX-5 had a flat engine cowling that ran directly out in front of the windshield. My eyes were nearly level with the cowling, making it easy to line up the nose of the airplane with the horizon. This helped me to know when I was flying straight and level. Despite this, that Robin bobbed up and down, like the bird in the song. I didn't know how much to move the stick, and it took a while to get the feel. I thought it was excessively sensitive.

Next, Roy said I was going to make some turns. He explained that I had to coordinate the stick and rudder, which was meaningless to me because I had never done it. I thought that when you turned you simply pushed on the rudder; when you wanted to bank you pushed on the stick. But in that first lesson I learned that a pilot must use both controls simultaneously—the ailerons and a tiny bit of rudder.

At first I skidded the airplane, then I gradually began to sense the skids and slowly learned coordination of ailerons and rudder. We went up and down a good deal, but we turned. Soon Roy had me making fairly steep turns, but the horizon kept getting away from me and I couldn't figure out why. Like most students on a first flight, I had preconceived ideas about how to use the controls; I was partly right and partly wrong.

Generously, Duggan stretched the 30 minutes I had bought. As he landed, I followed the control movements with hands and feet. "You did fine," he told me.

Whether he was trying to make sure that I continued as a student, or whether I truly did well, I don't know. Duggan was a

barnstormer, selling rides, but he also taught flying, and an important part of his income was from students. Making a living this
way was tough. He often went for days without a dime coming in.
He needed every student he could get.

By the time Duggan left that fall, I had almost six hours of
dual instruction. I earned $40 a month at the hardware store, and
I spent most of a month's salary on flying. I even had to borrow
to pay Duggan. It was probably to my advantage that I couldn't
afford much flying at any one time. The little air time I got was
spread over weeks, giving me time to think about what I had
learned. Learning to fly is complicated. An important part is the
time spent mulling over what you have learned.

Roy encouraged me to make flying my profession. One of
his sales pitches stands out in my memory, perhaps because it hit
home. One day I was raking hay with a horse in a field near where
he kept his plane. After a while I couldn't withstand the tempta-
tion, so I tied the horse to a fence and walked over to the airplane
to talk with him.

"Want to go flying?" he asked.

"I can't now. I have all that hay to rake, and I have to look
after the horse."

He looked disgusted as he reached into his pocket and
hauled out a roll of bills. It looked big to me, but at the time,
even a dollar bill looked big. His roll was probably mostly one
dollar bills, perhaps twenty of them.

"Rudy, you sure ought to keep on with this flying. I may
not be the richest guy in the world, but I didn't have to sit on a
hayrake seat and look at a horse's ass all day to earn this."

Roy Duggan was a superb instructor who explained theories of flight and practical aspects of flying in the most complete
detail. I carried some of the principles he taught me throughout
my flying career.

To him an airplane accident was uncalled for: it simply
should never happen. "Airplanes aren't dangerous," he told me in
his blunt way. "It's always the idiot flying them that makes them

dangerous." He'd put his attitude across firmly. Grinding his teeth, he'd tell me, "That is the way it is." In later years even Roy Duggan had accidents with airplanes, but he lived through them.

When Duggan taught me to fly, there were few instruction books on flying and aviation equipment. Those that were available were too expensive for me. Roy told me to write a penny postcard to every manufacturer of aviation devices advertised in magazines.

I sent cards to magneto companies, engine companies, carburetor manufacturers, and propeller manufacturers. I wrote to Curtiss, Command Air, Eaglerock, Waco, and other companies that made airplanes. The resulting reams of free aviation material I received gave me a technical knowledge that I couldn't have learned in any other manner. Studying those pamphlets was almost like going to ground school.

When Duggan flew away that fall he left me with good memories and vague but determined hopes to continue flying. To my astonishment, that December I received a letter from him. A businessman, George Arnold, wanted to buy an airplane and hire a pilot. He was looking for a beginner who needed to build flying time more than he needed a big salary.

Arnold wanted someone to fly between the Northwest Angle of Minnesota and the end of the railroad at Warroad, Minnesota, hauling fillets of walleye pike and northern pike to market and bringing supplies and passengers back and forth. Arnold had several enterprises, including a store at Penasse on American Point in the Northwest Angle. He also ran the northernmost post office in the country.

How could I take the job? I hadn't even soloed. It sounded wonderful but I was apprehensive. Duggan invited me to live with him and his wife, Christine, in Minneapolis while I finished flight training. "If you can pay the cost of renting an airplane, I'll charge you a dollar an hour for instruction until you solo," he generously offered.

My dad gave me the money. Sister Inga and my mother fussed, but I went to Minneapolis. I stayed with the Duggans on

Portland Avenue. Daily, we drove the short distance to Wold-Chamberlain Airport. Duggan arranged for use of an open-cockpit biplane—a Tank-powered Waco on skis. The Tank engine was a conversion of the OX-5 by the Tank Brothers of Milwaukee. It had air-cooled cylinders that replaced the water-cooled ones, eliminating the weight and bulk of radiator, hoses, and fittings. The engine also had two magnetos rather than the one found on standard OX-5s.

Duggan taught me how to navigate. Much of the navigating in those days was pilotage, which is recognition and locating of landmarks that can be identified from a map. Since much of Minnesota is laid out in straight section lines, it was a simple process. Sometimes we had to fly across wooded regions with no recognizable landmarks. In such situations he taught me to use dead reckoning. With the relatively short flights we made, we could easily draw a line on a map, set a compass course, and allow for any crosswind. We could determine the amount of crosswind from the drift of the airplane. Generally, we didn't miss our destination by much. When weather limited visibility I learned to follow railroad tracks or roads.

Among other techniques, Roy had me practice slow flying, which gave me a feel for the airplane. At speeds just above a stall, a pilot must use controls carefully. Even a shallow turn can bring on a stall. I learned to ease in a little power on turns to prevent this. Some of the early planes were vicious when they stalled, for a stall could suddenly turn into a spin. Spins in many planes of the era were difficult to stop.

I flew the open-cockpit Waco on skis from the rear seat while Roy instructed from the front seat. I made several takeoffs and landings. By then I had logged a total of eight hours and ten minutes of dual time. On one go-around just after I landed, Roy yelled for me to hold for a moment and climbed out of the airplane. I wasn't sure what he had in mind until, with a big grin, he waved me off. He was soloing me!

No pilot ever forgets his first solo flight. I was both

frightened and elated. Roy had always been in the airplane to correct my mistakes, but now, suddenly, I was high in the sky, dependent only on myself.

The flight went well at first. I had seen a twin-engine Northwest Airlines Lockheed go in for a landing ahead of me. I was on my downwind leg, turning the base leg for landing, when the Lockheed suddenly appeared close behind me.

It was January, and most of the airport was snow-covered, used by planes on skis. But a couple of runways had been plowed free of snow for Northwest Airlines' Lockheed 10-passenger planes.

The nearness of the big plane alarmed me. I didn't land, but went around. This was an unfortunate encounter for a student on his first solo flight. Northwest made several passes at the runway, while I circled a short distance from the field, waiting. Finally the Lockheed left the area, and I landed on the snow of the open field without difficulty. I learned later that the Lockheed crew had had trouble lowering their landing gear. They eventually made a normal landing.

Today when a student pilot solos, his instructor cuts his shirt tail off, a recent tradition. There was no such foolishness in the 1930s. Money to buy shirts was hard to come by, and if anyone had suggested ruining mine, they'd have had a fight on their hands.

I was a happy 18-year-old. I was a pilot, even though I had less than 15 minutes of solo time. My solo flight occurred only 32 years after Orville Wright's historic 59-second first powered flight in 1903. Man learned to build and fly efficient, complex machines of the sky in an amazingly brief time.

Today we think of the Curtiss-Robin as primitive, but in the mid-1930s any halfway dependable airplane was considered one of the wonders of the world. To my teenage eyes, the boxy 1920s and 1930s airplanes were complex, lovely, and graceful. For years I marveled that I could get into an airplane and with roaring engine and spinning propeller, climb into the sky and circle, swoop, and climb again, all the while, godlike, looking down on the earth far below. A new world opened to me when I became a pilot.

Duggan arranged for use of a Fleet biplane powered with a 5-cylinder Kinner engine. In it, he showed me how to get into and out of a tailspin. He then showed me how to do a loop. My loop wasn't very good, but I did get the idea. I became airsick, so we landed, and that ended my flying instruction while I lived with the Duggans.

Whenever I think of the Curtiss Robin airplane in which Roy Duggan started teaching me to fly, and other sturdy and honest Robins that I flew, I'm reminded of another Curtiss Robin that made a famous flight. In July 1938, this nine-year-old bird (with a 165-horsepower Wright J6-5 engine) lifted off Floyd Bennett field in New York and disappeared into the clouds at 5,000 feet. The pilot had said he was headed for California. He flew by compass for more than 28 hours until his West Coast destination lay below. He landed—*on the west coast of Ireland!* Douglas Corrigan, the pilot, has ever after been known as "Wrong-way" Corrigan.

Those of us who knew and flew the dependable Curtiss Robin weren't really too surprised at the magnificent performance of his rugged little airplane. Despite the dependability of the Curtiss Robin, my next few months of experience with one came close to shaking my resolve to be a pilot. It wasn't the fault of the airplane.

Flying at the Northwest Angle

AFTER DUGGAN soloed me, I returned home to Roseau. About a month later, I heard the exciting roar of an airplane engine. I ran out the door and watched a ski-equipped, Challenger-powered Curtiss Robin land on the snowy field in front of our farmhouse.

Flying it was good old blunt-spoken Duggan. He opened the door and stuck his head out and yelled, "How does that sound to you?" pointing to the idling engine as it barked out its characteristic sound.

"Fine," I yelled back.

"It sounds like hell," he shouted, shaking his head as he shut it off.

He was right. It was a Curtiss Challenger radial engine, a model that always ran rough, although it was reliable. The well-used airplane he flew had recently been purchased by George Arnold, and I was to be its pilot. Duggan warned, "Arnold doesn't know that you've just soloed. I told him you had about

50 hours flying time. Don't spill the beans. He's tickled to death to have the plane and an experienced pilot."

My salary was to be $50 a month and room and board. I was to fly from Minnesota's Northwest Angle, a true wilderness area at the northernmost point of the state. On maps, it's that little segment of the United States that seems to be inside Ontario, Canada.

It was a wild, almost lawless community separated from the United States. The waters of huge, 45- by 90-mile Lake of the Woods connect it to Minnesota. Only pioneering types were rugged enough to live there. More than half a century ago, when I flew over the northwest tip of the Angle, I could see oxcart tracks embedded in the soil—remnants of the old fur brigade canoe route from Montreal. Here, fur was unloaded from Red River oxcarts and placed in canoes. Those tracks must have been more than 100 years old.

A few folks lived there, with several trading posts on the islands. To travel out of the Angle, they had to cross treacherous Lake of the Woods. In winter when the lake froze over, residents used cars, sleds, and horses to travel on the ice. Periodically, all of these plunged through thin ice. The lake is so big that pressure ridges develop in the ice, some up to 30 feet high. Propeller-driven sleds used by the residents were powered with a variety of airplane engines—OX-5's, Hissos, various radials, and even some rotary engines from World War I, the Gnome and LeRhone. It was often necessary to chop through the ice pressure ridges to travel down the lake even with these wind sleds.

And summer boat transportation was slow because of the great distances. Because of the isolation, there was no sure way to get to medical help when needed. Nor was there any quick communication system, for there were no two-way radios there.

When Duggan arrived at my home with that Challenger Robin, he wanted me to leave for the Northwest Angle immediately. I threw some clothes into a suitcase and climbed into the plane with him. I sat in one of the two passenger seats in the back, for there was only one seat in the front, for the pilot.

"Let's change seats. You need to fly it," he yelled back after he had taken off for the 70-mile flight. Somehow we changed seats while airborne, and I flew to the Northwest Angle and landed. Of course, I used up ten times the space on landing that I should have. Everyone was thrilled to have the airplane, the first owned by anyone in the Angle.

We stayed the night. The following day George Arnold wanted to go to Roseau. Duggan flew the plane, and landed us in a farmer's field not far from my home. Before he and Arnold went to town Duggan said, "Rudy, you'd better take her up."

They were hardly out of sight when I cranked up the engine and taxied toward a corner of the 40-acre field. I sat and debated for a minute, unsure of myself. After all, I had only 15 minutes of solo time, and I had barely flown in this airplane. But I was young and eager and anxious to get the flying job.

I poured the coal to her, the skis slipped across the snow, bounced lightly a time or two, and I was off. I circled, thrilled to be flying alone over my hometown. Every house, every street, every tree, was familiar, yet everything looked different from the air. In that early winter of 1935, the village of Roseau, population 1,200, lay quietly under a blanket of sparkling snow. From each snow-covered roof a chimney poured bluish-white wood smoke from a stove within.

Beneath me, the village lay in neat squares. The Roseau River ran diagonally across the town, flowing from southeast to northwest under its cover of ice. That little stream eventually wound its way to the Red River of the north and flowed on to Hudson's Bay.

Across the river and two blocks east was the old brick school where I spent many years. I looked down at it from my roaring airplane, and saw the broad stone steps that led to the big double front doors. Although I could not read it from the air, I knew that carved in stone above the door was the date A.D. 1912. I broke into a broad grin as I realized that high above the old school and traveling at 100 miles per hour, no teacher was going to say, "Please be seated and work on your algebra."

I turned back, getting ready to land. My smile slowly disappeared as I circled. The problem I now faced was equal to any algebra problem. I had to get the noisy Robin safely back to earth. Duggan had taught me that speed was a necessity for safety—the only sure way to prevent a stall—so my tendency was to use too much speed. On my first pass I whizzed down and realized I would not stop in time even if I did touch down.

I went around again, and repeated my approach, somewhat slower and lower. Again it appeared that I would run out of space, so I gave her the coal and climbed out again. On the third pass, my approach looked good. To my intense relief I touched down and slid to a stop with room to spare.

When George and Roy returned, they were pleased that I had flown the plane. George still had no hint as to how green a pilot he had hired.

Roy went home to Minneapolis and I flew George back to the Northwest Angle, landing on the ice of the lake without difficulty. Next day I flew him to Roseau. From there he took a bus on to Minneapolis and I was on my own.

As soon as he left I cranked up and headed back toward the Northwest Angle. Ten miles on the way the engine started to bark, stop, backfire, and run terribly rough. I had no idea what kind of terrain I could land on in an emergency, but I was sure looking. I headed for a little clearing by a country schoolhouse, but before I reached it the engine smoothed out, and I continued on.

Back at the Northwest Angle, I started commercial fishing with Joe Risser, about my age, who was to help me with the airplane and I was to help him with the fishing. We'd shove a wooden device known as a jigger through a hole we cut in the ice, then repeatedly pull a rope attached to a metal pick on the jigger. The pick rode against the ice. Pulls on the rope sent the jigger farther and farther across the lake under the ice. When it was far enough, we'd cut another hole in the ice, and retrieve it and the line. Next we'd pull 1,000-foot gill nets under the ice, using the rope we'd strung with the jigger. (Years later I introduced the jigger to some Interior Alaska fishermen who had been stringing gill nets between holes in the ice with long poles.)

Joe and I pulled the nets daily. On our toboggan was a box with a kerosene lantern in it. We'd put the fish in with the lantern to keep them from freezing until we could haul them to the fish house, where we filleted them, dipped them in water, and froze them. Our product was a beautiful fillet completely encased in ice. We packed the fish in wooden boxes. When we had enough for a load, I'd fly the fish to the terminus of the Great Northern Railroad at Warroad. On my return flight, I hauled merchandise for the trading post.

I needed an extra hand when I started the Curtiss Challenger engine. First, I had to crank the inertia starter located at the base of the engine outside the cabin. It was like cranking a cream separator—tough going. As I cranked, it set a flywheel spinning faster and faster. When I judged it was going fast enough by the pitch level of the whine, I yanked the crank out and quickly leaped into the airplane. Next, hurriedly, I pumped the Lunkenheimer primer to feed fuel into the cylinders. Then, before the inertia flywheel ran down, I engaged the engine. Once the engine was turning over, I cranked an electric magneto booster, which produced spark to fire the engine. The engine usually started on the first try.

Sometimes Joe started the Robin by hand by pulling the prop through while I primed and stood ready with the magneto booster. I had to be careful not to crank the booster before Joe was clear of the propeller. The booster produced an untimed spark, and it could cause the engine to fire in advance, causing the prop to kick back.

Flying in the Angle was never boring. My youthful fascination with flight and my enthusiasm for airplanes grew. Luck helped me survive the many lessons I learned.

Shortly after my arrival, locals Kenny Carlson and Pete Frolander asked me to fly them to Angle Inlet, a long hike, or a short flight. I piled them into the rear of the Robin, took my place in the front, and took off. At the time I had landed the Robin only three, maybe four, times. They didn't know this, and I never told them. By the time the plane quit sliding on the ice after my landing, they had to walk probably half a mile. But they didn't care. It was the fastest they'd ever made the trip, and they were pleased. They were the first paying passengers I ever flew.

Then, a few worms crept into my apple of life. Days after I arrived at the Angle, the Robin started having engine failures. I'd be flying along when suddenly the engine would cough and quit. Fortunately, the first few times it happened I was above the lake, and I landed on the ice without any problem. After the first few failures, I always flew where I could land if the engine failed.

At the time, an airplane engine was an utterly strange device to me. I had no idea why it was quitting. Eventually, whenever I started on a flight I would wonder how many forced landings I'd have before I reached my destination.

One morning Joe and I were flying to Warroad with a load of frozen fish. We had flown only a few miles when the engine coughed once, then quit. I landed on the ice without difficulty. We had a faulty pair of pliers that jumped to the wide-open position when we squeezed them. They would barely work on the fittings I thought I needed to take apart.

We struggled with those pliers. It was cold, and I was upset, not knowing why the airplane engine had quit. My solution was to drain some fuel, thinking there was water in it. Joe helped me use the balky tool, and when we were finished I was so disgusted with the pliers I said to Joe, "Throw those lousy pliers away," and he flung them into the snow.

When we were about 100 feet in the air, again the engine stopped dead. I landed, but we needed the pliers, so we trudged back the half-mile or so and searched for them in the deep snow. We drained fuel and took off again, this time with the pliers in the airplane. Near Warroad, we flew over a bay in which many two-foot-high muskrat houses projected above the ice. The engine failed right there. The only place I could land was among these little frozen domes of snow-covered grass. It seemed almost impossible to miss them all, but somehow I managed. We drained fuel again.

After many weeks, I arrived at an explanation for the engine failures. Water had gotten into the fuel tanks, probably when someone refueled without filtering the gas, and it had frozen. With partly filled tanks, I could hear the ice clunking around in both wings. Occasionally the ice would jam against the outlet, blocking fuel flow to the engine. When I landed, the airplane assumed a different attitude, the ice would move, gas would flow, and the engine could start again. Draining the gas would never have removed the ice chunks, but it took a long time for me to realize that.

Nevertheless, I continued flying the airplane as best I could. I considered Arnold's Challenger-powered Robin a hot performer, and it was, compared with the OX-5-powered Robin Duggan flew. It was a later model, and the Challenger six-cylinder, air-cooled radial engine produced 185 horsepower at 1,800 rpm. It cruised about 100 mph and flew very well.

In those days, it was common for pilots to show off with spectacular flying. Barnstormers always roared over Main Street as low as they dared fly when they arrived at a town, quickly catching the attention of people on the ground. They then performed loops, rolls, and other exciting maneuvers.

I was eager to try that kind of flying, so one morning I took off with the Challenger Robin and held the airplane within two or three feet of the ice as it built up speed. I then pulled it into a ridiculously steep climb, a show-off special. I got up about 200 feet and the engine stopped dead. The airplane stalled, and the nose fell. I had enough sense to shove the stick forward and hold it there until I thought the airplane was flying, then I pulled back slowly. I was lucky. The nose gradually came up, but I was so close to the ground that the backs of the skis rattled on snow drifts as I leveled off. I had come close to piling that old Robin right on her nose. I decided it would be better to know a little more about what I was doing before pulling any more such stunts.

Soon after that, I learned another lesson. Before taking off one morning I found about an inch of dry snow on the wings, horizontal tail surfaces, and fuselage. It was so light that when I blew on the tail, the snow flew off almost like feathers. I decided there was no need to brush the snow off the wings, because I was certain that as I taxied over the rough drifts, the bouncing and the wind would knock all the snow off.

I fired up and taxied down the ice-covered river toward the lake. I was going pretty fast, expecting the airplane to fly. It didn't. The snow clung to the top of the wings. That changed the air foil so there was no lift. Suddenly the snow blew off the right wing. Immediately, it lifted into the air, raising the right side of the plane, and causing the tip of the left wing to hit. When the left wing walloped the ice it too shed the snow and suddenly developed lift. Desperately working the controls, I managed to get that old Robin under control and lift both wings into the air. It was a pretty wild 10 or 15 seconds. The lesson: always remove snow from wings, no matter how light.

The engine failures continued most of the winter. I didn't dare fly anywhere I couldn't land, because I knew that engine was going to quit.

Toward spring I flew 12 miles to Flag Island. Charles and David, the nine-year-old sons of the operator of McKeever's resort, begged their mother for permission to go for a ride with me. She was leery of my airplane. Putting on my best smile and with my smoothest sales pitch, I told her how safe it was. She relented, and I loaded the boys and took off.

We were circling over Flag Island when smoke suddenly poured out of the engine. It looked like the plane was afire, and at first I thought it was, for smoke came back at me through the instrument panel. That panel had more holes in it than it had instruments.

The poor mother must have nearly had a heart attack when she saw the smoke. I put down immediately, a mile or so out on the lake. By the time I landed the smoke had stopped.

I let the boys out and looked the engine over, but there was no indication what had caused the problem. I learned later that a piston had broken, and apparently the spark had set fire to the oil spray in the crankcase.

I arranged for a man with a couple of horses to tow me home. It was embarrassing for me, as I sat in the airplane while the two trotting horses pulled it the 12 miles back to American Point.

That ended my first flying job. George Arnold, disgusted, said he couldn't afford to keep the airplane. To him it had been nothing but trouble. He ended my employment, saying that by the time the engine was repaired, ice fishing would have ended for the year.

To me that old Challenger Robin seemed well named—It was one of the biggest challenges I ever faced. But nowhere could I have had better training for the bush flying that I was to do in Alaska. I learned how to handle an airplane in cold weather, how to preheat, tricks of snow flying, of winter flying—dozens of technical things one learns only by doing. And I sure gained a lot of experience with forced landings.

When the job ended, I could pass myself off as an experienced pilot. However, I didn't have enough experience to be sure of another flying job. Even many of the old-timers, truly skilled and experienced pilots, couldn't find work in that Depression year of 1935. An 18-year-old pilot could hardly compete for the few steady flying positions.

There was always barnstorming.

Barnstorming

IT COULD have been any rural midwestern town, quiet under the early Sunday morning sun. Abruptly, the peace was shattered as two airplanes roared just above the buildings of Main Street. Wearing goggles and helmet, I was flying an OX-5-powered Travel Air—a two-cockpit biplane. Roy Duggan flew a Stinson Junior with a 215-horsepower Lycoming radial engine. People on the street stared up. Cars stopped and passengers craned their necks. I hauled back on the stick and my plane climbed steeply into a chandelle—an abrupt climbing turn. Duggan also put his airplane into an eye-catching maneuver.

From 1,200 feet, I pointed my plane's nose toward the park in mid-city and dived, knowing that the engine's roar would blanket the town. Leveling off just above trees, buildings, and wires, I again climbed and laid the biplane on her side for a moment as I peered down, judging the effect of two screaming, diving airplanes on residents. To climax our arrival, we usually climbed above the town and looped, spun a few turns, snap-rolled, and performed wingovers and split-S turns.

After five minutes of wildly roaring about the sky, we flew to the outskirts of town and eased the planes to a landing in a farmer's field. When a crowd arrived, we sold rides for a dollar per person.

If business was good, we often remained in a town for several days. Commonly, we slept under the wing of the airplane, for there was never enough money to go to a hotel. We didn't have sleeping bags—I didn't know what a sleeping bag was. We used a blanket and a tarpaulin for bedding.

One cold night I dug a hole in a haystack near my airplane and crawled into it with my blanket and tarpaulin. Later, I was awakened by hay moving next to my face. I exploded out of the hole—and startled a feeding cow.

For several years, between 1935 and 1938, barnstorming and air shows provided a way for me to make a few dollars as a pilot. It was a fascinating life for a young, unmarried man without responsibilities.

Barnstormers were looked upon as irresponsible dare-devils. Most of us flew because we loved to fly. There were few prospects for a longtime career in aviation, and barnstorming kept us in the air. Adventure, not money, kept us aloft. The flash of wings in the sky, the feel of wind against my face, the sudden surge of power from an engine, the view of the world as if from the wrong end of a telescope—this was my passion.

Barnstorming started after World War I, when nearly 10,000 war-trained pilots became civilians. Simultaneously, thousands of war-surplus Curtiss JN-4D (Jenny) airplanes became available, priced at $300. An additional 1,000 surplus Standard biplanes, many powered with fine Hispano-Suiza engines, also became available.

At first, the swashbuckling barnstorming pilots were veterans of the great war (or at least claimed to be), and while flying their World War I Spad fighter planes over France, they may have even encountered the Red Baron. What could be more romantic than a silk-scarfed, helmet-and-goggle-clad young man, wearing breeches and polished leather knee boots? Add a flying machine and the scary thought of riding it among the clouds. The arrival of a barnstormer in a small rural community was often the high point of the summer for residents.

In the early barnstorming years, horses still provided much of the transportation in the United States. Model T Fords were beginning to flood the countryside. Commercial aviation was still a baby. Barnstormers often flew the first airplanes seen in small towns. Thousands of Americans first tasted flight on a brief ride with a barnstormer.

After a time, the offer of rides didn't attract enough business, so dollar-poor pilots devised hair-raising stunts to attract crowds. These included wing-walking, transferring from one plane to another in flight, picking up a passenger from a speeding car, and acrobatics. That usually brought a crowd. People loved the danger and risk. Barnstormers had been plying their trade for about 15 years when I joined their ranks. True barnstorming mostly ended with the start of World War II.

The barnstormers I worked with operated with some organization. Usually, we advertised in a local newspaper that we would offer airplane rides in that town on a certain day, usually a Sunday. Then we made as spectacular an arrival as we could. On other occasions, we flew to political picnics, county or state fairs— any large gathering. Sometimes we mounted skis on our planes and barnstormed winter carnivals.

Duggan watched over me for the first year to be sure I flew with good judgment.

Airplanes were still a mystery to many Americans in the 1930s. The heroics of World War I—Eddie Rickenbacker and his Spad dog-fighting Fokkers over the Western Front—still held a fascination for most. The enthusiasm over Lindbergh's 1927 flight, and the gradual enlightenment of Americans to aviation, brought us many passengers. The Great Depression was waning, although a dollar was still precious. The pace of life in the Midwest was slow. The excitement we brought to a small town was usually welcome.

After our slam-bang entrance, we would land and immediately kids would show up. They came on bicycles, afoot, or on horseback. They would sit around staring at the airplane and asking questions. They had no money for rides, but they were intensely interested.

Soon a few cars would arrive. The successful businessmen, bankers, and store owners of the area usually sat around outside the crowd as if they weren't very interested. I could almost determine the status of a man by where he stood in the crowd. The businessmen were usually our best customers. Our ticket seller would organize them, and our workday would begin.

For me, a pilot who didn't own an airplane, it was a tough way to make a living. I seldom had any money. We needed many passengers before we managed to get a few dollars ahead.

We used regular auto gas, which worked well in the OX-5 engine. Gasoline sold for 12 to 25 cents a gallon, depending on location. Sometimes, we'd boost the octane by putting mothballs (naphtha) in it. I didn't really know why it worked, but it seemed to.

The younger people were learning about airplanes and aviation, but occasionally we'd be stupefied by the ignorance of others. Duggan was once barnstorming with an American Eagle, a biplane that had ailerons on both the upper and lower wings— four of them. A man walked around and around the airplane, studying it carefully. Finally, he put his hand on an aileron and pulled it, making the other three move. He stood there slowly moving the ailerons up and down, up and down. The expression on his face was that of dawning incredulity. He turned to Duggan and said, quite seriously, "By God, you never could have told me that you could flap these things fast enough to make that machine fly!"

Aviation was still in its infancy, and even among

professional aviators misinformation was rife. It was a time of "air pockets," when many, including some pilots, believed that airplanes could fall into holes where there was little or no air. The phenomenon today known as a "wind shear" was a "vacuum" in the 1930s. Pilots still didn't know of the terrible danger of flying into thunderstorms. The jet stream—that high-altitude, swift river of air—was yet to be discovered.

Anything that drew a crowd was considered a godsend by a barnstormer. I once drew a crowd when I was barnstorming in the Red River Valley of Minnesota by flying backward. I discovered a husky wind at about 1,000 feet that was blowing almost as fast as the cruising speed of my airplane. I slowed to just above stalling speed so I was flying slower than the wind. The airplane backed up, the wind pushing it. It was fun, so I flew backward across town and the airport several times.

When I landed, a dozen cars had arrived at the airport. The locals had seen me fly backward. It was the most spectacular flying they had ever seen. My potential passengers proposed all kinds of theories to explain it. I overheard one man saying, "He was flying in air so thin that his propeller couldn't get a good grip." Others had equally zany ideas. I didn't explain. I was too busy hauling passengers. Those people figured that any pilot who could fly an airplane backward was super-skilled.

On another occasion, pure chance again brought me a rush of business. I was at Lake Bronson in northwestern Minnesota. Many people went there to swim. With an OX-5-powered Waco 90, a two-cockpit biplane, I landed in a farmer's field next to the lake and a crowd of Sunday swimmers. Immediately, a couple of adventurous young fellows wanted a ride. I put them in the front cockpit, took off, and circled low over the beach and swimming area. Suddenly, my passengers became excited. They clapped their hands as they peered down.

I looked down—into the roofless women's dressing room. Women grabbed towels and ran for cover.

My two passengers told their friends, and I did a great

business. All the young men wanted a ride. I circled that bath-house all afternoon and seldom stayed in the air for more than five minutes. All enjoyed it, except perhaps the women in the bathhouse.

When there was no special attraction to get passengers to my airplane, there could be periods of inactivity. I often sat in a farmer's field all day chewing on a straw and talking to kids. There were always kids.

Once when I sat and parried kids' questions near Red Lake Falls, Minnesota, one challenged, "I'll bet my uncle is a better pilot than you are." At the time I didn't think that anyone was a much better pilot than I was, so I just gave the kid a nasty look and didn't answer. After a while, the kid spoke up again. "My uncle is a lot better pilot than you are."

"Who is your uncle?" I finally asked.

"My uncle is Charles Lindbergh. He's coming here today in his airplane," the kid answered.

I didn't believe him at first. Then I remembered that Lindbergh had a half-sister who lived there. I decided I'd stay to see if Lindbergh really did show up. It would have been a high-light of my life to talk with him, for he had long been my hero.

I waited. Just before dark I had to leave. I had no lights, and I had to return the airplane. As I took off, a Monocoupe landed in the field I had just left.

Fifty years later, on September 5, 1985, I saw a tiny item in the *Roseau Times* under "50 years ago." It read, "Col. and Mrs. Charles Lindbergh flew their little plane in to Red Lake Falls for a visit with Col. Lindbergh's sister." I've always regretted that I didn't wait a few more minutes.

During my first summer of solo flying, in addition to barn-storming, I flew into the Northwest Angle a number of times, hauling passengers and freight, trying to make a dollar wherever I could. A border patrolman said to a friend of mine, referring to me, "That kid ought to be watched: he's probably smuggling stuff into or out of Canada, and I'm going to nail him."

My friend told me, and I boiled about it for some time, for I knew the border patrolman and he had never approached me. I had done nothing wrong, and he was blabbing in a way that I felt could hurt my reputation.

Before dawn one morning I took off with my OX-5 Travel Air and climbed to a good altitude. I flew to this man's house and dived on it full speed. The curved windshield in front of the cockpit was Plexiglas, and I dived so fast that it started to flatten out. I roared about 10 feet above the chimney, then immediately left the vicinity so my plane couldn't be identified. To my knowledge the guy never said another word about me.

We were forever trying to persuade businessmen to buy an airplane for us to fly. Commonly, there was a three-way split on the income from an airplane. The owner got a third, a third went to the airplane for fuel and maintenance, and the pilot received a third. That was the arrangement Duggan had with the OX-5 Robin.

But barnstormers were always broke. I once flew a Challenger Robin to Grand Rapids, Minnesota, with a friend from Duluth as my ticket seller. When we landed we didn't have enough money between us to buy gas to fly the airplane. There was barely enough for one ride.

A potential passenger arrived, and we gave him our sales pitch. "I'll make you a sporting proposition," he offered. "We'll flip a coin, double or nothing." If he won, he was to ride for nothing. If I won, he would pay two dollars for his ride.

We tossed the coin and I won. I took him on as short a ride as I dared, half-expecting to run out of gas. As soon as we landed, the ticket seller and I went to town with a can to buy two dollars worth of gasoline.

Most people who flew with me enjoyed the ride, but once in a while a passenger who was truly fearful would get talked into my airplane. Once, when I was flying a Cessna AW, a fellow wanted to take his girl for a ride. She didn't want to go. He talked persuasively for a long time and she reluctantly agreed.

As the wheels left the ground, I looked around and saw that woman sitting bent over with her head almost down by her feet. She refused to look out the window. She saw me looking at her and yelled, "Don't go any higher." I wasn't over 20 feet up, and I nodded and said, "OK."

She sat up and looked out. She thought it would be safe if I didn't go any higher. I very gradually climbed out and she didn't know the difference. Most people who have never flown aren't familiar with the view from high in the sky. She was pleased when we landed. She thought we hadn't flown high enough to be in danger.

Once a woman started to scream on takeoff and continued to scream as I climbed out. She was hysterical. I immediately landed and refunded her dollar.

It seemed that everyone who went up was a first-timer in the air, and I could never understand that. Barnstormers had worked most of those little towns for years. Yet first-timers kept buying rides. Sometimes there'd be so many people standing in line to buy tickets that I'd load passengers, take off, circle, and land, having to cut the rides short to get them all in the air before dark.

I once landed a Robin on skis at a little town in the Minnesota Arrowhead during a winter carnival. During that one short winter day I took in $103 and still flew back to Duluth. At a dollar each, with two passengers per ride, that was a lot of flights. My one-third share of that day's flying pay was more than two weeks wages for a day laborer.

Usually the businessmen who invested in the airplanes we flew had only enough money for beat-up, worn-out airplanes. And so we had a lot of engine trouble. I had so many forced landings, especially with OX-5 engines, that I began to think it was a normal part of flying.

In later decades, the eight-cylinder, optimistically rated 90-horsepower, water-cooled Curtiss OX-5 engine—built in two

V-banks of four cylinders each—would become famous. Even an exclusive OX-5 club was formed, limited to pilots who had flown airplanes powered by that engine. It was a slow-speed engine that turned a maximum of 1,400 rpms; half of them that I flew wouldn't turn up more than 1,300 rpms, and some were considerably slower.

The OX-5 was a World War I engine, used for many years in almost every airplane built. These engines were cheap, readily available, and about the only thing in the 90-horsepower rating. By the time I started flying, many of them were worn out. We used to buy used Curtiss OX-5 engines for $25 from Marvin A. Northrop Airplane Company in Minneapolis, a pioneer in the aircraft parts business. Or we'd send to Northrop for parts; often the parts would come off an engine that was worn out, and the part itself might be badly worn.

The OX-5 had exposed rocker arms that bounced the valves up and down. Among the many refinements developed for the OX-5 was the Miller overhead, in which little rotating wheels at the ends of the rocker arms were supposed to make the arms last longer, keeping the tappet clearance correct.

Whenever we got a Miller overhead, usually someone else had worn it out and the little wheels didn't rotate. Commonly, there were flat spots on the wheels. We turned the wheels around to where there wasn't a flat spot and jammed them so they wouldn't rotate. Usually this worked all right for a while.

My maintenance of OX-5 engines left a lot to be desired. I'd hear of someone with an old OX-5 that had been run out, and maybe it would be thrown out behind a barn. I'd run over there to see if I could find any parts I needed. These used parts were responsible for my many forced landings. For its time, the engine was reasonably reliable, but it had the potential for a lot of trouble. The average nonmechanical pilot flying the OX-5 not infrequently found himself looking frantically for a place to land because his engine had conked out.

The OX-5 had about 90 pipe-and-hose water connections.

Its one Burling magneto sat at the rear, directly below the drive shaft of the water pump. That water pump always seemed to leak. I made several forced landings because of water from the pump dripping on the magneto and carburetor.

The magneto had a safety gap: two points close enough together so if there was a surge of power, the current drained off by jumping between them. When drops of water lodged in the gap, the magneto shorted out, stopping the engine. It took a while for a pilot new to the OX-5 to learn about this nasty trait. Often, the water drop had evaporated by the time the plane had landed, so there was no easy way to diagnose the problem.

Commonly, too, a water leak dripped on top of the carburetor. There, a float with a needle stuck up. The hole for that needle wasn't water tight, so leaks from the engine, or rain, could run into the float chamber through the needle hole.

Once, after an OX-5 engine with an especially bad leak had quit on me a time or two, I tied a piece of inner tube above the carburetor. That solved that problem for a while. Such makeshift repairs were common with worn-out OX-5s during the late 1930s.

The Curtiss OX-5 manual warned, "The carburetor is unusually sensitive to water and foreign matter." For the OX-5 carburetor, it was a daily procedure for a pilot to drain water from four plugs (we called them jet wells) which had leaked through the float pinhole.

After that first barnstorming summer in 1935, which left me without any money in my pocket, I went to North Dakota to work with a grain-threshing crew. I drove a bundle team from sunup until black dark. For that work, I received $2.35 a day and I managed to save about $150. When I returned home, Duggan told me about an OX-5 Travel Air 2000 available for $300. Two friends, Carl Nordvall and Russell Quanbeck, each put in $100, and on October 5, we bought the airplane. Duggan picked it up and flew it to Roseau.

It was a nice-looking machine, but it was unlicensed. In those days that was of little concern. I climbed in happily, and it flew beautifully. That was the first airplane I had at least part ownership in, and it was great fun. I hauled passengers, and for a couple of weeks spent all my money on Red Crown automobile gas for that old OX-5 engine.

Now that we had our own airplane, my buddies and I plotted how we were going to make some real money. We decided we were going to Texas to hunt coyotes from the air. Two weeks after acquiring the plane, on a bright, crisp fall day, Russell Quanbeck crawled into the front cockpit, I settled in the rear, and we took off, heading south for Texas. We had flown two miles when the engine quit cold.

With my practice at dead-stick landings, I eased her down in a farmer's field. (A dead-stick landing refers to the propeller as a "stick." In a dead-stick landing the engine is stopped and the propeller is "dead".) When I took the top cowling off the engine, I could see no obvious problem. Others who knew more about engines arrived and managed to get it running again. I had placed the cowling on the ground. When one of the guys got into a car to go to town, he ran over and broke the cowling.

We decided I'd better fly the airplane back to the field next to my home. We would take the engine out and have Art Lien, a mechanic from Roseau who later became a well-known Alaskan aircraft mechanic, help us overhaul it.

I gave the propeller a swing and the engine started, running fine. Russell began to climb in but I told him I'd better fly it home alone, just in case. I took off and was soon lining up for an approach to the 20-acre field I planned to land in. From my experience it was a small field. I studied it, trying to decide what the wind was doing, and at low altitude I laid that airplane over in a steep bank. At that critical moment the engine quit.

That airplane just walked right into a tailspin. I had enough presence of mind to cut the switch and keep the nose down to gain flying speed so I could try to pull out. The nose started up, and the airplane was absolutely level when it hit the ground. The impact drove the wheels up through the fuselage, and the propeller, which had stopped crossways, broke off at the hubs. I was in the rear cockpit, with the safety belt around me.

At impact I flew forward, striking my head on the plywood instrument panel. The panel was backed by a length of three-quarter-inch steel tubing. My head broke through the quarter-inch plywood and put a bow in the steel tubing. The impact of both my head on the plywood and the plane striking the ground also broke the glass out of all the instruments. The tail skid ended up about four feet above the ground, directly above the hole where it had impacted; an impression of its full length and depth remained in the earth.

As the plane rebounded, my weight tore the seat from its fastenings to the fuselage, and I ended in a heap underneath the wrecked instrument panel. Still conscious, in shock, I leaped out of the plane and ran across the field like a jackrabbit. Then, in about 15 or 20 seconds, I became totally blind. I wandered in circles. I heard people coming, but I could see nothing.

My eyesight gradually returned after three or four minutes. I walked dazedly to my home, about 200 yards away. My forehead was swollen, and my head looked as if I'd been hit with a shotgun because of all the little pieces of glass embedded in the skin.

My mother called the family doctor. When he arrived, he wiggled my head and looked me over, but he didn't say much. I got the impression he didn't approve of flying. My mother was frantic, my father philosophic.

The next day, in spite of a big bandage around my head, I felt pretty good. I was relieved that I had no serious injury. I didn't know until years later that I had cracked my neck vertebrae. The cracks healed and left bone bulges that later showed up on X rays.

It was then commonly believed that if you had an airplane accident, the sooner you got back into a plane the less apt the experience was to scare you. Too young to have enough sense to let the crash affect me, and despite a stiff neck and bandaged head, I immediately climbed into and flew another OX-5 Travel Air 2000.

Parts of the broken Travel Air 2000 were stored in the family barn for 45 years. In the mid-1970s I sold them to a man who planned to rebuild the airplane. I hope he finished the job.

The barnstorming years were among the most colorful in early aviation, although it was a phase that didn't last long. My contribution was minor. By late 1938, clouds of World War II were on the horizon, and flying positions were opening up. No longer did we have to live hand-to-mouth.

I've always been grateful for my years as a barnstormer. Pilots in that profession taught me much about flying and about airplanes. In the 1930s, pilots usually added to their knowledge of flying through talk with other pilots, and experimentation. Books and magazine articles then available were usually written by theorists who had little or no experience, or by sensationalists. In any case I couldn't afford them.

Some of those barnstorming old-timers were true eagles. From them, I received a practical education I could not have obtained any other way—an education that served me well during the rest of my flying career.

Forced Landings

A FEW OF the many forced landings I have made stand out in my memory. In one, I was very lucky. I was 19 years old that July of 1935, and I had been hauling passengers with an OX-5 Travel Air at a town about 65 miles from Roseau. The airplane was slow, and cruised at 85 or 90 miles per hour, so I usually allowed plenty of daylight to fly home. On this day business was good, and darkness forced me to quit flying while I still had willing passengers.

When the last passenger climbed out of the plane, Bill Morse—ticket seller, parachute jumper, and future pilot—climbed in. I took off and followed the highway toward home.

Mechanic Art Lien had recently built a revolving beacon atop our movie theater. I was following the dimly seen highway when, suddenly, I saw that beacon in the distance. Man, I thought, I'll just head straight home. I left the highway and headed across country. When I was 15 or 20 miles from home that damned OX-5 quit cold. I had a couple thousand feet of altitude. It was too dark to see any more than where there were trees and where there were no trees.

I brought the plane around to a treeless space and felt my way down. The pitch of the wing wire whistle told me my speed. When I judged I was close to the ground (the airplane had no lights), I pulled the stick back and flared. We touched down and rolled to a stop.

I sat in the cockpit for a moment, congratulating myself for a safe landing. I then got out to walk around the front of the airplane. I couldn't do it. The airplane's nose was so close to a barbed wire fence there wasn't room for me to squeeze through! Just beyond the fence was a ditch. That scared me. I hadn't seen the fence or the ditch.

Lights came around a corner. A farmer who had heard my engine quit was driving around in his car trying to find us. He took us to the nearest town, where we called for someone to retrieve us with a car.

Next day, Roy Duggan, Art Lien, Bill Morse, and I returned for the plane. We stared in amazement at what we found. The field I had landed in was a veritable boulder pile. How I had missed every rock I'll never know. Some were so big they had barely been missed by the trailing edge of the lower wing as we rolled on our landing. The four of us worked half a day to pry from the ground and roll away enough rocks for a halfway decent runway for takeoff. Even then, Duggan did the flying: he felt it was too ticklish for me to tackle.

I never got used to forced landings. The many times in my early years of flying that I had an engine quit in flight and was forced to quickly seek a place for an emergency landing affected my flying for the rest of my career. The dead engines, of course, resulted from the poor quality of the equipment I flew.

I learned to react quickly to an engine's first cough. Why was it quitting? Was it ignition, fuel, or mechanical failure? A quick sweep of hand and eyes across my instrument and control panel usually told me whether the engine could be revived.

Another quick glance at the altimeter would tell me how much time I had to find a place to land. I'd search below, trying to remember the wind direction. Then I'd select a spot and maneuver to land upwind. Sometimes I was forced into dangerous downwind landings, but usually, in the farmlands where I flew, I could find a reasonably decent landing site. From the time I flew George Arnold's Challenger Robin with its frequent engine failures, my wariness saved my life many times.

Merle Buck was an old-time barnstormer whom I got to know before I learned to fly. He flew a four-place, 1928 Cessna AW airplane. Only 40 of these airplanes with wooden wings and a metal-tubing fuselage were built. They were fabric covered, and powered by a 110-horsepower Warner Scarab radial engine. Compared with the three-place, 185-horsepower Challenger Robin I often used for barnstorming, this was a very efficient little airplane. It carried three passengers at less cost than the Robin carried two.

Buck barnstormed with the Cessna primarily because of its economy. He had a gift for being able to make anything run. How he did it was the amazing part; I once saw him stop a leak in a carburetor with chewing gum.

I had known Buck for some time, bumping into him here and there at various airfields as we crossed trails barnstorming. He was probably as fine a pilot as ever barnstormed. He wasn't short of nerve, either. But when Merle Buck got through with an airplane, it was badly in need of maintenance. I learned this the hard way.

I found an angel in the summer of 1938—a businessman who was willing to buy an airplane for me to use barnstorming. With his money, I bought the Cessna AW that Buck had been flying. I went to Minneapolis to ride back to Duluth with Buck so he could check me out in the airplane. Buck had modified the upper cylinders of the Warner engine by drilling holes in them and screwing in petcocks. They could be primed for starting the engine.

Just before we were to start the engine to fly to Duluth, he got the fire extinguisher out of the airplane and squirted with it into these petcocks. In those days fire extinguishers held carbon tetrachloride.

"What on earth are you doing? Does that stuff burn?" I exclaimed.

He grinned. "This isn't carbon tet. It's gasoline."

"How do you get away with that?"

"Easy. I've had the plane licensed three times and inspected too. No one ever checks the extinguisher."

I've often considered what would have happened if someone, not knowing what Buck's extinguisher contained, tried putting out a fire with it. The Warner started easily after he had primed it. We took off and headed for Duluth.

I was interested in acrobatics, and I had been doing a few. We were flying along about 500 feet above the ground. "Is this airplane good for acrobatics?" I asked.

"Yeh, it's fine," he answered.

"Spins, loops, everything?" I persisted.

With that he stuck the nose down and looped that Cessna right there. We were just above the trees. Holy Moses! Even in my reckless young head, that seemed risky. He acted as if there was nothing to it—like banking to the left or right.

To be sure that the plane was safe for acrobatics, I wrote to Cessna asking if their AW model was approved for acrobatic flight. "We don't know of any airplane better suited," they responded.

Changing cylinder heads on the Warner engine required simultaneous expansion of the cylinder head and contraction of the cylinder. It was supposed to be done at the factory.

The cylinder heads in Buck's Cessna were so old and worn that they blew frequently. He always carried several spares in the airplane so he could replace them. Usually he'd catch them before they came all the way off. He showed me his technique for replacing the heads by dunking them in boiling water to expand the metal.

We often had a campfire and a big kettle in a farmer's field. I would put the cylinder head into a kettle and boil it so it would expand. The cylinder had to be cold (to make it contract) to fit the head. When possible, I used ice to cool it. When the temperatures of head and cylinder were right, the head would fit back on the cylinder.

I flew that Cessna all summer in 1938, barnstorming. The old Warner occasionally blew a cylinder head. Like Buck, I carried extra heads and cylinders, all of which I'm sure were beyond tolerance limits. However, the boiling water and ice trick worked. I was slowly learning about maintenance.

On one occasion I flew the Cessna into a little town in northwestern Minnesota where a county fair was under way. There was an airplane in a pasture beside the road, and I landed next to it. The pilot flying the plane was Merle Buck, and he had the field tied up. The first barnstormer arriving at a fair usually made a deal with the farmer who owned the best field available for exclusive landing rights.

But Buck said, "No problem, Rudy. You can fly here with me." So I started flying passengers. I was doing well until, with three passengers aboard, that worn-out Warner engine failed as I was leaving the ground. A fence loomed ahead. The airplane had enough speed for me to inch the wheels over, but the tail hit a post and was damaged.

I landed, stood on the brakes, and skidded to a stop in a farmer's nearly ripe stand of oats. I refunded my passengers' dollars, and they left, thankful, I guess, to be alive. I stood sadly looking at the damage to my airplane. The tubing at the leading edge of the horizontal stabilizer was broken and would require welding. Fabric would have to be replaced.

The elderly farmer who owned the oats soon arrived. To him, airplanes were about like spaceships are to us today. "Look what you've done to my oats!" he shouted.

"Gee, I'm sorry. I couldn't help it. My engine stopped."

That didn't mean anything to him.

"Look what you did to my fence!" he shouted, when he discovered the knocked-down post and wire.

"Yeah, but I couldn't help it," I said, weakly. "There was nothing I could do." He simply couldn't understand why I had hit his fence and torn up his oat field.

"You're going to have to pay for this mess!" he shouted.

"I'm going to be here for a few days. Would it be all right if I fixed the fence for you?" I offered.

"No, sir. You're not gonna fix it. I am," he said. "And you're gonna pay for it."

Fortunately, I had flown a few passengers and I had a little money. I asked, "How much do you want to fix the fence?"

"Two dollars," he said, as if it were a fortune. Maybe it was to him. Two dollars was a day's wages for a laborer at the time. The guy didn't seem so unreasonable after all.

But my airplane was still perched in his oat field. With Buck's help I got the tubing repaired, and he helped me put new fabric on, including applying aircraft dope, which shrinks and tautens the cloth. I forget why the engine quit, but I remember Buck helping me to get it running again. Finally the airplane was ready to fly.

With me was my ticket seller, Tommy Cassutt, who was then a youngster enthusiastic over flying. He later became a military pilot, then an airline captain. Tommy and I were loading the plane, ready to leave, when the cranky farmer again appeared.

"You can't take off in this field," he said in no uncertain tone.

But I explained, "I have to. There's no other way to get out."

"Can't you just kind of jump it over the fence?"

"If I ever get this airplane as high as your damned fence you'll never see me again," I said.

"Don't get smart with me, young man," he said. "I'll seize your airplane."

"It's not mine. You can have it," I snarled.

But he really didn't want it. Walking off, he shook a finger at me. "You can't take off in my oats!"

I told Tommy, "We've got to go. Now." But the wind was wrong. A high-voltage wire hung across the south end of the field. A light breeze blew from that direction. "Jump in. We'll give her all she'll take," I said. "I'll try it downwind."

We roared down the field, oats and stalks flying. She wouldn't fly. There was too much drag. I had to chop the engine before we reached the fence. "Tommy, jump out and take the train to Crookston," I said. "I'll meet you there."

Tommy leaped out and I took off, upwind this time. I managed to get the old Cessna off the ground and just cleared the high-voltage wire by "pulling on my bootstraps." Once in the air, I circled and looked down. The farmer came boiling across the pasture. As I watched, he strode up to Tommy, anger in his every motion. "Poor Tommy," I thought.

I flew to Crookston. That night when the train arrived, Tommy got off wearing a big grin. "That guy was sure sore at you," he said. "He chewed me out. Then I said, 'You think you're mad at him, look what he did to me. I don't have anywhere to go, and I don't have any money. I'm as sore as you are.'"

At that, Tommy said the farmer put his arm around his shoulder as if they had a mutual enemy. They walked to the farmer's place and the old guy drove him to the depot. All the way they commiserated with each other, agreeing that I was a real bastard.

I felt badly about it, and hoped that those knocked-down oat stalks managed to straighten up.

My many engine failures since I'd started flying made me feel as if I were jinxed. In six years, before starting to fly in Alaska, I logged 49 forced landings from the engine quitting in flight. I survived because I flew in farming country, where I could always find a field to land in. Or I flew over frozen lakes, where the ice offered a landing field of unlimited size. For most of the rest of my flying career, when in a single-engine airplane, I went out of my way to follow a route offering the most emergency landing spots.

I had some engine failures when I flew multi-engine planes. But in those incidents, the engines went out one at a time, and I was able to remain in the air. I suppose that I was overly cautious, for I often added 10 or 15 minutes to a trip because I chose a longer route to remain near a place to land. Some companies would probably have frowned at that had they known. But my caution gave me a chance to save the plane, or at least the occupants.

I hated to fly across any extensive stretch of water with a single-engine airplane. Even when I flew multi-engine airplanes, I had a yen to stay over land, and to fly where a walk-away-from emergency landing was possible. I did have engines stop when I was over ocean and far from land a couple of times.

In Alaska a fellow pilot who had noticed my sometimes-erratic flying routes once asked, "Are you afraid to fly over water?"

"Damned right I am. I even look for the narrowest place to cross the Yukon River," I answered. I didn't tell him how I acquired my phobia.

A good example of my engine-failure jinx occurred in 1937 with a Velie 65-horsepower, radial-engine-powered Monocoupe. It was owned by my friend Erling Mickalson, who had built the Bergholt Sport Monoplane. "You've got to fly it, Rudy. It climbs like a homesick angel," Erling claimed. Over the years I've flown a lot of planes that supposedly had that heavenly persuasion: most such traits were in the imaginations of their owners.

I climbed into this homesick angel and discovered that it performed no better than the old OX-5-powered planes that I had been flying. One day when I was flying it, the engine quit. Down I went into a beautiful field of ripe wheat. When the wheels hit that wheat I thought I was going to nose over, but I managed to prevent it. The Monocoupe had a straight bar across the axle between the wheels, and it sliced the wheat off clean about a foot above the ground. The grain looked as if someone had landed with a mower.

I was on my guard immediately, fearing the wrath of the farmer. The wheat farmer's house was half-a-mile away behind a row of high trees and he didn't see me or my plane. But there was no way I could have taken off in that high wheat, even if the engine had been running, so I hitchhiked to town and told friends of my dilemma.

Four of us took a pickup truck and some planks to retrieve the Monocoupe. Manhandling the plane backward along the mowed section where I had landed, we then cut the fence to get it to the road. We laid the planks across the ditch beside the road, and pulled the plane across. One of the fellows hurriedly patched the fence. We lashed the tail of the airplane to the bed of the pickup and towed it to town.

I wanted to go back and do a first-class job repairing that fence, but I was afraid the farmer would catch me. I've often wondered if he ever figured out what happened to his wheat and his fence.

The longer I flew the more wary I became, because occasionally I saw others killed or maimed by airplanes. A spinning airplane propeller once hit me, and after that I treated every propeller as if the engine it was fastened to were ready to start. The incident happened in 1936 at Crookston, Minnesota, when I was teaching Junius Holte, part owner of the airplane we used to fly. Junius had spent little time with the aircraft, an OX-5 Waco 90 biplane, and I didn't blame him for the accident.

The regular magneto switch for that airplane had been replaced with a simple old-fashioned knife-blade switch. When the switch was closed, it grounded the magneto and the engine stopped. When the switch was open, the engine was hot, ready to start. The airplane had to be started by pulling the eight-foot wooden propeller through. Normally, with an OX-5 engine it was necessary to pull a propeller through several times to prime it. On

Junius's airplane this was done with the switch off (knife-blade closed).

Junius sat in the rear cockpit. I called, "Switch off." He gave the proper reply, "Switch off." But he was confused. The knife-blade switch was really open ("on").

I gave the propeller a tremendous swing, thinking I was priming the engine. It was the first time I ever saw an OX-5 start on the first pull without a few priming pulls. The throttle was wide open. The engine immediately ran up to about 1,300 rpms as the plane stood with wheels blocked. What happened next took place in an instant, but I remember it as if it had occurred in slow motion.

I was standing perhaps a foot from the propeller, and its wash started to pull me in. My first thought was to put my hand on the spinner (the streamlined nose piece on a propeller), but there was no spinner—just the nut with cotter keys which would have made instant hamburger of my hand.

The only way I could get away was to bend my knee slightly for leverage. This put my leg in line with the spinning propeller. The wooden propeller hit me and instantly shattered. We later found about 12 inches missing from each end. The pieces were tossed a good 100 yards. I backed away. Junius was glassy-eyed, frozen, shocked because he had heard and felt the impact of the propeller on me.

I walked to the cockpit and called, "Hey, shut it off. I got hit by the propeller." He didn't respond, so I reached in and closed the switch.

By the time I reached his father, who was a doctor, a few blocks away, a blood blister had raised on my leg that was so large the nurse and doctor couldn't get my pants off. It was as big as a large grapefruit.

I lay in bed for a few days, used a cane for a couple of weeks, and my leg healed. I still have a few tiny scars above my knee. I guess if that prop had hit the kneecap, I'd have been crippled for life. One result was that for about five years I could not wear the accepted uniform of pilots of the era—breeches or pants tucked inside 18-inch-high laced leather boots. Tucked-in pants or a too-tight sock caused the leg to swell.

Sometimes our forced landings included a bit of humor. Once Roy Duggan, flying out of Milwaukee in the late 1920s, had an engine failure and landed in a big strawberry patch. The strawberry plants suffered only minor damage. The owner was upset at Duggan. He berated Duggan while Duggan repaired the plane's engine.

Roy tried to explain that the engine had failed, and that without the engine, the airplane couldn't fly. But the man insisted, "You'll have to pay for damages."

Roy had no money, but he agreed to sign a contract guaranteeing payment. The man's wife arrived with pen and paper and they wrote a detailed, official-looking contract that included Duggan's name and address, the N number of his airplane, and the date. The owner of the strawberries signed it, his wife signed it, then Duggan carefully read it. "This is only fair," said Duggan as he put it on the wing of the plane and signed it.

Then Duggan carefully folded the contract and put it in his pocket. He shook hands with the couple, then took off.

Air Shows

CROWD OF 2,000 AT OTIS AIR SHOW
Stunt Flying by Duluth, Waseca and Bemidji Pilots Thrilled Large Crowd

The thrill of the day to most of the estimated 2,000 people who witnessed the air show at the Otis airport on Sugar Lake Sunday was the long tailspin performed by Rudy Billberg of Duluth in a Challenger Travelaire bi-plane which carried the ship dangerously close to the ground before Billberg straightened it out.

    The Travelaire was one of ten planes which were at the Otis landing field to stunt for the crowd and to bring visitors from Duluth, Bemidji and Waseca. . . .

—Front page of the Grand Rapids,
Itasca County (Minnesota),
INDEPENDENT, August 5, 1938.

WHEN BARNSTORMING got slow, pilots often put on an air show, where they would sell rides, perform acrobatics, and stage parachute jumps. Occasionally, really hazardous stunts were performed, but usually they looked more dangerous than they were. Wing-walking or hanging from the wing or landing gear was usually performed by professionals who had their act down cold. Whatever was offered, air shows usually attracted crowds.

There are many stories about the air shows of the time. One that has always tickled me was recounted by barnstormers I knew, about a parachute jump staged by Verne Roberts. Roberts flew as a barnstormer at air shows or wherever there was a large crowd. I never met him, but like most midwestern barnstormers of the time, I knew of him.

A grandstand stood on the outskirts of Bemidji, and next to it was a racetrack. Beyond the racetrack was a florist's farm with acres of flowers. Just beyond that was a cemetery.

During one particular auto race the grandstand was full of people. Roberts had advertised that during the race Captain Hayfoot would make a parachute jump near the grandstand. Immediately afterward, Roberts and his airplane would be available to fly passengers.

He flew over the grandstand, did a few loops, and roared around low, attracting attention. Within minutes everyone was watching him. He then climbed high for Captain Hayfoot's parachute leap. He reached 2,000 or 3,000 feet, then pushed out a dummy stuffed with hay and attached to a parachute. The parachute didn't open. As hundreds watched, the dummy and the streaming chute plunged into the cemetery. Of course people didn't know it was a dummy: they thought it was a live Captain Hayfoot, and he had just smashed into the graveyard.

En masse, the crowd left the grandstand, ran across the racetrack, trampled acres of flowers, and crowded into the graveyard to see what remained of Captain Hayfoot. Roberts circled long enough to see the damage done to the flowers and cemetery by the trampling crowd. When last seen, he was flying southwest. Among barnstormers it was known that Roberts was afraid to return to Bemidji.

I participated in many air shows in the Midwest during the 1930s. Often Duggan and I would put one on. We would advertise, and maybe circulate handbills telling of parachute jumps or other spectacular events we had planned. Often there were motorcycle crashes, in which a motorcycle would crash through a tiny board wall built in front of the grandstand. Sometimes the wall was set afire just before the motorcyclist did his thing.

The handbills would call us the "Flying Aces" or some other silly name, describing us as "skilled acrobatic pilots." I wasn't really very skilled, and the acrobatics were not great. What they amounted to was absolute wildcat flying that scared people half to death. Of course many people came half fearing we would kill ourselves and half fearing we wouldn't.

What acrobatics I knew I learned from Roy Duggan and others. Precision, perfection, smoothness, and coordination were not yet visible in my performances. I think that most of the time I looked like a disaster about to happen. The people loved it, but it wasn't as dangerous as it looked. Precision acrobatics came to me later; I taught it in a government training program of pre–World War II.

We did it for the money, of course, and for the love of flying. Even today, when I think of air shows, I envision flashing wings, the high-pitched whine of airplane engines, and the pungent odor of aviation gasoline. Air shows now feature fantastic demonstrations by tremendously skilled pilots flying airplanes specifically designed for aerobatics. Modern pilots perform maneuvers and fly with a precision that we could scarcely have envisioned in the 1930s.

Fortunately for us, at that time the average person didn't recognize great flying skill or precision flying. We simply flew in a way that appeared as if at any moment the airplane was going to fall out of the sky and crash. We looped and spun and snap-rolled and dove, making a lot of racket. The crowd kept waiting for someone to crash, and they were thrilled. They especially loved low-level flying, and we gave them plenty of that.

Once in a while I'd make a few dollars. In 1937 I did especially well at the Tri-State Fair at Superior, Wisconsin. I barnstormed and did acrobatics, and by the end of the fair, money was burning a hole in my pocket. So that fall, I decided to explore the Far North. The lure of Alaska had hold of me even then. A friend and fellow pilot, Milt Nelson, and I drove to Seattle, sleeping in his panel truck at night. We caught a ship to Juneau and arrived about the time all the salmon canneries were closing. We looked for a flying job, and, fortunately, there were none. If I had landed a job I wouldn't have been qualified: the wet weather and float flying among the great forested mountains of southeastern Alaska would have been utterly foreign to me. I returned home and continued flying in the Midwest, but Alaska was still on my mind.

I started flying some of the lighter planes when they became available. The Piper Cub, for example, was so much easier to handle than the big, clumsy, older airplanes that I liked to use it at air shows. One of my favorite demonstrations was a long tailspin. I would climb, not too high, and spin 12 or 13 or so turns— just letting her grind right down—until I was close to the ground. Then I would straighten and pull her out. People liked that. I almost hit the ground a couple of times through carelessness, but usually it was not a dangerous maneuver. Once I spun down behind a little hill out of sight of the crowd, and by the time I flew out from behind the hill, people had started to run across the field to view the crash.

During one air show I slow-rolled a Challenger-powered Travel Air 2000—a two-cockpit biplane. Originally it was powered with a 90-horsepower engine, but the Challenger produced 185 horsepower and made the airplane a good performer. I was at perhaps 900 feet when I rolled the plane on its back in front of the crowd. I hadn't bothered to clean the cockpit, and there was all sorts of junk on the floor. Dust, mud, dirt, paper, gravel, a tin can or two, screws, nuts, and I don't know what all cascaded out. Some of the dust and dirt got under my goggles and into my eyes. I was in instant trouble. I finished the roll absolutely blind. I was able to rub my eyes enough to see a little, so I could land. That was probably the closest I ever came to completely losing control of an airplane. I never rolled an airplane again without making sure the floor was clean.

Most of the 1920s and 1930s biplanes that I flew had no airspeed indicator, and I learned to fly them by sound and by feel—the sound of the wind in the wires and wings, and the feel at the seat of my pants. That was a normal part of learning to fly then, and a part that has changed in more recent years.

Once in a while I flew a biplane with what we called a Johnson airspeed indicator. Bolted to a strut, it was a gadget with a lever on which was a blade that caught the wind, with numbers that ran up to about 90 miles per hour (not many OX-5-powered planes could fly any faster). Air pressure pushed the lever to the appropriate spot. It wasn't very accurate. The only time I ever looked at it was when I wanted to see how fast I was cruising. For landings, when flying speed is critical, I learned that sound-and-feel was more accurate.

Some of the air show barnstormers I knew were truly precision pilots—eagles, in my view. Some later became airline pilots. John Walatka, who eventually became a much-loved and well-known bush pilot in Alaska, was an acrobatic pilot who flew with the grace of a ballet dancer. My first meeting with John is still a vivid memory: I was sitting cross-legged on the ground near Roseau, dreamily chewing on a timothy straw and waiting for a friend to return with the OX-5 Travel Air we were taking turns flying. I couldn't hear the OX-5, but I suddenly came alive when I heard the familiar throbbing bark of a Curtiss Challenger engine. Jumping to my feet, I quickly located the visiting plane. It was a Curtiss Robin headed straight toward our field.

The Robin wasn't up very high, perhaps 500 or 600 feet. Instead of entering a normal traffic pattern, it flew directly overhead. As I peered up at it, the plane suddenly executed a flawless snap roll. This brought me wide awake, for I hadn't thought of the Robin as a snap-roll–type airplane, nor would I have dared do a snap roll so close to the ground.

The ship landed, taxied up, and three men got out. They asked me how to get a ride to town. Two of the men were slightly inebriated businessmen. John Walatka, the third man and the pilot, was the one who caught my eye. John was six or seven years older than I, with large bones. He was well padded, but not fat. He walked like a rag doll about to collapse. I had never seen a man appear so completely relaxed. All of his joints seemed about to unhook. At first I thought he too had been drinking, but he hadn't. Maybe a nip, but no more.

I soon learned that he was in no way about to collapse—he was in complete control. And as time passed, I also learned that he was a superb pilot and a sought-after airplane and engine mechanic. Less than a year later, in the spring of 1936, John invited me to Bemidji, where he was manager of the airport, and I leaped at the opportunity. He let me live with him. I helped with chores around the field, and he allowed me to use his J-2 Cub to fly passengers, to teach students, and to practice for my transport license. In this way, I could earn a little money to live on. We developed a good working relationship.

John was a compulsive practical joker, and I became wary as a wolf. It was not uncommon to find the tail skid of my plane tied to a fence; or, after I had cranked my heart out trying to start an airplane engine by pulling the prop through, to find that the spark plug wires were disconnected. When I would find the problem, I'd often hear his laughter from around a corner.

At the time, the Works Progress Administration (WPA) was building a hangar at the Bemidji airport, and workmen left their lunch boxes on a bench in a large tool shed near the hangar. John thought it was great fun to take out the lunches, drive a nail through the bottom of the boxes into the bench, and then replace the sandwiches. At lunchtime the men grabbed their buckets, usually on the run, only to be almost jerked off their feet. Everyone knew who did it, but John was a big man and no one did more than protest.

I was sitting on that same bench one day, leaning against the wall with my legs pulled in close, eating an apple. I wore a newly pressed pair of pants with a sharp crease sticking out probably three inches in front of my shin. Suddenly, I heard the sound of a shot. I looked around and saw John straightening up from beside the bench vise with a .22 rifle in his hand.

"Look at your pants," he called, with a crazy grin on his face. I grabbed the cuff area of my pants leg, and sure enough there was a clean bullet hole through the crease. I was shaken, and let out a few choice adjectives, ending with, "Damn you Walatka, you'll pay for this one."

I bided my time. One day John was to meet with the city fathers on airport business. He went to town and bought the fanciest necktie that money could buy. He put it on and returned to the field. I caught sight of him as he ran up to various WPA workers with his thumb holding out the tie. "How'dya like that. Ain't it snazzy?" he asked. I knew my time had come.

I ran into the shed and sharpened my jackknife to a razor edge, then came out and waited. Soon he arrived, walking fast with his thumb under the tie. He yelled even before he got to me. "Hey Rudy, look at my tie. How do you like it?"

"Boy, that's a beauty," I said, as I walked up and took hold of the tie, presumably the better to see it. I quickly ran my left hand up to the knot, and with a swift thrust of my right hand I cut the tie off right below the knot. I remained alive only because I was quick and could run faster than John. Fortunately, he didn't hold a grudge. I went back to work the next morning.

I remember an air show in North Dakota during the 1930s in which a pilot flew who was regarded as the North Dakota acrobatic champion. He was a fine pilot, and I wished I could fly like he did. But John Walatka, who also flew at that show, outflew him in every way. John sometimes appeared reckless and devil-may-care, but when it came to flying, he wasn't at all careless: he could make an airplane perform as few could. He was a born eagle.

Roy Duggan was also an excellent acrobatic pilot. He was not as wild as I was. His moves were precise, smooth, coordinated, and carefully planned. He was a Tex Rankin type, who flew perfect acrobatics that seemed less spectacular to the average viewer.

I almost made a parachute jump during the summer I worked with John at Bemidji. We planned an air show one weekend at some sort of a gathering, and figured our audience would like to see a jump. Although John had jumped five times, I had never used a parachute. "Why not let me make the jump?" I suggested, and he agreed.

We couldn't afford to buy parachutes but were able to rent them from a St. Paul company which sent them out by train. A day or two before the two parachutes arrived (jumpers wore two: one as backup), I managed to obtain use of an airplane in which I could haul passengers and make a few dollars during the air show.

When we used or borrowed an airplane, we usually paid the owner in one way or another. Sometimes it was a share of the income from flying passengers. Sometimes we'd repay an owner by giving him flight instructions, for many of the planes we used were owned by nonpilot businessmen. With borrowed airplanes we checked them over carefully before flying. I would make an exterior check, and where possible I had a mechanic make an interior check of hidden cables, fittings, and the engine. Engines of the time were exposed and easy to get at. Most engine work in the field consisted of pulling the propeller through as a compression check, changing spark plugs, sometimes retiming magnetos and changing magneto points. Daily we drained carburetors and a bit of gasoline from fuel tanks, to eliminate settled water and dirt.

Rusty Elliot, a developing young pilot, came to me and suggested that he make the parachute jump for the $10 fee. After all, he pointed out, I would be making money flying passengers.

Ten bucks was about a week's wages for many workers in those days. This was logical, so I agreed to forgo the jump in his favor.

On the day of our air show, the weather was nice, although a little windy. When time came for the parachute jump, John Walatka took Rusty to about 2,500 feet and Rusty leaped out of the airplane. He was using a 24-foot parachute, the size commonly used in those days, which lands a person reasonably hard. He descended near the edge of a pine forest. I thought I saw his parachute deflect slightly, maybe from a downdraft pouring off the trees. Moments later when Rusty landed, we all went to help him pick up the chute.

When we reached him Rusty was lying on the ground. His back was broken. For months, Rusty lay over an arched frame while his back healed. Eventually he recovered and resumed flying. But within a year, he crashed an OX-5 Travel Air, killing himself and his passenger.

Era's End

"DO SOME EIGHTS!" the flight inspector yelled from the front seat of the roaring Tank-powered Waco 10—the same biplane I had soloed in. I really didn't know how to "do eights," but I picked a couple of crossroads not far apart and flew a figure eight around them, which seemed to satisfy the inspector. Next, he had me do a couple of touch-and-go landings, and then he asked me to land and bring the plane to a stop.

"The eights were fine. You been practicing your spins?" he asked, as we stood beside the plane.

"Oh yes," I answered. And I had. Before taking the flight test I had practiced spins and what I thought were figure eights. I had also practiced dead-stick landings, although I felt I had more than enough experience in that category. But I had practiced mostly on my own. Duggan wasn't always around, and I didn't have anyone to teach me the maneuvers on which I was to be tested. Later I discovered that the figure eights I flew for the inspector were accidentally acceptable.

The Air Commerce Act of 1926 required the licensing of pilots and mechanics and the registration and certification of aircraft, and it regulated air traffic. In the 1930s, however, enforcement was lax, mostly because of low staffing of the Civil Aeronautics Authority (CAA, now the Federal Aviation Administration).

Then, pilots could earn three types of licenses: private, which required 10 hours of solo time; limited commercial, which required 50 hours of solo time; and transport, which required 200 hours of solo time. The transport license was equivalent to the commercial license of today, and pilots who had it were automatically licensed instructors. There was no separate instructor's rating, as there is now.

I had 50 hours of logged solo time in licensed aircraft—and much more time that was not logged in unlicensed planes. I had been barnstorming for some time, but technically I could not legally fly passengers. It was time for me to become legal. I decided to try for the limited commercial, which allowed a pilot to fly passengers for hire within 10 miles of his base airport. This would allow me to earn money so I could continue to fly.

"Take her up and do some spins," the inspector said, handing me a parachute. I looked the chute over, and fiddled with it. I didn't know how to put it on.

"So you've been practicing your spins," he said, sarcastically, shaking his head. Pilots were supposed to wear a parachute whenever doing spins. "Show this guy how to put this parachute on," he told another pilot who was standing nearby.

Wearing the parachute, I climbed the Waco 10 high above the field. I pulled the plane's nose up until the airplane quit flying. When the Waco stalled, it fell off on one wing and started to spin. I let it whirl around twice, and then straightened out. Precision was required—I was expected to come out flying in the same direction that I had been before the spin. I landed, and the inspector just nodded and wrote out a limited commercial license for me. It was August 3, 1936. For the first time I could legally fly passengers.

Flying from Roseau, which I had listed as my base, was limited, and soon I decided to interpret the law in my own way. I figured I could haul passengers within 10 miles of any place I landed and consider wherever I landed as temporarily my base. So I went wheeling all over the country hauling passengers again, having fun, and building time.

Eventually, I decided to try for the transport license. Again, I had had very little training for the flight test. I rented a Taylorcraft and hired an instructor to show me some of the maneuvers I needed to know.

A rather arrogant inspector came through Bemidji, flying a new Fairchild 24 provided by the Department of Commerce. One evening I volunteered to shove the Fairchild into a hangar for him. Wouldn't you know, I pushed that brand new airplane into a two-by-four and tore the fabric. I believe the inspector thought I did it deliberately.

The next day I approached him about taking the check ride. "Go shoot a few spot landings," he said. "I'll watch to see if you're qualified to take the test."

I took off with the Taylorcraft as he stood near the runway. On my first approach I saw I was far short, so I gunned the engine to bring the plane to the proper spot.

Johnny Walatka was standing near the inspector. Wanting to help me out, he said, "Well, by God, he's clearing his engine," which was something we had to do in those days. It kept the engine from loading up with too much fuel.

"Clearing it, hell," said the inspector. "He's wearing it out!" When I landed, he said, "You'd better practice some more."

There was nothing for me to do but practice. But he did agree to give me the written part of the test. While I sat waiting for him to arrive to administer the test, I read a newspaper, and for the first time I could recall, I saw a weather map in that paper. "Weather map" was listed as a subject in my upcoming test, so I studied it for some time.

Sure enough, one of the sections of the test directed, "Draw a weather map." I drew the map I had just seen in the newspaper and I passed the test with a good mark.

Returning to Roseau, I tried to practice maneuvers, but it was difficult without an instructor. Some weeks later I ferried a new Taylorcraft to Minnesota from Ohio for a fellow, and he allowed me to use it to take the flight test.

I flew the T-Craft to Fargo, North Dakota, where there was a permanent flight inspector. He was hardboiled, and I was young, naive, and a little afraid of him. We got into the T-Craft and I took off. We flew various maneuvers. Some I didn't do well. When that happened, he took over the controls and demonstrated how the maneuver should be flown. "Now you try it," he would say. I tried it, and it went well.

We landed and walked to his office. He sat behind his desk with a sour look and typed out my license. Once he looked up and said, "If you'd stayed home and practiced instead of running all over hell hauling passengers you'd have done a better job." The pilots' grapevine had kept him informed of who was flying where and when. He had known all along about my illegal flying.

He handed me the license, saying, "I guess you won't hurt yourself." I grabbed it and ran before he could change his mind. That was on June 28, 1937.

During the 1930s many pilots flew without licenses, and no one really thought about formalities. We also commonly flew unlicensed aircraft. We had our own code, and as far as our experience, education, and knowledge allowed, we flew safely. An unlicensed airplane didn't necessarily mean it wasn't airworthy. It simply meant that the Department of Commerce hadn't inspected it. Usually the pilot didn't have enough money to fly it to where it could be inspected. Slowly, as the CAA expanded and as aviation developed, unlicensed airplanes and pilots became things of the past.

By 1938, it was clear that the barnstorming era was ending. Flying was a growing industry, and many barnstormers were finding steady work as transport pilots, crop dusters, or flight instructors. Americans were now more familiar with airplanes. An airplane in a field beside the road wasn't the curiosity it once had been.

My father was working in Duluth, and I decided to move there. He was no longer superintendent of schools, but had been appointed to the railroad and warehouse commission, a state job, which kept him in Duluth. My mother lived there winters, but had to spend summers at Roseau helping my brother run the farm. I hung around the Duluth Airport until I was able to use an airplane to haul passengers and do a little flight instructing.

I could have become a smuggler. Once, in Bemidji, I was eating in a restaurant. A stranger sat down next to me. He knew my name and that I was a pilot. He talked around and around a subject, speaking softly so no one else could hear. He represented a fur company, he said, and wanted me to fly some furs between Canada and the United States. "Big money for you, with no risk," he wheedled. I never did understand whether the fur was to be flown from Canada to the United States, or vice versa. Not interested in the possibility of going to jail, I firmly said no.

About then I flew a man from Duluth to Lake LaCroix, on the Minnesota-Canada border. Flying a Luscombe on skis, I landed on the ice in front of his beautiful home. His wife and young daughter ran out to the plane to meet him.

A week later, Joe Brickner, a federal game warden, came to the airport and wanted to know what my Lake LaCroix passenger had in the way of freight, and what I had brought back. I told him the man had no freight and I didn't fly anything back, but Joe didn't believe me and hung around watching me for weeks. When he finally realized I wasn't flying contraband across the border, we became friends and he continued to come to the airport simply to visit.

In 1939, I married Bessie Hagen. I had met Bessie four years earlier, when I was flying passengers one fall at the Roseau fair on a field just north of our farm. I went home for lunch, and my sister Helen introduced me to Bessie, a 15-year-old girl whom she had just met. Of course, a girl that age was just a child to a man of 19, but I didn't forget her because she was really pretty. With our family living part time in Duluth, Bessie and Helen spent a lot of time together because Bessie lived in Duluth. By then Bessie was no longer a child—she was a beautiful young woman, and I fell for her hard. We started going out together. On one of our first dates I took her for an airplane ride. On another date, I flew acrobatics with her in the plane. She seemed to enjoy herself.

We were married a year later. I flew us to Otis Lodge, a popular resort on a little lake near Grand Rapids, Minnesota, where we had a one-day honeymoon.

I started to teach Bessie to fly, but soon our daughter, Cathy, was on the way. Flight training ended, and Bessie never did learn to fly. She is, however, an excellent navigator, and she knows what to do around an airplane. She could always get more stuff in an airplane than I could, so she has always been the official loadmaster.

For half a century, Bessie has been my love and my partner. She has put up with my fiddle-footed ways, staying with me when I jumped from one job to another or from a good job to unemployment. I have repeatedly worked myself into top aviation positions—check pilot, captain, station manager. But these representations of success eventually paled for me, for I dislike regimentation and repetition. I left many a position of security for the unknown, seeking fresh adventures, new fields to conquer, other challenges. Dozens of times Bessie has packed our possessions for our moves with a smile, meeting our new challenges head-on.

At Duluth, I became acquainted with Harry Peterson, an aircraft mechanic, and the flying opportunity of a lifetime presented itself. The federal government was starting a Civilian Pilot Training (CPT) program—the result, I think, of some forward-thinking people who suspected we were on the verge of a war in which many pilots would be needed. Harry proposed a partnership: he would buy the airplanes and, in conformance with the CPT program, we would train students from scratch to a commercial rating.

The students for our school came mostly from a junior college in Duluth. The government paid all costs, and 10 students were assigned to each instructor. The first airplane that Peterson bought was a new, 50-horsepower Luscombe. It had two-place side-by-side seating, was all metal, and aerobatic-approved. I went by bus to the Luscombe factory in Trenton, New Jersey, to get the plane.

I took off from Trenton airport with the brand spanking new Luscombe—it even smelled new—and set a compass course for Minnesota. After about 45 minutes, none of the landmarks checked out with my maps. I suddenly realized that instead of flying west, I was flying south—the compass was faulty.

I returned to Trenton and the Luscombe factory and told them that the compass hadn't been swung and needed compensating. No one at the factory knew how to do it. Roy Duggan had shown me this simple procedure. One of the Luscombe mechanics helped, as I propped the tail on a box and swung the compass by adjusting tiny internal magnets. The compass indicated the proper reading at various headings, and I again took off for Minnesota. Crossing the Alleghenies, I gained my first experience in mountain flying.

After a day or two I flew over a huge hangar at an airport. A hurried map check showed me to be at Akron, Ohio, and over the Goodyear blimp hangar. The compass was still off: I was flying too far to the south.

As I approached Gary, Indiana, late one afternoon, I flew into an increasingly heavy snowstorm. It became obvious that I wasn't going to make it to an airport. I found a farmer's field that looked promising, and set her down. My experience as a barnstormer made it easy. The farmer rushed out, excited at seeing an airplane land in his pasture, and he insisted that I stay the night with him.

The snowstorm had passed by morning, leaving five or six inches of loose snow on the ground. I was able to stomp enough of it down in front of the Luscombe so the airplane could lift off, and I flew on to Madison, Wisconsin. A cross-country flight by small airplane was unusual in those days—so unusual that I was interviewed on a Madison radio station for about 15 minutes shortly after my arrival.

From Madison, I followed a high-tension line across Wisconsin, found an airport at a little town, landed, and tied the plane down for the night. I was wondering how I was going to get in to town to find a room when a tall, friendly fellow came along, who introduced himself as Max Conrad and drove me to a hotel. The name meant nothing to me until a few years later when the famous Armistice Day blizzard struck the Midwest. Dozens of duck hunters were stranded on the Mississippi flats. Conrad, flying in terrible weather, found many of the hunters and directed aid to them. He saved I don't know how many lives at great risk to his own.

Later, he became a famed transoceanic flyer, known as "the flying grandfather." During his years as a pilot, Max Conrad logged 52,929 hours in the air—some sort of a record, I'm sure. He was one of the true eagles I met over the years.

I reached Minneapolis the next day, near dark, and telephoned Harry Peterson to tell him I planned to stop for the night. He urged me to fly on to Duluth, despite the darkness. "We'll put out lanterns for you," he promised (there were no lights at the Duluth Airport).

I found the dimly lit field with a dozen or so lanterns around it and carefully landed. It doesn't sound like much today, but in the late 1930s a brand new airplane was something to celebrate. I think every aviator at and around Duluth came to admire that little Luscombe.

As the CPT program grew, we acquired more Luscombes, with 65-horsepower engines; a Wright-powered, five-place Gullwing Stinson, which, as I recall, we bought used, for $1,800;

and a metal-fuselage, fabric-wing Meyers biplane, powered with a 145-horsepower Warner engine. We used the Meyers for teaching acrobatics, and we flew in that open-cockpit plane even during winter. The cold was bearable only because we wore heavy flying suits.

Roy Duggan had been flying mail, passengers, and freight in the Lake of the Woods country of northern Minnesota for several years. He got wind of the CPT program and showed up to get in on it. He had gone to Ohio to fly the Meyers biplane back for us. Upon arrival, he was full of four-letter adjectives, calling the aircraft the "Goddamned no good Meyers no purpose biplane."

The airplane *was* underpowered, but for our use it was satisfactory. That airplane flew many hours of inverted flight. To keep the engine running when we flew the Meyers upside down, we had to continuously work a hand-powered fuel pump. The Meyers wasn't alone in flying inverted; for more than a year, I believe I flew upside down more than right side up, as I instructed students in acrobatics.

It was a noisy operation. When our students practiced acrobatics solo, sometimes they extended the maneuvers beyond what they should have. We could hear engines screaming from 10 miles or more. We always stood listening until the engine sound was again normal.

Early in the program, Duggan and I went to Boston to take a course in navigation from Northeast Airlines. I've never heard the last of that trip. Duggan and his wife, Christine, and Bessie and I decided that since we hadn't had proper honeymoons, we'd go by way of Niagara Falls and make it a honeymoon trip.

The four of us traveled in my new Oldsmobile. More than 50 years later, Bessie and Christine still remind us that Roy and I, each puffing a cigar, walked ahead, while the two brides followed in our wake wherever we went on that "honeymoon." I suppose it wasn't very romantic.

While learning navigation in Boston, we flew all over New England on practice flights. When we returned to Minnesota, we taught both ground school and flying.

The government established new ratings, and Duggan and I went through a re-rating program. For the first time, we had special licenses to give flight instruction. I was appointed one of the first flight examiners to issue private licenses for the Duluth district. I also became a flight examiner for acrobatics, after taking several courses in acrobatics. I could check out acrobatics instructors. In that position, I had to fail a few students, including one girl, and I hated that responsibility. But if a student could not learn to fly, he or she had no business at the controls of a plane. Such a pilot is a hazard to all.

Some of the CPT administrators tried to devise a means of selecting a potentially good pilot before flight training. They reasoned that if this could be done, we would not waste time trying to teach the hopeless ones to fly. They developed a complex questionnaire. Those who completed the form had to reveal information about their hobbies, the books they read, their interest in sports, what kind of clothing they liked, and so on. I think the administrators hoped that if someone liked sauerkraut and beans, he or she would automatically make a good pilot.

It didn't work. The study revealed no traits in common that marked a person with aptitude for flying. It was just the opposite: good pilots were as diversified as any group could be, with no set behavior or interest patterns.

When the war started, many of our students went to Randolph, Kelly, and other military fields to continue training for military flying. I've never heard from any of those I taught to fly in those years. I did hear through the aviation grapevine of some who came back from World War II with many decorations for their flying exploits. I also learned of a few who were killed in action.

One day in the spring of 1941, a tall, slow-talking pilot walked into the Duluth hangar and introduced himself as Sigurd Wien. He had grown up in Cook, Minnesota. He was now flying in Alaska. I realized instantly he was the brother of Noel Wien, one of my heroes, and I was thrilled.

Sig had flown to Duluth to carry out an unpleasant errand. One of his pilots, a Minnesotan named Johnson, also from Cook, had been killed in a flying accident in Alaska. Wien had accompanied the body home for burial.

After we talked for a while, I asked, "Is there any chance of a guy getting to fly in Alaska?"

"Sure," he answered. "Why don't you come up and fly for me?"

I almost fell over. I couldn't believe it. I had long dreamed of flying in Alaska, and had even made one abortive try to do so. There was a saying in the aviation profession that Alaska's pilots were the world's best because they had to be. I wanted to be one of the world's best.

I stammered that I'd have to find someone to take my place at the school. And Sig said, "There's no rush."

Shortly after that, a letter arrived confirming that I was hired to fly for Wien Airlines* in Alaska. I wrote to Sig that I wanted to bring my family. I didn't know it, but in those days it impressed Alaskan employers when a man wanted to bring his family; it indicated that the guy planned to stay. He replied, "Come when you can." A boyhood dream was coming true.

---

* Between 1928 and 1985, airlines named for the Wien family were called Wien Alaska Airways, Wien Airways of Alaska, Inc., Wien Air Alaska, Wien Alaska Airlines, and Wien Consolidated Airlines. "Wien Airways" and "Wien Airlines" were commonly used to refer to these variously named companies.

The Alaska Years

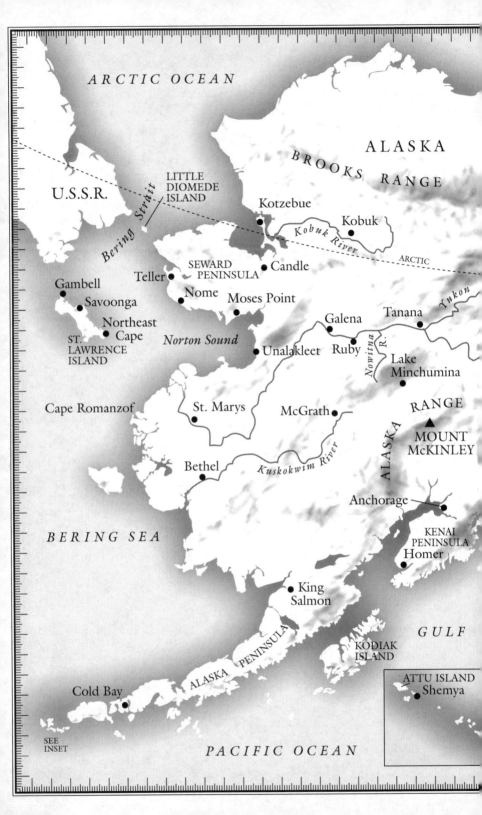

Alaska

IN 1941, THE interior Alaska town of Fairbanks was simple, uncrowded, charming. Log homes and buildings dominated. Weeks Field, the airport, was at the edge of town. The view of the great snow-clad peaks of the Alaska Range, 75 miles to the south, was breathtaking. The calm, dry climate was invigorating. Even today's bustling Fairbanks has a charm and a feel of the frontier that is lacking in most of Alaska's other larger cities.

Fairbanks is at the end of the railroad that runs from the coastal town of Seward. Mining and furs had long fueled the town's economy. In 1941, a military buildup was under way. Fairbanks was and still is the hub of myriad tiny settlements in the vast Interior of Alaska.

That fall, Bessie, 13-month-old Cathy, and I flew as passengers in a Northwest Airlines DC-3 from Minnesota to Seattle. I didn't have the slightest idea that soon I would be piloting one of these mammoth wonders of the air. To us the DC-3 was the height of aviation technology and luxury. From Seattle, we booked passage on the Alaska Steamship Company's SS *Denali*. It was Bessie's first time aboard a ship, but I was an old-timer, having ridden from Seattle to Juneau and back in 1937.

The coastal mountains rise steeply from the sea along the Inside Passage of southeastern Alaska, dense conifer forests crowding their lower flanks. Above treeline, the lofty peaks are rocky and snow-covered. Forested islands, big and small, sprinkle the channels and straits.

As we traveled, we gawked up at the rugged coastal ranges of British Columbia and Alaska. I had never flown in such mountains, and I wondered: what kind of air currents would I encounter among these great peaks? I had heard other pilots speak respectfully of mountain flying.

From Juneau, after waiting two days for good weather, we flew in a twin-engine Lockheed 10-A to Whitehorse, Yukon Territory. We stayed there overnight, and the next day flew on Pan American Airways' Lockheed 14 (predecessor of the Lockheed Lodestar) to Fairbanks.

Immediately, we were delighted with Fairbanks, a small town not unlike our home area in Minnesota. Trees and plants were similar. Life was slow-paced, pleasant. Everyone was friendly.

I found the Wien Airways office a short distance from Weeks Field and checked in. "You're to be stationed at Nome," said the manager. "We'll fly you and your family there as soon as we can."

I knew little about Nome, and innocently I assumed it would be like Fairbanks. I was beginning to realize that Alaska was a bewildering land of vast reaches, varied climate, and primitive conditions. I certainly didn't realize that it was one-fifth the size of all the rest of the states combined. Or, that only about 75,000 residents occupied the entire Territory.

At that time, there were only about 100 airfields and 200 airplanes in all of Alaska. The airfields ranged from narrow, crooked, over-a-mountain goat tracks, to large, improved river bars. None was paved. No government program existed to build airports in Alaska until World War II. Airplanes included mainly Stinsons, Pilgrims, Travel Airs, Cessnas, Fairchilds, Bellancas, and a few Lockheeds—all cabin planes.

After the flight from Whitehorse to Fairbanks, I began to understand the vastness of the muskeg and forest. Current maps revealed many blanks—unmapped areas—in remote regions of Alaska. I was to learn that in the Interior, where I spent most of my years, temperatures can skid to 80 degrees below zero Fahrenheit in winter, and sizzle at more than 100 degrees in summer. Mosquitoes can be so abundant that they can kill an unprepared pilot forced down in the wrong place at the wrong time.

Huge herds of caribou wandered the mountains and tundra. Moose, too, lived in great numbers in this wild land. Black bears, polar bears, and brown/grizzly bears—the latter the largest of earth's land carnivores—are still abundant in Alaska. Silver-scaled salmon pour into many coastal streams annually in a proliferation of nature that seems unreal. Yet there are thousands of square miles of barrenness—high, rocky peaks that scrape the sky, and 10,000-year-old glaciers. The glaciers—rivers of ice—in their blue-ice splendor flow slowly down many of the mountains.

Daylight hours in summer are almost continuous, and in December at Fairbanks there are but four hours of light each day. Things Alaskan seem bigger and more violent than anywhere else. It is a challenging land that can break even the strongest, and a land of opportunity for the bold.

Two or three days after our arrival at Fairbanks, Wien pilot Bill Lund arrived from Nome. He flew a four-place Cessna Airmaster powered with a 145-horsepower Warner radial engine. We were to return with him to Nome, our new home. It was late October, and it had turned cold. All of the small ponds near Fairbanks were frozen over, and fresh snow lay on the higher peaks. Bill loaded us into the Airmaster and took off.

As we flew over the frozen landscape, I reflected on how that October day in 1941 was a mere 16 years after the first commercial flight between Fairbanks and Nome. The bold pilot of that pioneering flight was Noel Wien. He flew a Fokker F. III, a huge, single-engine monoplane that was 12 feet tall at the middle of its two-foot-thick cantilevered wing. Wien sat in an open cockpit in front of the wing and next to the 240-horsepower, six-cylinder, water-cooled BMW engine. That airplane could haul 1,200 pounds, and it flew at 90 miles an hour. In the cabin, separated from the pilot, the five passengers sat on upholstered chairs and a sofalike bench. The plush cabin had a carpeted floor, with glass flower-holders on the walls.

The airplane, built in Holland in 1921, had flown passengers for KLM airlines in Europe. For $9,500, Wien had purchased it in New York for Fairbanks Airplane Company. Disassembled, this European plane was shipped to Fairbanks via the Panama Canal. The Fokker had no brakes.

On June 5, 1925, about an hour before midnight, Wien coaxed the huge ship into the air and headed for 530-mile-distant Nome. He followed the Tanana River to the Yukon River. He then flew down the Yukon. He navigated by following rivers and locating other prominant land features on a map. There was no radio. There were no landing strips, as such, between Fairbanks and Nome.

His brother Ralph rode as mechanic in the after cabin with the passengers—a mining engineer and two women—and 500 pounds of baggage. Noel expected to find sandbars along the Yukon River in case he had to make an emergency landing. In fact, he planned to land on a sandbar at Ruby, on the Yukon River, to refuel. But the river was high, and the sandbars were all covered with water, including the one at Ruby.

Half an hour beyond Ruby, wondering where he could land to refuel, Wien flew into a storm. Remembering a small, cleared spot near Ruby, he turned back. He had no choice but to land in that clearing. The big, heavily loaded Fokker touched down in the clearing, which Noel soon learned was a baseball field. It then ran uphill, over the top of a rise, and started downhill. Having flown airplanes that had no brakes, I can imagine the helpless feeling Noel must have had as his plane ran into a soft spot and slowly nosed over onto its back. The Fokker's propeller was broken and the rudder damaged, but no one was injured.

The passengers went on to Nome by boat. Noel and Ralph Wien sent to Fairbanks for a new propeller, repaired the rudder, and with help from Ruby residents, righted the airplane. In a couple of days Wien took off and flew nonstop to Nome, where he landed on the parade ground of abandoned Fort Davis, an army camp established to provide protection for early gold diggers.

Noel Wien had broken trail. That Fairbanks-Nome flight was one of Alaska's great pioneer flights. To that point, fast travel time from Fairbanks to Nome in summer had been 15 days by boat. The three passengers who had traveled by boat from Ruby to Nome arrived one day after Wien's airplane.

Noel flew the Fokker nonstop back to Fairbanks. Two years later, in 1927, with a Hisso-powered Standard, he started regular air service from Nome to Fairbanks. After six months, he purchased from explorer Sir Hubert Wilkins the Detroiter II, a four-place cabin biplane, the fifth Stinson airplane built. With this plane he provided the first year-round air service between Nome and Fairbanks.

On our way to Nome with Bill Lund, I sat in the copilot's seat with a map on my lap. For the first couple of hours we followed big rivers, first the Tanana, then the broad, silty Yukon River, as had Noel Wien. Never had I seen a land with so few signs of man. Below me, here and there were dogsled trails. Occasionally, smoke rose from tiny log cabin villages on the riverbanks. Stretched out before us lay America's last wilderness frontier, and I was excited. But I was also apprehensive. I was accustomed to surveyed land where section lines ran north and south and east and west—to seeing highways, railroads, and towns every few miles. Here were great forests, treeless tundra, huge river valleys, and, in the distance, snow-covered mountains with sky-scraping peaks.

In about two hours we arrived at Galena, a small Indian village on the north shore of the Yukon River. Bill landed on a big gravel bar near the village. The temperature was minus 30 degrees Fahrenheit and the bar was frozen solid—a perfect landing place.

After Bill refueled, we left the Yukon valley and flew across the Nulato Hills, the last barrier between the Interior and the Bering Sea. These are low but extremely rugged mountains. Peaks rise to about 3,400 feet, and they are slashed by heavily timbered deep canyons and steep ridges.

Being a flatlander, fresh from Minnesota, with a vivid memory of 49 in-flight engine failures, I peered into the canyons and looked at the steep ridges with much trepidation. "What on earth do you do if an engine quits when you're over this country?" I asked Bill.

He smiled grimly, shook his head, and shrugged.

"You must have top-notch equipment," I ventured, "and keep your engines up."

"We try," he said, noncommittally, "and we don't expect engine failure."

He wasn't speaking for me. I didn't see how I was going to fly in this rugged country.

We arrived at Nome five hours after leaving Fairbanks. This gold-rush town, 150 miles south of the Arctic Circle, lies on the south side of the mostly treeless, windswept Seward Peninsula. Constantly battered by Bering Sea storms, the sad-looking frame houses and other buildings appeared as if they had been sandblasted. Little paint remained. Many of the buildings had been hastily erected in the early 1900s. Some leaned, others sagged. Most looked as if they needed replacing. Even today, the sidewalks are boardwalks. In 1941, the streets were dirt—mud, at spring breakup. It was the bleakest town in the bleakest area I had ever seen. Even the poorest rural village I knew in Minnesota looked prosperous and comfortable by comparison.

Mining was the lifeblood of Nome. More than $100 mil-
lion worth of gold had been wrested from Nome area mines in the
four decades before our arrival. Mining had changed from one- or
two-man operations with crude equipment to large-scale dredging
efforts run by big companies. There were perhaps 30 working
mines on the Seward Peninsula in 1941.

Because Wien Airways had yet to find a place for us to live,
we had to check in to the Patterson Hotel. Our room overlooked
the Bering Sea. Seven big ships were anchored offshore a couple
of miles. Nome had no harbor. Lighters—small boats—were
busily hauling freight ashore. There would be no more ships for
eight or nine months, because ice on the Bering Sea prevents
winter maritime traffic.

An icy wind constantly blew from the Bering Sea, and the
curtains in our room at the ramshackle Patterson billowed out
from the closed windows. Nome was a town of drafts. The doors
of most buildings in Nome, including the Patterson, were warped,
fitted loosely, and were often stuck.

After I looked about, I realized I had moved my family
into a truly primitive frontier town. There was no plumbing.
Water was delivered house to house in containers. Instead of flush
toilets, every home had a honey bucket (chemical toilet). To me,
most of the houses looked like shacks. Food and other living costs
were astronomical. I was running low on money, and if we had to
remain long, the hotel room was beyond our means.

I was discouraged and depressed. If we'd had enough
money, I'd have turned around and gone back at least as far as
Fairbanks. Happily, I didn't leave. Wien Airways soon found a
comfortable little house for us on Steadman Street, and Nome
grew on us.

When I started working for Wien, I thought that I would
be flight checked very carefully by the company pilots. After that I
expected to be gradually broken in to Alaskan flying. It didn't
work that way.

Within a day or so after my arrival in Nome, Sig Wien took me with him on a flight to Deering, a small Eskimo community 140 miles north. We flew in the Cessna Airmaster in which Bill Lund had flown me and my family to Nome. Sig pointed out landmarks, this mountain and that, this river, that creek. He knew them all. I assumed I was on a round trip with him, but in his typical closemouthed way, he had a surprise for me. We landed at the Deering field, which was surrounded by tundra. The short, narrow, dirt runway was covered by enough snow to make landing a little touchy.

On the ground at Deering, Sig and I unloaded a couple of passengers and some freight. On this, my check ride with my new employer, I hadn't even touched the controls. Then Sig pointed to a Stinson Gullwing powered by a 245-horsepower radial Lycoming engine. "Take that and make a few landings," he said.

The Gullwing—named for its graceful wings—was popular in Alaska then. It was a strong airplane that could haul a good load, and it was very stable in the air. I know of no other airplane of the time that was nicer to ride in. Its takeoff performance wasn't as good as some, but it was passable. I gave the airplane a good walk-around preflight inspection, wiped frost off the wings, checked the fuel, and took off. It was a ratty-looking plane, as beat-up looking as some of the junk I had flown in my early flying years in Minnesota. To compensate, the engine ran well.

The runway at Deering was shorter than I was used to. I came in under power, settling pretty well and making good three-point landings, stopping with plenty of room. I thought I was doing fine as I made half a dozen touch-and-go landings.

As I taxied off the runway, a man came over to talk with me. He was perhaps five feet eight, mild-mannered and calm. He seemed concerned. "You're slowing that Gullwing too much," he said. Then he introduced himself. "I'm John Cross, and I fly around here too."

John Cross was a name I knew. He was an eagle who flew in Alaska's Arctic for many decades before and after World War II.

Few arctic pilots have been so admired and loved. "Give her a little more speed on final," he advised.

"Yeah, but I gotta be able to stop," I answered.

"Try it," he said in his soft-spoken way. "You'll stop. You need that extra 5 or 10 miles an hour on final. Better that you run into the willows at the end of the runway at 5 miles an hour than fall out of the sky in a stall at this end."

He was right. I shot more landings and used a higher (and safer) approach speed, and I stopped in plenty of time. It wasn't necessary to slow down so much, or to land under power. So I was learning, and I was pleased that a really experienced Alaskan flyer was willing to give advice. Any pilot could have learned from John Cross.

After I had finished doing landings, Sig said, "Fly the Stinson back to Nome, will you Rudy?" He needed to fly the Cessna out of Deering.

"Oh, there are three passengers for you," he said, as a by-the-way.

"I don't know this country. What if I can't find Nome?" I blurted.

"Don't worry about it. These guys have mined here all their lives. They can show you the way," Sig promised.

I laid out the route to Nome on a map and worked out the proper compass course, then I loaded the three miners.

"You're new, aren't you?" one asked.

At my answer, he asked, "Think you can find Nome?"

"Sig says you guys know the way if I get lost," I half joked.

The instant we left the ground the guy in the front seat with me pointed and said, "Fly that direction." Then one of the guys in the back said, "No. Fly a little to the right of that." The third guy disagreed with both. "Look, I've flown this route with Sig lots of times. He always flies that way," he said, pointing off about 30 degrees from the route recommended by the second miner.

I followed my compass course and grinned to myself as the three miners argued about which direction we should fly. When we were about halfway, one of the guys in the back called up, "Why do you keep turning?"

I hadn't turned at all: I'd glued the proper course on the compass to the lubber line and hadn't deviated three degrees. In flight, as a plane passes geographic features, often perspective changes and it can appear that the airplane is turning.

The three miners were still arguing when I landed at Nome. Lesson one on Alaskan flying: don't count on passengers helping to find the way to a destination.

The next day, I was sent on a flight to Cape Prince of Wales with two passengers.

"Where do I land? What do I look out for?" I asked.

"Land on the beach—it's pretty good," I was told by the other pilots. "Sometimes the crosswinds are bad. What you really have to look out for is Cape Mountain, just southeast of Wales. A pilot or two, flying along the south side when winds were strong from the north, have been driven down onto the ice by the downdraft."

"It drove them onto the ice?" I asked.

"Yeah. They crashed," came the answer.

"You have to kind of watch for an updraft there too, so you don't get boosted into the clouds."

I knew virtually nothing about mountain flying and the winds encountered around mountains. I started on this trip with a lot of concern. I got over Cape Mountain and there was a strong north wind—just what I had been warned about. I stuck my nose into it and the plane started dropping. I turned back as quickly as I could.

I tried to go around it, but I didn't know how far out to sea I should go. If I had known, I could have gone out half a mile or so and I would have been away from the downdraft. But I didn't know. I had been warned, I took heed, and I returned to Nome with my passengers.

Bob Long, Bill Lund, and the other Wien pilots chided me.

"All your ratings didn't get you through, huh?" one said.

"Nope, by God, they didn't," I said, and let it go at that.

At the time there was much subtle pressure exerted to push pilots into the kind of flying they shouldn't do. It was dollars talking, of course. Small flying services in Alaska have often been economically marginal, with every dollar being important. Also, I was the newest pilot, and tradition called for the old hands to try to scare hell out of me. I heard some hair-raising tales from them about the dangers of flying from Nome. I had been around enough pilots to know that the stories were aimed at disconcerting the new kid on the block. I acted impressed and almost scared, shook my head and said "by golly" a few times, and went on about my flying.

Gasoline, available at most trading posts, was expensive in the villages along the Arctic Coast. At Kobuk, a village northeast of Nome, for example, the trader sold a box of two five-gallon cans of fuel for $10. That sounds cheap today, but in 1941 that was high-priced gasoline. We were encouraged to load up heavily on fuel at our starting point, thus eliminating the need to buy at the outposts. To survive, small airlines had to take advantage of every cost-saving device.

The day after having turned back, I flew the two passengers to their Cape Prince of Wales destination without difficulty.

My first six months of flying in Alaska were difficult for me. It was different from any flying I had ever done. I knew nothing about the venturi effect of high winds in mountain passes, how winds falling off a mountain can actually push a plane down, or how winds pushed upward from a long slope can lift a plane high into the sky. But I learned.

I also learned about bush residents who, with two-way radios, frequently called in and asked for a plane to fly out to pick them up. For someone who lived maybe 200 miles from town and 50 miles from the nearest neighbor and wanted to fly to town, the circumstances were usually urgent.

A woman up the coast from Nome radioed in one day requesting an airplane. "What's your weather?" she was asked.

"It's clear. Nice weather. Perfect," she answered. She was a damned prevaricator, and I risked my neck to find that out.

I took off in a Gullwing Stinson, and I wasn't very far from Nome when I had to choose between going under a low overcast and flying across the mountains, dodging clouds and peaks—a real iffy situation—or flying on top of the overcast. I had had 10 hours of dual instruction in instrument flying, so I knew the basics. I also knew how to use the radio range, the signal from Nome that instrument pilots used as a guide.

I followed out the northeast leg of the Nome radio range and climbed on top of the clouds, a foolish move with a single-engine airplane. I timed myself, saying, "OK, judging from the ground speed I was making at the beginning of the flight it will take me 90 minutes to get to the place from where the woman called. It'll be clear when I get there." I still believed her, even then.

When I was over the place where the woman lived, there was no sign of the ground. There was no hole in the clouds. I flew beyond, and found no change. I returned to Nome, arriving as a nasty storm was about to hit. I barely made it to the airport.

When I got in, I asked one of the other pilots about the woman and her radio call. "Oh hell, you can expect that," he said. "When they want to go, they want to go. They'll tell you anything to get you to come for them, and they figure you'll get there some way."

John Cross wasn't the only veteran Alaskan pilot to offer me valuable advice. Another pilot that I met at Nome, and who had a positive effect on my Alaska flying, was Gordon McKenzie. He flew for Mirow Flying Service, a Wien competitor.

McKenzie learned to fly with the British Royal Air Force in World War I. He barnstormed in Washington state before moving to Alaska to fly for several pioneer airlines—McGee

Airways, Star, Woodley, and Mirow.

I was still wide-eyed and fresh to Alaska when I met Gordon. He was rough and tough, but outgoing and a happy-go-lucky back-slapper with a Scottish brogue. He was an exceedingly skilled pilot, and he knew the Nome-Anchorage route by heart.

Once, shortly after I arrived at Nome, I was holding on a flight to Fairbanks because of bad weather. In those early years I felt guilty when I didn't fly in bad weather, an attitude that soon changed. In roared Gordon in a Lockheed Vega, a hot airplane, and he was flying right on the deck. After he landed and got out, I walked over and said, "I'm supposed to fly to Fairbanks and don't know whether to buck this weather."

His answer was straightforward. "You won't make it."

Gordon's superior skill, quick thinking, and action once probably saved his life and that of his passenger. One day in 1942, McKenzie left Anchorage in a fast, narrow-geared Mirow Flying Service Lockheed Vega. He had one passenger, Al Polet, who lived in Nome. In the rugged Rainy Pass country, the usually reliable Pratt & Whitney Wasp engine failed. The choice of landing places was limited. Only the short, rock-strewn river bars of high altitude were available.

Gordon selected the bar that seemed best. He saw at once that a straight-on landing would be disastrous. The plane was certain to flip onto its back at high speed. He made a quick, and I think courageous, decision. Just before touchdown, he kicked the rudder to turn the Vega sideways. Thus, when the plane hit, the landing gear, not stressed for side load, was torn off, and the barrel-like fuselage of the Vega slid rather than tumbled. The fuselage, though broken in half, rumbled to a stop with neither man hurt.

I gradually started to learn what I needed to know from the various flights I made and from advice offered by Sig Wien, Bill Lund, Bob Long, John Cross, and Gordon McKenzie. I learned the names of the mountains and what they looked like from every side. Eventually, they became individuals, almost with personalities. I learned that when I saw a plume of snow flying from the tops of certain peaks, I didn't want to fly close because air turbulence would be bad. I learned that Nome weather can change unbelievably fast, as does any coastal weather.

I liked the freedom of the country and the people and their attitude. This was a land where a pilot was truly appreciated—not for the stunts he could fly, but for his ability to get in and out of short runways, for finding his way in bad weather, for providing a much-needed service for isolated people.

In the early 1940s, Nome was a true outpost, and there I learned a simple but basic lesson: real freedom lies in wilderness, not in civilization. If a man wanted to wander about downtown Nome with a pistol on his hip, hardly anyone would comment. There was some hard drinking, but Bessie and I stayed clear of the waterholes so it seldom affected us. I enjoyed clumping along the wooden sidewalks. Of course, in spring we had to wear rubber boots to cross the seas of mud that were called streets. I enjoyed becoming acquainted with the free-thinking, generous, hospitable people. I liked contemplating the wide difference between the two primary winter travel modes—dog team and airplane. Most people remained in town all winter. There was a stability and a friendliness that both Bessie and I liked.

Unfortunately, the stability didn't last.

Alaskan Bush Pilot

ONCE I BEGAN to know northwest Alaska and various routes from Nome, I was assigned longer flights. Two 1941 trips I made to Fairbanks from Nome, both with a Gullwing Stinson, were especially memorable.

One flight was with an engine that was missing badly. I was flying without freight or passengers. "You want me to fly that thing to Fairbanks [530 miles] with a bum engine?" I asked the mechanics, incredulous.

"We know what's wrong with it," they said. "It won't stop. We promise."

It was December, when daylight hours were short. I flew that sputtering airplane with my heart in my mouth. From the sound of it, I expected the engine to stop any moment. I made it to the village of Ruby just before dark, landed, and spent the night there.

In the morning, I was readying the plane to fly the rest of the way to Fairbanks when Catholic bishop Walter Fitzgerald trotted up and asked if he could accompany me.

"No, Father, I can't take passengers," I said. "The engine is missing terribly. The company sent me without passengers, and I don't dare take you."

He chuckled and said, "If you're going to fly in that airplane, I don't see any reason why I shouldn't." He helped me prepare the plane for departure. It was clear he expected to go with me. He was very persuasive.

I was weakening, and he knew it. Finally, he wore me down and I let him climb in. We clattered off the Ruby runway and headed for Fairbanks. "If you have any influence with the powers above, Father, now is the time to use it," I suggested, my heart speeding up every time the missing engine slowed.

"I'm not worried," he said. He sat relaxed, hands folded across his lap as he peered down at the snowy world.

It helped to have that priest with me. He was a fine companion, and I had to admire his nerve. That spitting, rough-running engine didn't seem to bother him at all. I was greatly relieved when we touched down at Weeks Field with the engine still sputtering away.

The other Nome-Fairbanks trip I recall was in November. With three passengers and some freight aboard, I left Nome in the dim arctic light of the low-lying winter sun. For three hours, we skimmed over frozen tundra and jagged mountain peaks and then into the rolling valley of the Yukon. The passenger who occupied the front seat next to me continually chewed on a long 1886 cigar. He didn't light it, just chewed.

The new runway under construction at Galena was covered with six inches of fluffy snow. I landed gingerly but without difficulty, taxied in, unloaded some freight, refueled, and took off. I didn't know this, but in taxiing through the loose snow, the disk brakes must have become hot and melted some snow. A few drops of water found their way into the brakes on one wheel. The moment I took off that water froze.

Assuming that all was well, I flew along the Yukon River.

A headwind had developed during the day. As the wind became ever stronger, it slowed our progress, and I realized that if we were to reach our destination it would be a close race with darkness. To be safe, I decided to spend the night at Ruby. Don Emmons, a pilot who flew for Archie Ferguson at Kotzebue, had been snowed in there a day or so earlier. Someone had plowed snow from the runway so he could leave.

I found the 1,100 feet of newly plowed runway, but it was only 40 or 50 feet wide and there were three-foot-high berms on each side. I set up for a normal landing and the plane dropped smoothly. Near the ground I flared, and we touched down near the end in a fine three-point landing. The instant the wheels touched, I was in trouble. Because of the frozen brake, the plane lurched to the left. I tried frantically to straighten her but she did not respond. In that moment the narrow width of the runway was used up.

Whack! The airplane hit the berm, tipped over onto a wingtip, and slid for several feet. Then she tipped up on her nose, coming to rest with the nose in the snow. The propeller was bent, the right wingtip mangled. There we sat, still belted into our seats, staring out the windshield at the snow-covered ground. I looked at the cigar chewer next to me; only about an inch of frayed cigar stuck out of his mouth. In spite of the circumstances I had to grin. I wondered if the rest of the cigar was crumpled in his mouth or if it had been rammed down his throat. I think the greatest damage caused by that accident was to my ego. Here I was, the new pilot, and already I had broken an airplane! I felt terrible.

I thought that a Wien pilot would come to get us in a day or so, but I was too optimistic. We waited nine days for an airplane. I worried about Bessie and Cathy being alone at Nome. During those nine days there was no question in my mind that I would be fired.

When I broke that Gullwing at Ruby on November 2, 1941, I was
Continued on page 103

The home-built Bergholt Sport monoplane was built by
Erling Mickalson, with Rudy Billberg's help, in Roseau,
Minnesota, in 1929-30. Mickalson is in the cockpit.
Photo courtesy of Jennie Mickalson

Rudy Billberg soloed in this Tank-powered Waco 10 in
1934. His instructor, Roy Duggan, stands by the plane at
Wold-Chamberlain Airport, Minnesota.

This OX-5-powered Curtiss Robin was the airplane in which
Rudy Billberg received his pilot training from Roy Duggan.

FLY!

─IT'S IN THE AIR─

An Afternoon of Genuine Entertainment with the Flying Aces

| Licensed Airplanes | | Licensed Pilots |

U. S. FOREST PATROL STINSON *Airport ELY, MINNESOTA*

Special Trips Anywhere | **Flight Instruction**

Program to include Acrobatics, Smoke Trail Demonstration, Parachute Demonstration (not a live drop) and a special exhibition of flying an airplane on its back.

Electric Voice to Keep You Posted

FREE-- No Admission Charge

Scenic Rides, Open or Closed Ships, $1.00

Left: In the rear cockpit, Rudy Billberg pilots this Travel Air 2000 in 1938. This plane was powered by a 185-horsepower Challenger engine, and he used it for acrobatics and passenger hopping.

Above: This poster advertised an airshow/barnstorming afternoon at Ely, Minnesota, in 1937. Rudy Billberg, twenty-one years old, was one of the "flying aces" entertaining the crowd.

Top: Rudy Billberg stands by the Luscombe 8A with a 50-horsepower Continental engine that he flew from Trenton, New Jersey, to Duluth, Minnesota, in December 1938.

Above: Bessie and Rudy Billberg, shortly after their marriage in Duluth in 1939.

Above: Roy Duggan on the float of a Travel Air 6000 with a Wasp 450 engine he flew in the late 1930s at Warroad, Minnesota. *Photo courtesy of Roy Duggan*

Below: A frozen brake put this Gullwing Stinson on its nose as Rudy Billberg was landing at Ruby, Alaska, in 1941. Billberg, standing in front of the plane, was on his first job as a pilot in Alaska, flying for Wien Alaska Airlines out of Nome.

Left: John Walatka in his Stinson Reliant at Dillingham, Alaska, in the 1940s.

Below: An American Pilgrim 100A similar to the one flown by Rudy Billberg in 1942 hauling freight for the Northway Operation during World War II in Alaska. There is only one known Pilgrim surviving in the world. It's at the Alaska Aviation Heritage Museum in Anchorage. *Photo courtesy of Peter Bowers*

Eight of the pilots who flew on the Nabesna-Northway run for Morrison-Knudsen Construction Company during the summer of 1942. From left: Merle K. ("Mudhole") Smith, me, John Walatka, Frank Barr, Don Emmons, Jack Scavenius, Frank Krammer, and Herman Lerdahl. Of those who flew on that operation, only Roy Duggan, Rudy Billberg, and Grenold Collins survive. *Photo courtesy of Johanna Walatka Bouker*

Two of the airplanes used in the Northway Operation: a Boeing 80A Trimotor biplane (in the foreground) and a Hornet-powered American Pilgrim. The planes hauled materials for construction of the airport at Northway.

Noel Wien at Nome in 1925, with the huge Fokker
airplane, at the conclusion of the first commercial flight
between Fairbanks and Nome. *Photo by Schoenmaker.*
Courtesy of the Alaska Aviation Heritage Museum, Anchorage

25 years old. An interesting exercise for a man in his seventies is to read the diaries he wrote as a young man. My diary entries for that day were filled with dire predictions about my future as a pilot. They were melodramatic and also clearly romantic. To me, the Alaska so colorfully described by Jack London, the Alaska of my boyhood imagination, was still very real.

My diary entry for the day I had left Nome in the Gullwing read that "the 245 horses pulled us majestically into the air," and, "I was flying among the pilots upon whose courage depends the very life of this far north land."

And after the accident, I wrote, "The picture and hopes of a bright future were in a few short seconds covered by a black terrifying veil. What will happen now? Will the faith of my company be shattered? Will I lose my job? If so, what will become of my family? We have not much money left."

After a few days of depression and anxiety, I decided there was nothing I could do about my situation. I settled down and began to look around at Ruby, a typical Yukon River village. My diary entries reflect my changing thinking:

"Every day as the ice thickens, more and more dog teams race back and forth on this winter highway of the North. It would be interesting to know where they came from and where they're going.

"The roadhouse here usually has from three to a dozen Alaskan sourdoughs sprawled around the lobby. The main topic of conversation is gold mining. I'm surprised to find little interest in trapping or hunting."

Alaskan roadhouses were a pleasant surprise. They are actually hotels or inns, wayside stops with rooms and food. The atmosphere is homelike, and meals are served family style. The warm living room or lobby usually has a huge stove, often a converted boiler, or a 100-gallon barrel made over to accept cordwood. Usually the walls are decorated with a few trophy heads of Alaska's big game, antlers at least. On the floor are bear or wolf skins. Near comfortable chairs are books and well-worn magazines. Usually the guests know one another.

In the early years of flying, pilots were always especially nice to the cooks at roadhouses, for during winter it was necessary for the oil from an airplane engine to be drained into closed containers and kept in the kitchen overnight. Then, in the morning, the oil had to be heated before being poured back into the engine. In deep cold, oil won't flow; if an airplane engine isn't drained, it's a terrible job to heat the engine so it is warm enough to allow the oil to flow and to start. As a result, in early morning, Alaska roadhouses all had a similar odor—a mixture of warm oil and boiling coffee.

More from my 1941 diary: "The yarns unwound by the old-timers are very amusing. If they see you are interested, they spin them faster and faster until I believe it gets beyond their control. The results become elaborate and well-fabricated tales.

"When the sun sets and supper has been served on the long dining room table, the boys again congregate in the lobby to smoke and chew 'spittin' tobaccy,' of which they expectorate huge gobs into honest-to-goodness brass spittoons. This goes on for a time, and out of it grows a poker game that sometimes lasts until the sun brings forth the light of a new day."

During the nine days I awaited rescue at Ruby, my feelings for Alaska and its people deepened. I filled my diary with random thoughts:

"People of the North are very friendly souls. They take life easy and time means nothing to them. Northerners think nothing of waiting a week or two for a plane to take them wherever they want to go. During this period they get to know everyone in the village. I believe this to be the principal reason that they are a friendly people.

"I think that people live long and have better health here simply because of the absence of terrific rush and nerve-racking noise so prevalent in American cities. These people really take time to enjoy life and relax.

"Today I was told of an old prospector who is worth

several hundred thousand dollars, but pinches his pennies as though he were on the verge of starvation. As the story goes, this man purchased two hams at the local trading post. After six months he had used only one and returned the other, saying it was moldy and unfit to eat. The merchant begrudgingly refunded the money. The prospector went on his way, happy.

"Upon examination, the merchant found the ham to be OK. He cut it in half, displaying the two halves on the counter. In less than an hour the prospector returned. He spied the two halves of ham on the counter and remarked, 'Now there is a fine ham. I'll take it.'

"The merchant, who had upped the price of the ham, wrapped it up and the prospector left. Everyone was happy."

The United States mail was still being hauled by dog team from Ruby to Cripple by Scotty Clark. His was one of the last, if not the last, dog-team mail contracts in Interior Alaska. He returned from a two-week trip hauling mail while I was there. I was simply thrilled at this use of sled dogs. During the 1930s, airplanes took over most of Alaska's winter mail routes. My stay in Ruby gave me a new awareness of the changes wrought in Alaska by the airplane.

We spent much time sitting around the roadhouse watching a fellow build a dogsled in the lobby. I was fascinated by his work. A good dogsled has no nails or bolts—it's all lashed together with babiche (rawhide). With a really good dogsled a musher can stand on the runners at the rear, and the front of the sled can be twisted to a 45-degree angle without damage. A rigidly built sled will quickly break when loaded and pulled on a rough trail. The runners of a properly built dogsled toe in slightly, which helps the sled to track properly behind the dogs and keeps it on the trail.

The young man building the sled carefully explained all of this to me, with demonstrations, and I made notes in my diary. Years later, when I had my own dog team and sled, this early introduction was very useful.

As the days dragged on, I felt especially badly for my three passengers, who should have been in Fairbanks long ago. "Don't worry about it," one of them said. "We'd still be on the trail if we'd gone by dog team." Because aviation was still new to Alaska, people were delighted to be able to fly, regardless of inconveniences. Even if it were cold in the airplane and occasionally turbulence slammed passengers around, flying was still light years faster than a dog team. As one of my passengers pointed out, by riding in an airplane it was possible to get to a destination in hours instead of weeks. Ground travel in virtually roadless Alaska was painfully slow in both summer and winter. "The aviation," as some referred to flying, was radically changing life in Alaska.

Finally, Bill Lund showed up and flew us away from Ruby. Eventually a repair crew found the still-frozen brake on the damaged plane, and no blame was attached to me for the incident.

On December 7, I was in the Nome office waiting for a flight when Bill Lund rushed in, out of breath. "The Japanese have just bombed Pearl Harbor," he shouted. I didn't know where Pearl Harbor was; at first I thought it was somewhere in Alaska.

Alaska went on a wartime footing, although martial law (recommended by some) was never proclaimed. Private flying stopped, and unused small planes along the coast were ordered dismantled. A few company-owned transport planes were taken over by the military, but the single-engine equipment used to serve bush communities continued operating just as it had. War changed the aviation world: suddenly there was a demand for pilots, lots of them. Within six months this affected me and my flying.

Nome was ordered blacked out at night. A speck of light showing from a window or door invariably brought a warden with a message to "douse that light." In December, daylight in Nome is brief—only four or five hours, depending on cloud cover. On night errands the town was so dark we bumped into telephone poles, stumbled off the sidewalk, and bumped into unknown

buildings. I remember going into two or three stores before finding the shop I wanted. I still chuckle over the drunk who, when
chided for lighting a cigarette on the street, snapped at the
warden, "How in hell are we going to fight a war if the enemy
can't find us?"

Gold mining was stopped because the equipment and
manpower were needed for the war effort. In Fairbanks,
Anchorage, Juneau, and other major towns, outside electrical or
neon signs were switched off, for a dimout was in force.
Occasional air raid alerts brought complete blackouts. Rubber
tires, hip boots, sugar, meat, and cooking oils that were rationed
in the states (Alaska was still a Territory) were not rationed in
Alaska because the population was only 75,000 and amounts used
were relatively insignificant.

We all listened to Nome's civil defense radio station.
Everyone was required to have emergency gear, including two
weeks' worth of food, ready for immediate evacuation. We kept
ours piled in the entryway of our house. Several big bobsleds
parked around town were hitched to ready-to-go Caterpillar tractors. If Nome were invaded by the Japanese, Nome residents
planned to take to the hills. Mining shacks were scattered across
the Seward Peninsula, and people could have survived at least for a
time in them.

Fairbanks and Anchorage hummed with military activity.
Anchorage, headquarters to General Simon Bolivar Buckner's
Alaska Defense Command, became a war-oriented city like no
other in North America. Soldiers dominated, and housing was
impossible to find. Homeowners rented out rooms and beds by
the hour. Commercial and military airplanes roared about. Tiny
Merrill Field at Anchorage, named for pioneering bush pilot
Russell Merrill, became the busiest airport under the American
flag. For a time, Merrill Field averaged more than 10,000 landings
and takeoffs per month. In 1942, Merrill saw more operations
than did New York's La Guardia Airport.

We grew accustomed to the threat from the Japanese,

although we lived in fear. That spring, pilots were told to keep their eyes on the Bering Sea during flights. We were to report smoke immediately. Presumably, that would identify an approaching invasion force.

I continued to build flying time as a bush pilot. I quickly learned that people in remote villages depended on bush planes and pilots for everything from mail to medicine. In emergencies, an airplane could mean the difference between life and death. On a day-to-day basis, it provided the stuff for a more comfortable life. I still have a battered and faded four- by seven-inch notebook in which I logged my 1941–42 flight time, making notations of freight hauled and orders from bush residents. The entries include:

January 10. Near Kotzebue, saw a large herd of reindeer milling on the spit. Apparently wolves were after them, although from my altitude I could not see them.

At Kotzebue, I landed on the sea ice. The little town consists of a line of small buildings along the beach, of which half were almost drifted under with snow, some showing only their roofs. Almost all the people reach the doors of their houses through outside tunnels large enough to walk upright in. Some of these tunnels are 15 to 20 feet long.

February 5. Georgiana Koolook to come from Candle to Kotzebue.

Boy at Nome to come to Kotzebue. Catholics to pay. Ask Father McHugh.

Blankenship wants tickets on ice breakup.

Package at Kotzebue Signal Corps for Nome.

6 rolls film for Univex camera. Frank Davidovics.

Hauled 194 pounds freight from Deering-Candle. Tom Roust. Paid $9.70 cash.

R. J. Sommers to Nulato. Tell Mrs. Sommers to wait for Mr. Seely.

February 6. 249 pounds reindeer meat from Deering to Kiana. Engine and converter sent by Davidovics to Bud Thompson with Bill Lund.

Brought 24 pounds dogs' heads from Deering to Kotzebue hospital. Hirch is to make out government bill for payment. [This was in response to a rabies epidemic: examination of the brain of an infected animal detects the disease.]

Miss Coffman wants to know about some packages Sig was to have brought from Fairbanks.

Harry Brown, Kobuk, needs to go to Fairbanks on the 20th or 25th of April. Wants to know if we can take him direct and come back here to complete mail run. Must know next mail trip.

Get $10 worth of stamps (15, 50, and 1 cent) for Stewart.

Hauled 306 pounds sheefish from Kotzebue-Nome. 250 pounds for Polet.

Paul Davidovics wants at least 1 quart whiskey from Deering.

That winter I often flew from Nome to Kotzbue, 200 miles to the north, with the Cessna Airmaster or a Gullwing Stinson. I would drop off mail and pick up mail for the tiny inland Eskimo villages of Kiana, Shungnak, and Kobuk on the Kobuk River, and Selawik on the Selawik River. Kobuk Village, 150 miles from Kotzebue, was the most distant.

On my first flight to the Kobuk River villages, I went directly from Nome. I had never been in the area, and I couldn't find a detailed map. I had a book called *ALASKA*, a Federal Writers Project publication of 1935. In it was a folded map, about 15 inches square, of the Territory of Alaska, with little detail. I found the Kobuk River without difficulty, but I couldn't see any villages. I didn't know whether I had reached the river above or below Shungnak. I flew upriver for a time, and suddenly I saw four or five people standing on the river ice. I could see no houses, tents, dog teams, or anything else. I circled and landed on the ice and snow of the river.

I turned around to taxi back to where the people had been, and, to my surprise, all but one had seemingly vanished. I later realized they had gone into their snow-buried homes nearby. I taxied up to the one person remaining, an elderly Eskimo woman. I shut the engine off, climbed out, and kind of tipped my hat, as it were, saying, "I'm Rudy Billberg and I fly for Wien and I'm . . ."

She stopped me right there.

"No speak English," she said, or words to that effect.

"I have a load of mail for Shungnak," I said helplessly, wondering how I was going to get directions from her.

"Shungnak there," she said, pointing upriver.

That's what I wanted to know. I took off and flew upriver, and in a few miles found Shungnak. To my amazement, the entire village turned out to meet the airplane. Nothing like that had ever happened to me in Minnesota. For many years, this was the custom at small Alaskan villages—virtually every resident arrived at the plane within minutes of my landing. The people would peer into the airplane to see its interior, who was aboard, how much mail there was, and what kind of freight I had.

Next they would politely ask, "Have a good flight?" The second question was usually, "Any news?" They didn't want to know about the war in Europe, or if California had slid into the sea. They wanted to know what was going on in other villages in the region. Everyone was acquainted with virtually everyone else within a radius of a couple hundred miles. Usually that involved only a few hundred people. A newborn baby's arrival, a marriage, someone getting injured or lost, a hunter bagging a bear, the arrival of a new teacher, an emergency flight to a hospital—this was news. Even a new litter of pups born to a valued sled dog was of interest.

Flying the Seward Peninsula and other parts of northwestern Alaska on skis, I didn't worry too much about engine failure. I could have landed almost anywhere. After seeing some of the violent winter storms that whooped across the region, I realized that if I were forced down, my troubles would start after I landed. Surviving on the tundra far from help wouldn't be easy.

I began taking emergency gear—a good sleeping bag, food, warm clothing, a tent. I had so much gear that some of the other pilots shook their heads and grinned. Later, I came to know pioneer Alaska aviator Sam White, and I realized that the survival gear I carried was basic. Sam always had enough stuff in his airplane so he could live comfortably if he went down, no matter what the weather or where he was. He wasn't going to just survive in an emergency—he planned to enjoy life. Mechanic Jim Hutchison at Fairbanks made a stove for him out of a five-gallon gasoline can. Sam then stuffed the stove full of survival equipment. He always carried a sleeping bag that was as big as the moon, as well as a little tent.

After years of flying in the North, I came to believe that carrying a tent was almost as important as having a sleeping bag. Because of the chill factor, a few knots of wind can considerably lower the effective temperature. The little tent I carried folded up as a seat cushion. During winter in the open tundra, or wherever there is wind, a snow wall or a snow house is almost essential for survival.

On many of those flights north of Nome, I also had to be prepared to do makeshift repairs to my airplane. Once that winter, I landed the Cessna Airmaster on the glare ice of the river at Marys Igloo, an Eskimo village. I was taxiing and the airplane wouldn't turn. That plane had heel brakes on the floor below the rudder pedals. I jammed the brakes, and the wheels slid. I kept trying to work one brake to swing the plane around, and in tromping down on that brake I broke the pedal. This left me with a brake on one side only. With the short runways in the region I couldn't fly that way, so I had to make an emergency repair.

In the village I found a six-inch strap hinge on an abandoned door, which I fastened in place of the broken pedal so it would depress the brake lever. It held long enough for me to finish my mail, passenger, and freight deliveries that day and return to Nome.

Some of the medical emergency flights I made that first winter in Alaska remain strong memories. The isolation of Alaskan villages was new to me. Before airplanes arrived, people either died or they didn't. Often, villages were so far from a hospital or a doctor that, without a plane, there was no practical way for a seriously ill person to be taken to help.

An old man named Samson at the Eskimo village of Noorvik was attacked by what was believed to be a rabid wolf. The animal leaped on his back and bit his neck. When I arrived with the mail, he was waiting to be flown to the hospital at Kotzebue. The flight was uneventful, but I was happy to get him there. I often wondered what would have happened to him if he hadn't had medical help.

Also at Noorvik, a woman developed abdominal pains, and I was to fly her to the Kotzebue hospital. The Kobuk River, which I used as a runway, was covered with rock-hard snowdrifts. As I took off, the skis clattered across the snowdrifts and we had some rough bounces for perhaps 30 seconds. That poor woman screamed with pain at every bounce.

Late that spring I landed at the Eskimo village of Golovin with a Stinson Gullwing airplane. I had to dodge several small snowdrifts that persisted despite the warm spring sun. Near the center of the strip was a small parking area. I stopped there and walked the remaining 300 feet to the village. As I rounded the corner of a building, I came upon the south beach, which was the main thoroughfare of Golovin. On a driftwood log high on the beach sat an elderly Eskimo woman. I walked toward her intending to inquire about the passenger I'd come for, but as I drew near I changed my mind.

I realized that I was looking at perhaps the oldest human I had ever seen. She didn't seem to notice me, but sat enjoying the warm sun while she idly poked at the sand with a short stick. Her face was a picture of great dignity, where time had etched the joys and sorrows of many years. How gracefully she must have grown old, for the beautiful lines revealed not the slightest hint of bitterness or frustration, but rather a calm and peace rarely seen. Her faint smile caused me to wonder about her thoughts. Surely she's recalling some pleasant time in the past, I thought, for at her age the perimeters of the present and future must nearly coincide as the mind seeks the distant horizons of the past. I left quietly and went about my business. I never learned her name or saw her again.

I had another unusual experience that spring, during one of my stops at Galena. At that time, the main landing area at Galena was a large, curving sand and gravel bar just below the village, which offered a smooth and spacious landing field except in times of high water. Flying a Gullwing Stinson, I circled the bar, which was already bare of snow although the Yukon River remained locked in ice. After determining wind direction by observing smoke from a village stovepipe, I landed and tied my plane down. The river ice seemed solid and unthreatening. While carefully studying the sandbar for rocks or driftwood that might endanger tomorrow's takeoff, I noticed that gravel was being hauled from the bar. A newly constructed road ran over the riverbank to the site of a new airfield being built north of the river. Confident all was well, I walked to the village to secure lodging for the night.

Tired after my day of flying, I fell into deep sleep at once. After several hours I awoke with a start and leaped to my feet. Wondering what could have alarmed me, I peered out the window. It was midnight. The river and the country, still light from the midnight sun, lay quiet and beautiful. No sound, not even the howl of a dog, broke the stillness, yet I was filled with uneasiness.

Could the plane be in danger? Since I was awake, I dressed and walked to the river bar. All was quiet; no wind or other danger menaced. But I untied the plane, climbed in, started the engine, and taxied up the new gravel road to the top of the bank. Here I retied the plane and then returned to bed.

When I awoke in the morning, I heard a roar. Running to the window, I was stunned to see the wild river, freed from its winter prison, rushing in the bright sunlight. The turbulent current pushed a mass of broken ice. The landing bar where I had originally parked the airplane lay under six feet of water and crashing ice. I could scarcely believe what I saw. I had heard about northern spring breakup, but I hadn't realized it could happen so dramatically. And I'll always wonder: Why had I awakened at midnight? While I slept, had I heard the cracking of ice far upstream? If so, why didn't I hear anything after I awoke in the night?

In early June, I flew Bessie and Cathy to Fairbanks. Nome seemed too vulnerable to attack by the Japanese. I wasn't worried about myself; I believed I could always get away from Nome in an airplane. By then I was flying the Fairbanks run almost full time.

The morning after arriving in Fairbanks, June 4, 1942, we awoke to learn the Japanese had bombed Dutch Harbor, a U.S. Naval station at Unalaska in Alaska's Aleutian Islands. The war was coming closer. Until I could find housing, Bessie and Cathy stayed with Sam and Mary White. Sam was a great pilot. We became close friends and remained so for more than 35 years.

Business picked up on the Nome-Fairbanks route, as it always does in the summer in Alaska. In addition, as a result of the Japanese attack on Alaska, there was a sudden increase in military freight and passengers on the route. I often stayed at Fairbanks for two or three days at a time flying other routes between my runs to Nome.

One day I was sent on a flight from Fairbanks to the east. The rugged Alaska Range and Wrangell Mountains were new country for me. I flew between and over the high peaks, craning my neck, awed by the magnificent scenery. I landed at Nabesna, about 250 miles southeast of Fairbanks. There I was startled to see a number of large airplanes. A big operation was brewing, and I wandered around, snooping.

In the distance I saw a familiar figure. Could it really be? I walked closer. My eyes hadn't fooled me. It was Roy Duggan.

With him, incredibly, was Johnny Walatka. What were my two old barnstorming cronies from Minnesota doing in Alaska? I had stumbled onto the Northway Project.

The Northway Project

IT HAPPENED over the canyon of the Nabesna River, near the rugged Wrangell Mountains. I was flying a Pilgrim, perhaps the largest single-engine airplane in North America at the time. I was loaded over the legal limit. I flew into a downdraft that was pouring off those great mountains, and that big Pilgrim dropped like a brick for 2,000 feet. About 500 feet above the ground, I ran out of the downdraft and hit bottom—it felt as if the airplane had struck the ground. I was sure the wings were going to tear off. Suddenly, I was flying in quiet air again. The incident scared the daylights out of me.

It was summer, 1942, and I was one of the pilots flying for the Morrison-Knudsen (M-K) Construction Company, of Idaho, on the Northway Project, which was an airfield-building effort at what is now called Northway.

As late as 1937, there was not a paved airstrip, a lighted field, or a radio beam anywhere in the Territory of Alaska. Weather forecasting was equally nonexistent for air routes.

Virtually all flying was by visual contact, in daylight, in single-engine airplanes. Pan American World Airways was attempting to fly a weekly schedule between Juneau and Nome. Their planes were equipped with two-way radios that communicated with ground stations along the route. The CAA had planned a network of airfields across Alaska, but there were no funds to build them. It wasn't until 1939–40 that the military, recognizing the possibility of war with Japan, commenced work on these airports.

By April 1940, General "Hap" Arnold had planned construction of airfields that would allow planes to leapfrog across Alaska from the Canadian boundary to Nome. This network of airfields included Northway, Tanacross, Big Delta, Tanana, Galena, Moses Point, and Nome. While these fields were being built by contractors, the Army Air Corps was constructing Ladd Field at Fairbanks and Elmendorf Air Base at Anchorage. Before the hurried efforts to build these airfields, there were roughly 100 airports in Alaska. Many were modified ball parks or hand-graded, rough, short, narrow runways in villages.

While airport construction progressed at a frantic pace, riverboats, dog teams, horse teams, and tractor and sled trains continued to haul vital supplies in the Territory. The major road in Alaska in 1940 was the Richardson Highway, which ran from Valdez on the Gulf of Alaska to Fairbanks in the Interior. Not until after the war started was a highway built to connect Alaska's two major cities, Anchorage and Fairbanks.

The Alcan Highway, now called the Alaska Highway, which runs 1,393 miles from Dawson Creek, British Columbia, to Delta Junction, Alaska, was another emergency wartime project. This road-through-the-wilderness—one of history's great engineering feats—was built in eight months in 1942 by the U.S. Army Corps of Engineers. For the first time a road linked Alaska with the South 48 states, providing an alternative route to Alaska for military equipment other than the then-hazardous (because of Japanese submarines) marine shipping paths. This great highway was built to follow a chain of airfields between Edmonton,

Alberta, and Fairbanks, and connected with other airfields being built in Alaska.

At Nabesna, on the flight that Wien had assigned me, I glimpsed my old friends Roy Duggan and Johnny Walatka. I ran toward them. When closer, I called out, "Roy?" "Johnny?" still not believing my eyes. They turned, saw me, and both whooped. Our meeting was one of mutual surprise and pleasure. We wrung hands and slapped backs.

"Why don't you go to work here?" they asked, after we had brought ourselves up to date on each other's lives.

"I hate to quit Wien. I've just gotten comfortable," I told them.

"What are they paying you?" they asked, slyly looking at one another.

"Three hundred bucks a month," I said. I thought that was pretty fair. I didn't tell them that sometimes the pay was slow in getting to me. During the previous winter while I was flying at Nome, I went broke and no check was forthcoming. At the Wien office, I told them I needed money to pay my grocery bill.

"How much is your bill?" they asked.

"Ninety bucks," I replied.

I was handed $90 and promised the rest of my salary soon. I always got every cent due me from Wien, but sometimes it took a while.

"What do you think we're making?" Duggan grinned.

Dying of curiosity, I shrugged and guessed, "Four hundred?"

"Nope. Double that," he chortled.

I couldn't believe it. No one made that much money. I'd never heard of such riches for flying.

"By God, I could go for some of that," I declared.

"We'll talk to Harold for you," they promised. Chief pilot for the Northway operation was Harold Gillam, one of Alaska's great pioneer pilots.

Before I flew back to Fairbanks that day, Gillam had hired

me. I was to start flying for him immediately. I hated to tell Sig
Wien, because he and his company had treated me well. But I
couldn't turn down $800 a month plus room and board.

Sig didn't like it, but he was gracious, and he understood
when I told him what my new salary was to be.

I showed up at Gillam's Fairbanks hangar the next day
and flew with Harold to Nabesna in the M-K Lockheed 10A.
He led me to a huge single-engine airplane—the 10-passenger
Pilgrim NC733N (see cover illustration). Other Pilgrims carried
12 passengers.

"Think you can handle her?" he asked.

"I don't know. How's it fly?" I said.

"Nicest flying airplane in the sky," he claimed. Gillam
owned several Pilgrims, and he had flown them on his Alaska runs
for nearly a decade.

The Pilgrim *was* a wonderful plane to fly. The pilot sat all
alone way out front—there was no copilot seat because the airplane was designed so one man could fly it. The controls were
ball-bearing-mounted and as smooth as silk. You peered down on
the engine and had marvelous visibility all around. With its long,
thick wing, its 575-horsepower Pratt & Whitney Hornet engine,
and long propeller, the Pilgrim leaped off the ground quickly and
handled like a big, high-powered, light plane. It was very stable in
the air and landed easily. The propeller tips traveled at or near the
speed of sound and made a terrible racket. The sound of a flying
Pilgrim was unmistakable.

Harold showed me where all the controls were, and gave
me a few tips. "Go ahead. Make a few touch and goes," he
suggested. I fired her up, taxied out, and poured the coal to her.
There was a lot more torque on takeoff than I was accustomed to
because of the big engine, but I was prepared for it and used a lot
of right rudder to compensate. Big engine bellowing, that empty
Pilgrim leaped into the air. I quickly discovered the fine flying
traits of that airplane. Of the perhaps 40 different types of planes I
have flown, if I were asked to choose a single-engine plane with

which to make spot landings, one that could pack a big load, handle wing icing, and that flew the easiest, I'd pick the Pilgrim.

Sadly, to my knowledge only one Pilgrim is left—N907Y, at the Alaska Aviation Heritage Museum in Anchorage. Until the mid-1980s, 907Y was a working airplane owned by the Ball Brothers of Anchorage. Its last work was to haul fresh salmon from beaches to a cannery in Bristol Bay.

The American Pilgrim, first built in 1931, was produced by American Airplane and Engine Corporation, in Fairchild's factory. It was a slab-sided, pot-bellied-looking airplane, with the windshield and cockpit almost on top of the engine. Pilots joked that it took off, flew, and landed all at the same speed. Actually, it cruised at 110 miles per hour, and, when empty, landed at 55 or 60 miles per hour. We used two Pilgrims on the Northway Project: 733N, the plane I flew most of the time, and 711Y, which I flew a couple of times. Both belonged to Harold Gillam.

The Northway operation, like so many Alaskan construction projects of the time, was a direct result of World War II. It was supposed to be secret. Nothing about it appeared in newspapers or magazines. Not until a year or so after the war did the Northway runway appear on maps.

President Roosevelt had promised airplanes to Russia on a lend-lease basis to replace those the Germans had destroyed in the fighting on the Eastern Front. The long flight of these planes from the United States to Russia began at Great Falls, Montana. From there the planes hopped to Edmonton, Fort St. John, Watson Lake, Whitehorse, Fairbanks, Galena, Nome, and thence across the Bering Strait, over Chukotka, Yakutia, and Siberia to Russia. The runways at Northway, Tanacross, and Big Delta were built for emergency landing, refueling, and waystops between Whitehorse and Fairbanks. Northway was 300 miles from Whitehorse and 150 miles from Fairbanks, on the then-building airway. It was also conveniently close to Nabesna, which could be reached from Valdez by truck and from which the airlift I participated in flew materials.

Russian pilots were flown from Russia to Fairbanks, where they picked up the lend-lease airplanes at Ladd Field and flew them to Russia. These Russians were often veteran combat pilots. Many had had their families killed and their villages and homes destroyed in the war by the Germans, and they passionately hated the Germans. One Russian who flew a fighter plane from Fairbanks to Siberia was said to have shot down a German fighter and then seen the pilot climb out of the wreckage. The Russian pilot allegedly landed nearby, ran down the German, and choked him to death.

The Russians had become hardened by war. When one of their pilots disappeared, lost in a lend-lease plane he was ferrying between Fairbanks and Nome, an American flyer offered to make an aerial search. "No thanks. He wasn't a good pilot anyway," a Russian official responded.

One cocky Russian landed a P-39 fighter at one of the waystops and at high speed taxied it among parked planes. The American operations officer caught up with him and gave him hell. The pilot, unimpressed, said, "I got eight Nazi planes. How many you got?"

On the way to Russia, the Russian pilots lost only two-tenths of one percent of the planes delivered to them at Ladd Field (about 16 planes). Bad weather, mechanical problems, and lost pilots accounted for most of these crashes. That's a better record than the five-tenths of a percent (about 40 planes) that the Americans lost (for the same reasons) while flying the much shorter route from Great Falls to Ladd Field.

In recent years, some of the planes lost between Fairbanks and Siberia during the war have been found in remote Alaska and Russia. In 1988, Nikolai Ivanov, a Russian and a professional hunter from Yakutsk, found debris of P-39 Kingcobra 24962 and a human skeleton in the thick taiga forest of the Mutula River Valley of eastern Russia (Yakutia). Russian records indicate that the plane was flown by Air Lieutenant Vasily Kovalev. Kovalev left Fairbanks in early March, 1943, flying the Kingcobra. On

March 24 bad weather dispersed the formation he flew in, and no one knew what happened to him until his plane and remains were found 45 years later.

In 1979, snow machiners discovered remains of two P-39 Kingcobra fighters near Birch Lake, 45 miles southeast of Fairbanks. Records show that the planes, being ferried to Fairbanks from Montana in February 1944, collided in the air and crashed. Both pilots parachuted to safety.

Between 1942 and mid-1945, at Ladd Field the United States turned over to the Russians 7,926 aircraft, including 2,619 P-39 Bell Airacobra fighters, 2,397 P-63 Bell Kingcobra fighters, 1,363 A-20 Havoc bombers, 732 B-25 North American Mitchell bombers, 710 C-47 Douglas transports (the military version of the Douglas DC-3), 54 AT-6 advanced trainers, 48 P-40 Warhawk fighters, 3 P-47 Thunderbolt fighters, and one C-46 Curtiss Commando transport.

The Lend-Lease Act allowed President Roosevelt to "sell, transfer title to, exchange, lease, lend or otherwise dispose of" defense articles to any country whose defense he thought vital to the defense of the United States. During World War II, the United States transferred about $50 billion worth of defense articles to 38 countries. The United States received back from these countries about $8 billion, plus returns in kind (similar goods) worth approximately $2 billion.

Construction of the Northway runway posed a special problem. There was no road to the runway site, there was no sizable river nearby on which boats or barges could haul supplies, and there were no major trails. In the rush of war, airplanes were the only practical way to get materials to the site. Building materials were trucked to Nabesna from Valdez, and from Nabesna, we flew them the last 60 miles to Northway. Demonstrating the wastefulness of war, by late 1942, materials for the runway could have been trucked there on the Alcan Highway.

Airplanes couldn't haul the 17-ton Caterpillar tractors and 12-ton scrapers used to build the field. That equipment was landed by ship at Valdez, then driven under its own power 275 miles along the Richardson Highway to Slana on what is now the Tok cutoff. From Slana it was driven southeast on the trail to the Jack Creek mine, finally arriving at Nabesna.

The heavy equipment was first put to use at Nabesna, where Morrison-Knudsen constructed the finest gravel runway in Alaska. It was 6,000 feet long and 300 feet wide, with two cross-runways of 1,800 by 250 feet and 2,100 by 100 feet. After these runways were completed, the tractors and scrapers chugged down the valley of the Nabesna River to Northway. On the way they scraped driftwood and other debris away and leveled two gravel bars for emergency runways. One of those emergency strips was to save my neck.

Morrison-Knudsen searched high and low for airplanes for this mammoth flying project. Eventually the company leased the two Pilgrims that belonged to Harold Gillam, two Boeing 80-A Trimotor biplanes, a Travel Air 6000, and a Stinson Trimotor. They were mostly battered bush planes scrounged in Alaska, Canada, and the Pacific Northwest, and we called these the "fatigue run" planes.

A Spartan Executive, a Vultee, and a Lockheed Electra 10A were also part of the fleet. They were executive-type planes in which supervisors, inspectors, and other bigwigs traveled. They also made passenger and parts runs to Anchorage and Fairbanks. We called flights made by these planes the "glamour runs."

That summer the six fatigue run planes flew what was probably the largest airlift in the world to that time. In mere months, from Nabesna to Northway we transported 5,000 tons of asphalt in 28,000 barrels, tons of sacked resin, as well as boilers, lumber, fuel tanks, and other materials—everything necessary for a paved runway with lights as well as living quarters and cooking facilities for military personnel.

On my first day, I had scarcely landed after checking myself out in Gillam's Pilgrim 733N when I was told to get busy. We were instructed to remain in our planes for 12 hours a day except during meals and brief rest stops. We taxied to the loading ramp where crews hustled the freight on board. Another crew poured gasoline and oil into the plane. Every airplane was loaded above legal limits; we flew with barely enough gas for the round trip. Because of the national urgency of the project, CAA inspectors looked the other way.

My memory is hazy, but it seems to me that the Pilgrim could pack five barrels of tar, each weighing more than 500 pounds, plus five sacks of resin of 100 pounds each. I believe the Pilgrim hauled some loads that weighed 5,000 pounds. My loads were so heavy that with the engine wide open, it took that old Pilgrim about three-quarters of a mile to gain enough speed to lift off. Northway is downhill from Nabesna. Once off the ground, I followed the Nabesna River, gradually descending the 60 miles to Northway.

At Northway, we'd land on a newly bulldozed, sandy runway. The resistance to our wheels was great enough that we stopped easily as we taxied to the unloading area. While a crew hustled my load off, I remained in the cockpit. Then I'd take off and roar back to Nabesna. When I had my 12 hours in, another pilot would take over and fly his 12 hours, for it was summer and light all the time. This 24-hour relay continued all summer.

It was a wonderful job. I enjoyed counting my money—it was the first time in my life I had truly gotten ahead a bit. The flying did become repetitious, so the little diversions that happened stand out in my memory.

One day I flew low past a bald hill along the Nabesna River. Below was a grizzly bear digging in the earth. He was big, fat, bow-legged, and hump-shouldered, with a golden coat that looked like a haystack. Next time I flew by, he was still there. I was empty, so I went down for a closer look. I was new to Alaska, and hadn't yet seen any grizzly bears. I got right on top of him. At the sight and sound of the big Pilgrim, he ran down the hill so fast he was almost tumbling.

I thought that was fun, but I didn't see him again that day.

Next day, though, there he was. The plane was empty so I went down for another close look, and he ran in a half-hearted way, looking back over his shoulder.

Finally, he caught on that I wasn't able to hurt him, and he stopped running when I flew near. He stood half crouched on hind legs, front paws ready to strike, and I could see him snarling in anger. Then I decided maybe I wasn't so damned smart: what if my engine conked out and he caught me on the ground? I quit chasing him.

A few days later, I took off from Nabesna with the Pilgrim groaning with an over-the-legal-load, as usual. I was flying along when suddenly smoke came from the engine. As I stared in horror, more and more smoke poured from one of the top cylinders, which was about three feet in front of the windshield. A hole soon appeared in the cylinder head. Fire and smoke erupted from it. Before my eyes, the hole enlarged. The engine ran rougher and rougher. The hole grew large enough so the flow of the air-gas mixture and suction were disrupted.

The engine was barely running. It would roar a bit, hesitate, cough, and run again. I looked frantically for the nearest emergency runway along the Nabesna River. With relief, I spotted one ahead. I didn't have much altitude, and I was going down fast.

It was nip and tuck. The old Pilgrim was almost stalling. I struggled to hold the nose up as long as I dared, clinging to altitude, trying to stretch my glide to reach that cleared sandbar. My wheels tore through the tops of willows next to the sandbar. The heavy airplane bulldozed its way through instead of tripping on the trees. I relaxed mentally, knowing I was OK.

Then I looked ahead and saw the big grizzly bear that I had buzzed. He was legging it down the middle of the runway, directly in front of me, trying to outrun me, hind claws almost combing his ears. The clattering, banging airplane seemed about to land on top of him. I hoped he would turn off one way or the other, for I was almost on him, tires banging across the gravel. He was so close that the propeller threatened his rear. He disappeared under the nose of the plane and I was sure I was going to hit him. I didn't see him again. I got on the brakes, and gradually brought the Pilgrim to a stop. I sat for a long time, grinning to myself, happy to have landed safely and amused about that bear.

I could see through the windshield that the cylinder was a mess. The Pilgrim wasn't going anywhere until the cylinder could be replaced.

Since the bear had disappeared from under the airplane, I wasn't sure where he was. I dug out my .22 Special, a handgun that I always carried in my pilot bag. I was apprehensive about climbing out of the plane. I felt safe in the cockpit, which was 10 or 12 feet above ground.

Gun in hand, I climbed down slowly, ready to ascend like a skyrocket if I so much as heard a bearlike sound. Once on the ground, with pistol ready, I got more courage and walked up the runway. I found tracks where the frantic bear had swerved under the wing and then had run into the brush. Curious, I followed them. Within a few hundred feet I realized what folly this was, and I began an immediate retreat. If the harassed bear returned, I would be in a real fix. That .22 Special would have been about as useful as a popgun.

Like a character in the funny papers, I moved slowly at first. The farther I got from the brush and the closer to the plane, the faster I moved. Back at the airplane I felt better. Nevertheless, until my rescue, I carefully watched the edge of the brush where the bear had disappeared.

Jack Peck, later a well-known Alaskan pilot, soon flew over and I told him by radio about the blown cylinder. In a few hours, Pilgrim 711Y arrived with a mechanic, a new cylinder, and other parts. I flew 711Y out to Nabesna, leaving the pilot and mechanic to repair 733N. I continued to fly my usual loads of freight with 711Y until 733N was repaired and back on line. The barrels of tar and sacks of resin aboard 733N were dumped overboard so the Pilgrim could take off from that relatively short runway. I'll bet the stuff is still there.

Once that summer, Harold Gillam assigned me to fly the Spartan Executive airplane that was based in Anchorage. I replaced the regular pilot, who had to have surgery. The all-metal Spartan, powered with a 450-horsepower Pratt & Whitney Wasp Junior, was a low-wing, fast, sleek airplane far ahead of its time. I flew passengers, light loads, important messages in swift flights in a big radius around the Territory. That assignment was all too short, for the regular pilot recovered and I was assigned another, far different kind of a plane.

The Spartan Executive that I flew came to an unfortunate end two years later. Piloted by Eddie Bowman, the Spartan left Anchorage on June 2, 1944, for Northway. Passengers aboard were M-K general superintendent Lou Steelman, paving superintendent Jerry Noonan, and master mechanic Curtis Clark. Thirty miles from Northway, flying over mountains at 10,000 feet, the engine quit. Unable to restart it, Bowman lost altitude at 2,000 feet a minute. He tried to level off and stretch his glide, but the plane wanted to fall off, so he had to resume his dive. He headed for the Tetlin River. He didn't quite make it.

As he tried to reach a gravel bar along the river, the plane sheared off treetops. The last tree dragged the engine and instrument panel out of the plane. The Spartan hit the ground hard. Steelman's left leg was broken. Clark had a broken rib and was badly scratched and bruised. Pilot Bowman was bruised and shaken up. Noonan, who was uninjured, administered first aid to the others.

Grenold Collins, flying an M-K Travel Air 6000 from Anchorage on the same route, discovered the wreckage. He flew to Northway, unloaded, and returned to the rescue. When he landed on a river bar a mile away, a wheel of his Travel Air dropped into a hole. The airplane somersaulted, smashing the propeller, a wing, and the landing gear. The radio still worked, so Collins called the Army at Northway. They sent a relief plane to parachute a doctor to the scene.

A bulldozer and scraper then ran across country 45 miles to grade an emergency runway on a Tetlin River bar. One of the M-K Pilgrims, flown by Herb Haley, picked up the survivors two at a time and flew them to Anchorage.

Gillam next assigned me to fly one of the strangest looking airplanes it has been my lot to fly. "It looks like a bunch of parts flying in formation," Duggan cracked, and he was right. The plane was a Sikorsky S-39-B, a five-seat amphibian powered by a 450-horsepower Pratt & Whitney Wasp Junior. Maximum speed was 120 miles per hour, and it cruised at about 100 miles per hour. The airplane was comprised of a wing with the engine mounted on top of it just above the cabin—perhaps not the best place for an engine. Oil from the engine sometimes dripped on the windshield. Two booms that looked like two-by-eights extended back to the tail surfaces. Supported under this by numerous struts was a boatlike hull and cabin with retractable wheels.

Bizarre as the airplane was, its paint job was even stranger: the airplane had belonged to Martin Johnson, the explorer, who had used it in Africa. In imitation of a zebra, it was painted yellow with black stripes.

My first trip with the Sikorsky was from Anchorage to McGrath, where Morrison-Knudsen was building an airport. I was based in Anchorage. Bessie, with Cathy, came to Anchorage and stayed in a hotel about a week, visiting me from our home at Fairbanks. I told Bessie I'd fly past the hotel so she could look out the window at the airplane I was now flying.

I guess she took one look and almost fainted. She knew a little about airplanes, and that contraption didn't look like anything she thought her husband should be flying. She doubted it would get to McGrath, and was on edge until I returned to Anchorage. With no telephone service in rural Alaska, a reassuring phone call was not possible. I flew to McGrath without difficulty, and began to shuttle between McGrath, Aniak, and Bethel—all villages on the lower Kuskokwim River.

Sometimes I'd haul a full load of beef, sometimes aviation

fuel, sometimes groceries, and sometimes passengers. Because it was wartime, we had to radio ahead to our destination to give our estimated arrival time, and to get clearance to land. The long, trailing radio antenna wire of the Sikorsky was weighted with a heavy lead ball. As I neared Bethel one day, I reeled out the antenna to call ahead and the whole works broke off, antenna, lead ball, and all—I was without a radio. I thought nothing of it, and flew on, planning to land as usual.

At Bethel, Morrison-Knudsen was building an airport on the east side of the Kuskokwim River. As I neared the airport, in the river off to the left end of the runway was an oceangoing ship. Approaching the runway, I flew right by the ship's stern. I reduced throttle for landing and looked over at the ship, and to my surprise, I was looking straight down the barrel of a cannon. Someone was in a seat there, cranking that gun around, keeping it lined up on me. I was puzzled by this reception but went ahead and landed.

I hadn't been on the ground two minutes when an Army colonel dashed up and absolutely roared at me. "What do you mean by coming in here without a clearance? Where did you come from? What is your business here?" My jaw dropped and I just stared at him.

"Answer me, dammit. We almost shot you down," he yelled.

I was bewildered. "Shoot me down. Why?" I asked, genuinely perplexed.

"You were flying an unidentified aircraft," he said, pointing at my bizarre-looking "collection of airplane parts flying in formation." "It looks Japanese."

Such foolishness really disgusted me. "By God, if you ever get a Japanese flying over here in an outfit like that, you'd have him right where you want him!" I blurted.

My explanation about the broken radio antenna made no difference to him. I wasn't supposed to come in without calling ahead.

"Where the hell was I supposed to go? I know I'm supposed to get clearance wherever I land," I said. "But I had to land somewhere."

I got another antenna hooked up, but I was still shaking my head when I left Bethel.

Harold Gillam sent a different pilot down to fly the Sikorsky, and I went back to Nabesna to fly the Pilgrim. I learned that my replacement landed the Sikorsky wheels-up on the McGrath runway, scraping the hull rather badly. I don't know what happened to that zebra-striped contraption after that.

I flew the Pilgrim until late fall. Finally, the Northway runway had enough paving so those of us hauling freight from Nabesna could land on it. On our first landings, almost every one of us who touched down on the smooth pavement with our overloaded planes found that our brakes couldn't stop us. All summer we had used our brakes mostly for turning, and we had counted on the sandy runway to provide braking action. If we hadn't taken off and gone around again, we'd have run straight off into the brush at the other end of that mile-long runway.

Even after having our brakes repaired, we had to land short on the paved runway. The brakes hadn't been designed to stop our planes with such gross overloads.

Soon after that, the Northway airlift ended, and most of us who had been hired for that specific job were laid off. Pilots who participated in the Northway Project when I was there included Roy Duggan, John Walatka, Grenold Collins, Jack Scavenius, Merle ("Mudhole") Smith, Jack Peck, Frank Kammer, Don Emmons, Frank Barr, and Herman Lerdahl. Lerdahl usually flew the glamour run in the Vultee, a sleek, low-wing plane that carried about 10 passengers. At this writing, only three of us survive—Duggan, Collins, and I.

Some of these pilots were well known in Alaska even then, and some went on to become famous later. I was the youngest and an unknown.

At the end of the Northway Operation, I was far more

qualified to fly in Alaska than when I had arrived a year earlier. I was beginning to know the country, and I had come to know many of the people in Alaska's aviation industry.

Today, half a century after their wartime construction, the runways from Edmonton to Nome are all still in use.

11

Noel Wien

"BUSH PILOT," a term that came into use in the 1920s, connotes derring-do. It hints of dangerous mercy flights, of ventures into uncharted wilderness. For those early pilots who deserved the title "bush pilot," it was all of these and more. Skill, courage, and dogged persistence were necessary to provide dependable transportation with the crude, fragile, and undependable airplanes of the time. For Alaska's early pilots, most runways were ball parks, river bars, and ridgetops. Navigation aids were nonexistent, as were accurate weather forecasts. Maps were incomplete and not designed for aerial use.

The pioneering years of bush flying had ended when I arrived in Alaska in 1941. Wien Airways, for which I flew, was owned jointly by Noel and Sigurd Wien. By then, airplanes were providing safe and regular transportation for everyday living, as well as the occasional emergency flight.

In Alaska, the transition from dog teams, horses, and riverboats to air service came swiftly. While pioneering pilots were blazing aerial trails in the North, airplanes were improving by leaps and bounds.

Noel Wien was the first in Alaska who could properly be called a bush pilot. He was the first to provide consistent air service. Wien was a talented, reticent, careful Minnesota farm boy from Cook, 250 miles from my hometown of Roseau. He learned to fly in Minnesota in 1921, and he started flying in Alaska in 1924, 17 years before my arrival.

Aviation transformed Alaska in those 17 years. Other pilots helped Noel Wien blaze those aerial trails, but Wien was the first to fly into and land north of the Arctic Circle. He was first to fly from Alaska to Asia, and first to fly from Anchorage to Fairbanks. Noel Wien established dozens of aviation firsts in Alaska. He was a genuine pioneer.

Imagine the year 1924 and the 1,000-resident town of Fairbanks. It had dirt streets, log cabins, and false-fronted stores. A trail used by dog teams and horses snaked 150 miles north to the Yukon River, the river route east to the Yukon Territory or west to the Bering Sea coast. Another dogsled and wagon trail ran 300 miles south to coastal Valdez. Model T Fords and other early autos painfully traveled these roads only in the summer. A just-completed 400-mile railroad connected Fairbanks with the southern coastal port of Seward. Steamboats carried mail, freight, and passengers on the Tanana and Yukon rivers.

Other trails, used in winter mostly by teams of up to 25 dogs hauling mail, freight, and passengers, spoked out from Fairbanks. Along the main trails, about a day's travel apart (20 to 30 miles), were log roadhouses where travelers and their dogs or horses found meals and overnight accommodations.

On July 6 of that year, 25-year-old Noel Wien flew into town in a two-cockpit Standard J-1 biplane. The plane was powered by a water-cooled 150-horsepower Hispano-Suiza (Hisso) engine. Wien carried a pilot's certificate signed by Orville Wright. He had followed 300 miles of railroad track from Anchorage. His was the first flight ever between Anchorage and Fairbanks.

Headlines of the *Fairbanks Daily News-Miner* proclaimed, *"PLUCKY AIRMEN BRING 'ANCHORAGE' TO INTERIOR WITHOUT STOP: FAST TIME MADE OVER UNKNOWN COURSE. PILOT NOEL WIEN WAS AT THE STICK, WITH MECHANICIAN WILLIAM B. YUNKERS AS PASSENGER."* (*Anchorage* was the name given to the Hisso Standard airplane).

Wien had flown mostly as a barnstormer in the Midwest and the South. When he arrived at Fairbanks, he had logged about 550 hours as a pilot.

A year earlier, Carl Ben Eielson had flown mail 275 miles from Fairbanks to McGrath. But his mail contract was canceled because he had piled up his plane. Three times. Eielson's greatest flying feats were yet to come.

Pilot Art Sampson was barnstorming in Fairbanks when Wien arrived. He left shortly. Before leaving, he told Wien that Alaska was not a good place for an airplane. "Nowhere to land," he warned.

Noel Wien decided for himself. As he flew, he watched for places to land, and he remembered them. During the rest of the summer, he flew paying passengers and what freight the little Standard could handle. Most of his flights were to mining communities within 100 miles of Fairbanks.

In the spring of 1925, he even made the first Interior Alaska rescue flight. In the Hisso-powered Standard, after a hazardous mountaintop landing, he flew Charles Opdyke, a seriously ill gold miner, 50 miles from Nome Creek to Fairbanks. That same year, he made the first commercial flight between Fairbanks and Nome with the great, unwieldy Fokker F. III.

Few man-made features marked Wien's routes. There were no fences, farms, church steeples, powerlines, section lines, or roads. There weren't even many villages. Because much of the landscape was still unmapped, Wien followed dog-team trails, rivers, and other distinctive landmarks. He found that Sampson was only partly right about places where an airplane could safely land. He knew sooner or later he would have forced landings; his experience with OX-5 engines was similar to mine. "Noel won't fly a straight line," passengers complained. They didn't realize that he was concerned with where he might land safely if the engine quit. When possible, he flew around big stands of timber, swampy tundra, and steep mountains, as I was to do some years later.

In the first years, he flew with a spare wooden propeller strapped to the fuselage. Noseovers and broken props were common, because of the crude surfaces of landing fields. His first airplanes had no brakes. Instruments included water temperature and oil pressure gauges for the sputtering Hisso, and an inaccurate altimeter. The Standard didn't even have a compass. At first, he flew only during the summer because his water-cooled engine couldn't handle the at least minus-50-degree temperatures common in Interior Alaska.

Noel, like all early pilots, was wary of the bush resident who assured him there was "a nice landing field" at such-and-such a place. Those became almost fighting words. What often was a nice landing field to a nonpilot was not a safe place to land an airplane. Few nonpilots knew how long a runway should be or how smooth it needed to be in order to be usable. Wind direction in relation to the long axis of an airport is critical. Few nonpilots were aware of this. The enthusiasm added to the lack of knowledge of bush residents who desperately wanted a pilot to land at their cabin or in their village led many a pilot to disaster.

Even after Wien had blazed trails and knew the aerial routes between Fairbanks and a myriad of villages, flying in Alaska wasn't easy. After 1927, when Noel first provided winter service, inside his plane even for short hauls he kept a plumber's firepot for heating the engine and its oil, a fire extinguisher (to keep from burning the plane up while heating it), a motor cover to retain heat in the engine while heating it, wing covers to prevent frost from forming or snow from building up on the wings while parked, a sleeping bag, a tent, emergency food, a gun for killing game, an axe, and snowshoes.

To maintain the stamina he would need for his hike out of

Alaska's untracked land when (not if) he was forced down, Wien jogged several miles a day. He didn't smoke. He drank only water and milk. In May 1925, as he expected, he was forced down. A strong wind blew him off course and into the Kantishna country where he ran out of fuel. He landed safely on a bar of the Toklat River, and in four days he hiked 80 miles across the tundra to Nenana, and in so doing lost 20 of his 165 pounds.

Alaskans took to airplanes like no other people in the world ever have. From the beginning, they flew 30 to 40 times as much as other Americans, measured in number of flights per capita or by the passenger mile. Today, Alaska has more than 10,000 pilots, one for every 45 residents. One aircraft is found in the state for every 50 Alaskans. There are six times as many pilots per capita and 12 times as many airplanes per capita as in the rest of the United States.

Only five years after Noel Wien established sky trails from Fairbanks, the Territory of Alaska (population 50,000) boasted 57 graded landing fields. Using these fields were 29 airplanes.

All Alaskans didn't immediately welcome airplanes. Contracts for hauling mail had long gone to drivers of dog teams, to horse teamsters, to stern-wheeled riverboats. Much of the economy of Interior Alaska revolved around ground transportation. Furthermore, in winter powerful sled dog mail teams broke trail, and others were able to use these trails—not insignificant in snow country with long winters.

Indians on the Yukon River netted and dried salmon to sell for sled dog food. They cut firewood to fuel the greedy steam engines of riverboats, which were big business. The roadhouses along the main trails depended on the business of mail teams, passengers traveling with them, and others with dog teams. Aviation threatened the livelihood of all of these.

Even in 1941 when I arrived in Alaska, aviation was not beloved by all. Shortly after I flew Bessie and Cathy to Fairbanks after living in Nome for the winter, I went to a Fairbanks bank and asked for a $200 loan to get my family settled in a house. The response was, "We don't loan money to sawmills, pig farms, and pilots." I had to get a co-signer for the note before I could get a loan.

Pioneer pilot Sam White once saw a sign at a roadhouse: "No drunks, Indians, or airplane pilots allowed."

I first met Noel Wien in 1941 when I arrived in Alaska to fly for the airline that he and his brother owned. My boyhood worship still lingered. He was quiet and unassuming, friendly, eager to help and give advice. I listened carefully, for I knew I was in the presence of a master of arctic flight. No early pilot had a finer reputation than Noel Wien. "Any commitment Noel Wien made was like a gold bond," fellow pioneer pilot Bob Reeve once said.

In 1966, near the end of his active flying career, Noel decided he wanted an instrument rating. For a man of his age, this was quite a commitment, because it involved many hours of hard study and practice. Since I was an FAA (formerly the CAA) flight examiner for the instrument rating at that time, Noel asked me to conduct the flight test. I was filled with pride at the chance to check out so distinguished a pilot, and he did a beautiful job. I believe I demanded more of him, and graded him more strictly, than most. I wanted no one to think he got the certificate because of who he was.

Years later a masterful biography of Noel Wien was published (*Pioneer Bush Pilot,* by Ira Harkey, 1974). I learned that Wien had been flying with only one eye since 1939; he lost the right eye when a piece of metal flew into it. Depth perception is critical to a pilot. How Noel managed to fly commercially for 16 years (until 1955) with one eye has to be one of the wonders of the aviation world.

In those early years, while some resented "the aviation," pilots became heroes to other Alaskans. Many Eskimos thought that "Sig Wien" was one word, and at least one child born to an Eskimo couple was named "Sigwien." Other pioneer pilots were often honored by having babies named for them. Many geographic features in Alaska are named for pioneer pilots, including Wien Lake, and the Walatka Mountains.

Wien Airways grew, absorbing several other bush airlines, and merged with Northern Consolidated Airlines. Eventually the company was called Wien Air Alaska. Until 1985, the company was a major airline that provided jet service along the West Coast as well as within Alaska. Economics, union problems, and perhaps mismanagement (not by the Wien family) resulted in the dissolution of Wien Air Alaska.

In 1962, Noel Wien was awarded an honorary doctorate of science by the University of Alaska, Fairbanks. Governor William Egan declared a Noel Wien Day in Alaska on July 15, 1974, to commemorate the golden anniversary of Wien's first flight to Fairbanks. Noel was Alaskan of the Year in 1975. The Fairbanks Public Library, built on the site of Fairbanks' onetime Weeks Field (which closed in 1951), is now the Noel Wien Memorial Library.

The convenience of whisking people and goods to distant places in hours instead of drudging for days and weeks on the trail made acceptance of aviation by Alaskans inevitable. And wonderful men—eagles—like Noel Wien helped make it happen.

On Noel Wien's sixty-fifth birthday, he and his onetime student, Sam White, who was then 73, practiced touch-and-go landings at Fairbanks in Sam's old Stinson.

On July 18, 1977, Noel Wien died at the age of 77, seven months after the death of Sam White.

Sam White

SAM WHITE was one of Alaska's unsung pioneer pilots. In 1928–29 Noel Wien and his brother Ralph, who was later killed in a flying accident, taught Sam to fly. Sam went on to a fabulous flying career in Alaska, including becoming the world's first flying game warden.

Noel Wien introduced me to Sam, and we remained close friends for the next 35 years. Sam was huge, powerfully built, and he had a booming voice. When I first knew him, he was a game warden for the Alaska Game Commission.

Despite his size and bluster, I soon learned that underneath he was a kind, just, and generous individual. I also learned that perhaps no man knew more about arctic survival in all seasons than Sam. I listened carefully whenever he spoke of this subject or of northern flying in general.

Sam's generosity and concern for others was legendary. An example occurred one cold winter day in the early 1950s. While living at Fairbanks, I received an urgent call. My friend Bob Buzby had left Anchorage in his new Piper Tri-Pacer to take his family to their trapping camp on the north slope of the Alaska Range. Bob was to have returned for more people and cargo, but he was two days overdue. The caller asked if I could get a plane and search for him.

Since I had no airplane of my own at the time, I went to Sam. He immediately loaned me his beloved L-5 Stinson. "Use it as long as you need it," he said. And he came to the airport and helped me preheat and start the engine. Then he loaded aboard his more-than-adequate emergency equipment. Within hours I took off, heading for the Alaska Range.

In 25 minutes I saw the Buzby cabin on a high ridge. Smoke curled from the chimney. I breathed a sigh of relief. But then I saw Bob's plane, perhaps 100 yards from the cabin, upside down in the snow.

As I circled to land, I saw another plane set down. It was Bob Hanson of Anchorage, a mutual friend, who was on the same errand I was. On the ground, we found that all was well except the upset plane. We loaded our ships for the necessary hauling that had to be done. Most of the family went to Fairbanks, and I flew them there.

Finished with the rescue, I tied Sam's plane to its moorings, unloaded the emergency gear, drained the oil, and drove to his house. After telling Sam of the rescue he sat down, much relieved. "By the way," I said, "Bob wants to know what he owes you for the use of your plane." Sam made his entire living with that airplane.

He jumped to his feet. "He owes me nothing," he roared. "Maybe you can do me a favor some time. If you can't, do it for somebody else." That was typical.

Sam White arrived in Alaska from his home state of Maine in 1922 to work for the U.S. Coast and Geodetic Survey. He mushed dogs, packed horses, paddled canoes, and walked over much of Interior Alaska in the next decade. He had been a hunting guide and lumberjack in Maine, and during World War I, he served with Lyman's Rangers, a hand-picked battalion.

In 1927, when Sam became a game warden for the Alaska Game Commission, market hunters (market hunting ended in 1925), trappers, and miners had decimated moose, caribou, and Dall sheep in some areas. Conservation laws were poorly enforced. Bush residents often deliberately set forest fires to clear away brush and grass. When asked why he wanted to become a game warden, Sam answered: "To hold back the killing and the burning."

At 200 pounds and six feet two, Sam became one of the most respected game wardens and commercial bush pilots in Alaska, and not just because of his size. He was a master woodsman, he was scrupulously honest, he was a superb pilot, and he understood the problems of bush residents.

White once faced down a trapper who aimed a .30-06 rifle at his belly. He quietly stared at the man, who, after a long moment, put the rifle down and meekly surrendered. Sam had caught him in a flagrant violation of the trapping laws.

He first flew game patrols with a Golden Eagle open-cockpit monoplane, powered with a LeBlond 90-horsepower, seven-cylinder radial engine. He paid $3,500 of his own money for that airplane when his annual salary was $2,800. The plane didn't perform well, so he sold it for $500. He then paid $3,500 for a Swallow biplane. The Swallow was a two-place open-cockpit plane with a maximum speed of about 100 miles per hour and it performed well. The plane had a three hour, twenty minute range, and it proved ideal for Sam's use. He flew hundreds of hours of patrol in it, often paying for the fuel from his own pocket.

With the Swallow, Sam proved that the airplane was practical for wildlife law enforcement in Alaska. It was a logical step from that to the many aerial wildlife management techniques in use today in Alaska and elsewhere.

From the air, Sam could spot traps set illegally close to a beaver house. He could tell when a trapper had traps out before or after trapping season. He could even tell when a trapper was illegally feeding moose or caribou meat to his sled dogs.

Illegally killed moose, caribou, sheep, or bears were easy for him to spot from the air, but very difficult to find during ground patrols. He also sealed (certified as legal) beaver pelts throughout his vast territory by flying from village to village. He did the job in weeks that way, instead of the months it would have taken had he used ground transportation.

Only Sam's stubbornness and determination kept him in the air, for he was in constant trouble over his plane with the bureaucrats for whom he worked. Once, he had to take two weeks' leave to re-cover and repair his own airplane after making a forced landing on an isolated lake while on warden business.

After World War II, Sam bought a government surplus L-5G Stinson. He removed the dual controls, moved and turned the oil cooler upside down so oil would drain back into the engine instead of freezing in the cooler. He rearranged the air intake, removed the rear seat, and installed a hammock seat. He added an eight-gallon center-section fuel tank, and added a left side beaching door so that on floats he could climb out from either side after reaching shore. He shortened and removed the curve from the control stick. And he added a flat, safety-glass windshield (the windshield cost him $1,200, installed, in the 1940s).

He flew that plane, N40013, for 21 years. Eventually he sold it, when his flying days were done. Within days it was destroyed by fire. "Died of a broken heart," White said of the burned plane.

Sam White had been flying in Alaska for a dozen years when I arrived in the Territory. In about 1941 he was ordered to ignore wildlife violations by military brass and he refused. He left his game warden job as a result. Politics were involved; war was coming and the military buildup in Alaska brought prosperity. He went to work for Wien Airlines in 1941, the same year I did, at double the salary he had received from the government.

During the 1950s, he flew his L-5G Stinson on charter for the U.S. Coast and Geodetic Survey and Geological Survey, mostly in northern Alaska. Then he went back to flying for Wien Airlines from a bush station at Hughes, on the Koyukuk River, a large lower tributary to the Yukon River.

No mention of Sam White would be complete without a few of his yarns. Each September, he flew his Stinson on floats to a certain lake to hunt moose. There, he pitched an eight- by ten-foot wall tent. The walls had been lengthened one yard, and when pitching the tent, he folded that extra yard under and weighed it down with camp gear, except on the back wall where he rolled out his sleeping bag.

In his tent one black night he awoke with the sensation of taking a half roll and then dropping back. He heard sniffing close to his head and quickly awoke. A bear had tried to shove its nose through the canvas. His loaded .30-06 lay at his side, but Sam didn't use the rifle. Instead, he let drive with his big fist, accompanied by a loud whoop.

Sam's fist sank into the bear's side clear to his wrist. The bear whooped in response, and made a great commotion as it fled. By then, Sam was on his feet, "flashlight and rifle pointing all directions at once," he said. It was a good blueberry year, and when Sam went out to check, he found evidence that he had certainly frightened the bear.

In 1953, Sam was flying for the Coast and Geodetic Survey from Stony River, an Indian village on the Kuskokwim River. Word came of an injured man upriver. Sam would have to land in a beaver pond to fly him out.

Sam flew to the L-shaped pond and landed. He decided it might be long enough for his 190-horsepower, Lycoming-powered Stinson to take off from, provided he used both lengths of the L. There was a problem, though: at the bend of the L on the outside of the curve was a beaver house, high enough so when he went around the corner he would have to lift the right wing over the house. The pond was formed by a 12-foot-high dam, which lay between high banks.

The injured man had jumped off a bank onto a log,

slipped, and landed astraddle the log. He was in great pain. The man's companions helped load him, then helped Sam pull the Stinson to the edge of the pond.

Sam shoved the throttle full. Water and mud flew, and he was soon on the step. By the time he reached the beaver house, he had enough speed to lift the right wing over it as he went around the bend. Next came the dam, with the water but a few inches from the top. Sam said he cleared that dam by about four inches. Then, he had a few bad seconds hanging on the prop before he gained enough flying speed to climb over the trees.

He flew to Bethel and the Native Service Hospital. A truck arrived for the injured man, and the driver remarked, "You'll be the first patient for our new lady doctor." At that, the distraught man pleaded, "Sam, take me back to the beaver pond!"

Sam even had an expectant-mother yarn. He was flying a Travel Air 6000-B. Passengers included a pregnant woman and Ole, a bachelor trapper. About 100 miles from Fairbanks, Ole tapped Sam's shoulder. "Sam, this woman is having pains. We've got to do something."

"Ole," Sam replied, "whatever has to be done, *you* have to do it. I'm busy flying this airplane." Ole spread mail sacks on the floor and the woman lay on them, ready for the big moment. When Sam finally touched down at Fairbanks, the baby still hadn't arrived. "I hit the ground running," Sam said, "and left every-thing up to Ole and the ground crew."

About 1943, Sam was aloft over the Yukon River in a Gullwing Stinson, hauling 22 five-gallon cans of gasoline, when one of the aircraft's ski harnesses broke and one ski suddenly pointed straight down. That triggered breakage of the second ski harness. He regained control at 900 feet and found himself flying with two skis jammed into vertical position, his airspeed barely 85 miles per hour. He beelined it for Circle, the nearest runway, while reporting his dilemma on the radio to anyone who could hear.

He didn't have enough altitude to circle but went straight in to the field, which was covered with two feet of hard-packed snow. The plane plowed a furrow down to and through the roots of the grass, stopped within 50 feet, and didn't flip. Four cans of gas split at the seams and gas gurgled out, but there was no fire.

When the plane stopped, Sam sat, still belted to his seat, with snow almost to his waist. He had shoved his right knee into the instrument panel and cracked his hip. An Indian man who had watched the landing shook his hand, saying, "Sam, you land like moose ptarmigan [big bird]. I think you come dead quick!"

Noel Wien arrived to fly Sam to Fairbanks. Seven weeks later he was flying again.

The law said that Sam had to stop commercial flying in 1961 when he reached the age of 70. Richard Wien, Noel's son, was the Wien Airlines executive who had to tell Sam he was through. Sam was like a second father to Richard, and he said, "Hardest thing I ever had to do."

During nearly 40 years of flying, Sam logged more than 11,500 hours aloft, high time for an early years pilot. (In 1966, when I issued Noel Wien's instrument rating, I believe Noel had logged just over 9,000 hours.) For most of the early years, flight time logged did not include taxiing time on the ground—only the time a plane actually spent in the air. That was changed in the 1950s I believe, when the CAA decided that pilots could log all the time an airplane was moving. Planes that Sam flew included his Golden Eagle and Swallow, Bellancas, Stinsons, Pilgrims, a Curtiss Thrush and a Curtiss Robin, a Fairchild 71, a Travel Air 6000B—all work planes of the early years. He made 11 forced landings, and had only two accidents.

Both Noel Wien and Sam White were giants of the air. Alaska has had many other aviation greats, but these two were special.

Sam O. White died at Fairbanks on December 14, 1976. He was 85. "If Alaska is a good place to live in, it's also a good place to die in," he once said.

Harold Gillam

ON NOVEMBER 9, 1929, famed pilot Carl Ben Eielson and his mechanic, Earl Borland, took off from Teller, on the northwest coast of Alaska, into a raging snowstorm. They were bound for the ice-locked *Nanuk*, off the village of North Cape, Siberia. Aboard the *Nanuk* were 15 passengers and $1 million worth of furs. Eielson's Alaskan Airways had been offered $50,000 to rescue the furs and passengers. Eielson flew the Hamilton Metalplane that Noel Wien, eight months earlier, had flown to the ice-bound *Elisef* on a similar errand.

Eielson and Borland didn't arrive at the *Nanuk*, nor did they return to Teller. The search for the lost plane and its famous pilot (Eielson had flown with Sir Hubert Wilkins on exploration flights in both the Arctic and Antarctic) and his mechanic made headlines for months. As an airplane-crazy 13-year-old I read every word of that story in the newspapers. I still remember the screaming headlines in late January 1930: *"FIND WRECKAGE OF EIELSON PLANE."*

Pilots Joe Crosson and Harold Gillam found the crashed plane. I had read about Joe Crosson for several years, for he was one of Alaska's best-known pilots. But I had not heard of Harold Gillam until the Eielson search. In my wildest dreams, I couldn't have imagined that I would meet both of these pilots and that one day I would work as a pilot for Harold Gillam.

Harold Gillam was not talkative, so I learned very little about his career from him personally. He was generous with flying advice when asked, however, and I took full advantage. Gillam was medium-sized, muscular, dark-haired, handsome. He was graceful, almost catlike, in his movements and always seemed relaxed. He was a fastidious dresser and was well groomed even when working around an oily airplane. In contrast to some of the early pilots I knew, he liked his airplanes clean and nicely painted.

Stories of Harold Gillam's legendary 15-year flying career have been told and retold. For years, I spent much time at the air-crossroads village of McGrath on the lower Kuskokwim River, which was a main stopping point on the mail and passenger route that Gillam served in the late 1930s. Longtime residents of McGrath spoke of Gillam almost reverently. They adored him.

Gillam, who served aboard a U.S. Navy destroyer for a time, was a qualified Navy deep-sea diver. He worked for the Alaska Road Commission maintaining highways for several years. He then started his own freighting company, and for a time hauled freight overland to remote mines using Caterpillar tractors.

He first flew in 1927. As a student pilot, he escaped death in the crash of a Swallow biplane in which his instructor was killed. But that didn't discourage him. He continued learning to fly. In 1929, when Ben Eielson and Earl Borland disappeared, Gillam had but 40 hours in the air and he had made only one cross-country flight. He didn't even have a pilot's license. Nevertheless, he begged Alaskan Airways to allow him to take one of their planes on the search. They allowed him to take an open-cockpit Stearman biplane.

The winter of 1929–30 was one of the stormiest on record

in the Bering Sea, with temperatures down to minus 40 degrees. On December 9, despite a heavy snowstorm, Joe Crosson and Harold Gillam, wearing heavy fur clothing, put extra gas and provisions in their two open-cockpit planes and left Teller, bound for the *Nanuk*, which was to be the base for the search.

In the air, Gillam followed the more experienced Crosson. Wind battered the two biplanes. Fog obscured the ground and Bering Strait, boiling up from open leads in the ice that covered the ocean. The two pilots were guided by the black open channels. In two hours they reached Siberia and followed the coastline north. It was near dark on that short arctic winter day when they landed at a Siberian Eskimo village to spend the night.

The next morning, they refueled and flew into a blizzard so bad that Crosson turned back. He lost sight of Gillam, and returned to the village where they had spent the previous night. Gillam didn't return. The following day, Crosson, convinced that the inexperienced Gillam was lost in the storm, flew for three hours along the coast. He found the trading village of North Cape, and offshore, the *Nanuk*. On the ice beside the *Nanuk* was Gillam's Stearman.

The low-time, inexperienced Gillam, flying alone, had bored through the storm to the ice-locked ship. Other pilots couldn't believe it when Crosson told the story. Crosson was one of the finest and most experienced pilots in Alaska. By luck, guts, or skill, Gillam had outflown him. For five weeks the two pilots lived on the *Nanuk* and watched the snow and wind, wind and snow, and thick fog. They couldn't even consider flying.

On January 25, flying their two planes together on their search, they found Eielson's crashed Hamilton Metalplane. The bodies of Eielson and Borland were not visible. Weeks later, Russian searchers found the two dead airmen as they dug through deep snow near the wreck.*

---

* The wrecked Hamilton Metalplane was returned to Fairbanks by the Soviets in March 1991. It is on display at the Pioneer Air Museum, Fairbanks.

Many of the stories I have read and heard about Gillam's flying in the 1930s were about his seemingly uncanny ability to fly in bad weather. Most of the tales, which I heard from several pilots, went something like this. Several pilots, weatherbound at McGrath or Bethel, or some other bush village, would watch the snow blow by, play cards, and tell each other the same old lies as they waited for the storm to end. Occasionally, they struggled out into the storm to check their airplanes. In the midst of the storm they would hear an airplane fly over, circle, and then Gillam's big Pilgrim would appear on the runway, taxiing through the snow. Gillam would bring the mail in, have the plane refueled, take the outgoing mail, and roar off into the blizzard, while the waiting pilots looked at each other in amazement.

That Gillam made such flights there is no doubt. No one knows how he managed it. It is known that he was one of the first in Alaska to equip his airplane with a precision altimeter, a directional gyro, a turn-and-bank indicator, and an artificial horizon. He once told Ray Petersen, longtime bush pilot, and later president of Northern Consolidated Airlines, "If you can't see because of bad weather, go on instruments at 200 feet. Eventually you'll see a reference point."

That's an incredible approach and an equally incredible statement. Barometric pressures change, sometimes rapidly. Even though an altimeter might indicate that an airplane is flying at 200 feet, the plane might actually be at 100 feet—or lower. Land elevation varies greatly. Even a small hill can poke up 250 feet. If Gillam couldn't see 200 feet, and he was flying at 100 miles an hour (the speed of the airplanes Gillam flew in the 1930s), he had virtually no time to react if a tree, a hill, or a mountain suddenly appeared.

The Pilgrim that Gillam flew for years when he was building his reputation as a bad-weather pilot was a wonderful, slow-flying airplane. It could even handle heavy wing icing. The pilot sat high in the front with superb visibility. All of this must have helped, but it still doesn't fully explain how Gillam managed to repeatedly bore through bad weather to safely reach his destination.

Gillam did have many accidents in his first years as a pilot.

He flew out of Cordova with, among other airplanes, a Swallow biplane, a Zenith biplane, and an Ireland amphibian. Within a six-month period in 1931, for example, he broke six airplanes, with varying amounts of damage. After flying in the Copper River country for several years, he had shown no profit.

He moved to Fairbanks and bought a used Hornet-powered Pilgrim. With that, his run of serious accidents mostly ended. In 1936, he contracted with the U.S. Weather Bureau to make twice-daily weather flights from Fairbanks. He had to fly to 6,000 feet at a climb rate of exactly 300 feet per minute. He would then descend in tight spirals. In the winter, he made flights before daylight and after dark.

Before each flight, Weather Bureau personnel attached recording instruments to the Pilgrim's struts, and up Gillam would go. On such flights, Tom Appleton, Gillam's mechanic, stood on Weeks Field and talked Gillam down with one of the first voice radios installed in an airplane in Alaska. Appleton listened to the Pilgrim's engine to determine the plane's location. In two years of year-round weather observations, only twice did Gillam fail to make his scheduled flights.

In 1937, famed Soviet flyer Sigismund Levanevsky was lost on a flight from Moscow to Fairbanks. A huge search was mounted. Alaska delegate to Congress Anthony Dimond recommended Gillam as the Alaskan pilot best qualified to fly radio equipment, fuel, and supplies needed for the search from Fairbanks to Point Barrow.

Gillam made regular supply flights to Barrow in a way that other pilots could hardly credit. Dan Cathcart, a United Airlines pilot, rode with Gillam on one of these flights. Cathcart said that Gillam left Fairbanks and climbed his Pilgrim high and flew above unbroken clouds for six hours, with no view of the ground. At the end of six hours, Gillam pointed the big pot-bellied Pilgrim down through the clouds and landed on the lagoon at Barrow. Cathcart had seen nothing to indicate where they were, no land, nothing. He was incredulous when the buildings of Barrow appeared nearby in the fog as Gillam landed. There had been no radio contact between the Pilgrim and Barrow.

I knew Oscar Winchell, who flew for Gillam for a time in the 1930s. Oscar told me another story about flying with Gillam above the clouds. On this flight there were mountains below, with no breaks in the clouds. Gillam circled a time or two, then pointed the nose of the airplane down through the dense clouds. When the airplane broke into the clear, it was directly over the airport. After Gillam landed, there wasn't enough gas in the airplane to taxi it to the hangar. "I don't know how he did it," Winchell said.

In the mid-1930s, Pan American Airways had the contract to fly mail from Fairbanks to Bethel. On that route, Pan Am earned the reputation as a "blue-sky" outfit because they didn't fly in bad weather. Mail delivery by Pan Am wasn't as reliable as it had been by dog team, although it was faster.

In 1938, Harold Gillam won the contract for that route. He flew it in his Pilgrim airplanes (he eventually owned three of them). Residents of the region have told me they could set their watch by Gillam's arrival. He established a 100 percent completion schedule. This was a route I flew hundreds of times over many years, and I know what the weather can be. I still don't understand how Gillam managed such an unblemished record.

As I flew that route, I often thought of Gillam in his Pilgrim, fighting weather, on that lonely flight from Fairbanks. Reportedly, he finished the Fairbanks-Bethel round trip many times while other pilots remained weatherbound. McGrath residents have told me that sometimes the old silver Pilgrim that Gillam flew came sneaking in just over the trees. Once, apparently, he taxied on skis 10 or 15 miles on the snow of the Kuskokwim River to reach McGrath when weather pushed him down to the ground.

When war came, the Morrison-Knudsen Company chose

Gillam as their chief pilot for the airport building project.

On January 5, 1943, Gillam left Seattle with the Morrison-Knudsen Lockheed Electra, bound for Anchorage via Ketchikan. Aboard were five passengers. A strong storm was battering southeastern Alaska. Other Alaska-bound flights from Seattle were canceled because of the storm. Gillam, after arguing with Boeing Field clearance officers, left anyway. He had recently received training for instrument flying.

At five that afternoon the Electra was overdue and unreported at Ketchikan. Gillam had radioed that one of his engines had quit, and that he was in trouble. The airplane had entered dense fog four hours out of Seattle. Gillam, on instruments, unknowingly flew on the wrong side of the radio range. The airways map he used was obsolete. He circled at 6,000 feet. Turbulence bounced the plane. Ice formed on the wings. Then, one engine stopped.

One of the surviving passengers later said that the airplane hit a downdraft. It dropped several thousand feet until it flew just above the trees. The Electra narrowly missed one mountain. Soon afterward, the right wing hit a tree and the Electra crashed.

The search for the plane was difficult. Weather was terrible, daylight hours in January are short, and no one even knew the general area where the plane had crashed. It seemed likely it had gone into the sea. The heavily timbered, snow-covered, steep peaks of Southeast Alaska are among the most rugged in the world. The Electra could easily have been buried under an avalanche or hidden by dense timber. Actually, it was within 15 miles of Ketchikan.

The only woman passenger, 25-year-old Susan Baxter, from Idaho, died of injuries within 48 hours. A month later, two of the least injured passengers were found on the shore of Boca de Quadra Inlet. They were bearded, ragged, frostbitten, and 50 pounds lighter than when they had left Seattle. The two other survivors, badly injured, had remained at the plane.

On the sixth day after the crash, Gillam had left the plane

to try to find help. His frozen body was found a mile or so from where the first survivors were found, on the shore of Boca de Quadra Inlet.

The CAA cited pilot error as cause of the crash.

Joe Crosson

WITH NOVEMBER 1932, a welcome Chinook came that warmed the land and brought smiles to the people of Fairbanks. With their summer work done, men from the mines, forests, and farms were thinking of their winter meat supply. With this in mind, Bob Buzby headed for the sheep hills south of Fairbanks. With him was Roy Madson, dredgemaster for the Fairbanks Exploration Company; Buzby's brother-in-law, Keith Harkness; and a cook named Bill Cory. They used the two dog teams belonging to Buzby and Cory. Buzby, a longtime friend of mine, had been born at Fairbanks in 1911 and lived on his parents' homestead at the present sight of Fort Wainwright.

The four mushed the dogs 45 miles to Wood River. They then traveled upriver 22 miles to Sheep Creek, where in a few days they killed the wild sheep they wanted. They left late one afternoon, heading home down Wood River, planning to remain overnight at Lynx Cabin. As they approached Lynx Cabin after dark, they saw a light coming upriver. It was Harold Meyers, a cheechako (greenhorn) with a bug—a candle in a can—lighting his way. Meyers had been at Lynx Cabin with Theodore Van Bibber, an early settler on Wood River. Van was sick and had sent Harold looking for help.

It was 6:00 P.M., three hours after dark, when the men reached the cabin. Van, more than six feet tall, a big strong man, was extremely ill. He was talking about dying, and that worried the hunters. They didn't know what was wrong with him, although they suspected appendicitis. He was having seizures that almost rendered him unconscious. They treated him by putting cold packs on his stomach.

After observing Van Bibber's condition for three hours, Buzby decided to go to Fairbanks with his dog team to arrange for an airplane to retrieve Van Bibber.

He was afraid to take the sick man to town in a dogsled because the rough trip might kill him. Keith Harkness was to accompany Buzby as far as Wood River crossing, about 20 miles. Wood River had much overflow (water on the ice). Often it was as deep as ten inches. Harkness was to walk back to Lynx Cabin the next day.

They took 15 dogs, nine of Buzby's and six of Cory's. Buzby asked Cory to put up a lunch, expecting him to put together a box with a frying pan, coffee, and some of the fresh sheep meat.

Buzby and Harkness arrived at the Wood River crossing at daylight. An old cabin, built by Sourdough Bill, stood on the bank. The two decided to eat and rest there. They then discovered that their lunch consisted of one sandwich each.

They had been wet all night as they crossed one overflow area after another. The temperature was dropping fast. They beat the ice off their sled, and at the crossing, found a foot of fresh snow that had drifted several feet deep in places. It was still snowing and drifting. The trip to Fairbanks was shaping up to be long and difficult. They saw that Harkness would have trouble returning to Lynx Cabin with moccasins through the overflow on Wood

River, so they changed their plan. Both would go to Fairbanks.

They left Sourdough Bill's cabin and encountered deep snowdrifts. Buzby forged ahead on snowshoes, breaking trail for the dogs. It continued to grow colder. They had 44 miles to go, and the traveling was very difficult.

They reached a cabin about 25 miles from Fairbanks, searched for food, and found virtually none. Each had a teaspoon of sugar and a teaspoon of bacon grease. The dogs were showing exhaustion. Harkness remained at the cabin to give them a rest, and to rest a bit himself. Buzby continued snowshoeing on, breaking trail. Keith planned to catch up.

Five or six miles beyond the cabin, Buzby came to a large, open, windswept flat. It was bitterly cold now, and growing dark. The trail virtually disappeared. He had to use a stick as he crossed the flats to poke through the snow to find the edges of the packed trail. There was no sign of Harkness, even though he should have overtaken Buzby by this time. Buzby realized they should have remained together. If either got into trouble, there was no one to help.

Buzby decided to return to the cabin to see if Harkness was in trouble. Within a mile, he met up with Harkness and the dog team. The dogs were reluctant to travel. In deep cold, the animals don't like to open their mouths to puff in the frigid air. It is difficult to get them out of a fast walk.

The men and dogs continued to struggle. They fought deep snow, bitter cold, exhaustion, and hunger.

Nine miles from Fairbanks, they reached Salchacket Slough. It was 11:00 P.M. At a small cabin, Buzby lit a fire in the stove while Harkness started to unhitch the dogs. Within a few moments he had five of them unharnessed. He stepped into the cabin to warm up and found Buzby asleep. Buzby had traveled for 48 hours without sleep. In the previous 36 hours he had eaten one sandwich, a teaspoon of sugar, and a teaspoon of bacon grease.

The two decided not to unhitch all the dogs. They brought all the dogs into the cabin, including those that still wore their harnesses. They rolled up in an old quilt they found on the one bunk. At 5:00 A.M. they awoke, half frozen, and lit a candle. They couldn't see the walls inside the cabin because of the steam rising from the 15 dogs. Frigid air poured through a hole in the cabin which they hadn't seen the previous night.

They reharnessed the five dogs Harkness had unharnessed, and took to the trail again. Buzby went ahead to break trail, while Harkness handled the gee-pole, a pole lashed to the front end of the sled and used for steering. As he steered, Harkness rode skis. They were within half a mile of town before they came to a broken trail. As they wearily pulled into Fairbanks, it was 9:00 A.M., and the temperature was minus 55 degrees.

Buzby phoned Mrs. Van Bibber, who worked as a nurse's aide at St. Joseph's Hospital. He learned that the only hangared (thus warm) airplane in town was a Fairchild 71 belonging to Pacific Alaska Airlines. Pilot Joe Crosson was in charge. Joe was tall, handsome, dark-haired, and friendly. There was no more capable pilot than Crosson, and Buzby was delighted when Joe agreed to fly to Wood River to try to pick up Van Bibber. Buzby agreed to accompany him to show him where Lynx Cabin was. Mrs. Van Bibber talked a Dr. Gillespie into going along too. Gillespie wasn't dressed for the cold, but he went anyway.

They had to hurry because of the short daylight hours. The airplane was already loaded with emergency gear, with snow-shoes in the back. The oil was quickly warmed and poured into the engine. A bit of snow was thrown on the hangar floor for the skis to slide on as the plane was pushed out into the frigid air. The Fairchild rose into the cold, leaving a vapor trail behind. Shortly, the plane was over Wood River.

Cory and Meyers had agreed to mark out a runway for the airplane near Lynx Cabin. Crosson flew back and forth examining the spot they had marked. "No good," he told Buzby. "We'll have to find another spot."

Crosson then searched up and down the river. The weak winter light made difficult the critical task of selecting a safe landing place for the big ski plane.

Wind normally blows downriver out of the mountains, and Crosson flew upwind slowly, searching. When he found a promising spot on the river ice three miles upstream from Lynx Cabin, he dragged by it slowly, turned, and dragged it again. He could find no really long, straight stretch in the winding river where he could land. This spot would have to do.

He never would have attempted a landing in that place if Van Bibber hadn't been depending on him. He came in slowly and touched down. The skis clattered across the hard snow, and the Fairchild came to a stop. While the engine continued to run, Buzby got out and placed two-by-fours on the snow in front of the plane's skis. Crosson then taxied the plane onto the boards. This kept the skis from freezing to the snow's surface.

Buzby and Dr. Gillespie headed for Lynx Cabin, and Crosson stayed with the Fairchild. He had to put the canvas engine cover on, and drain the oil to keep it warm. The engine cover reached to the ground, and Joe stood inside it as long as he could stand the fumes from the plumber's firepot. He put the oil on the firepot from time to time, and the firepot also kept the engine warm.

So there Crosson stood, guarding the plane from fire, watching the wind blow the canvas engine cover back and forth, hoping that the ill man would arrive before dark. He wanted to be able to see when he tried a takeoff from the short river runway he was perched on.

While Buzby and Dr. Gillespie hurried toward the cabin, Gillespie grew colder by the moment. He was in street clothes—not appropriate attire for the minus-50-degree temperature and Wood River wind.

They had almost reached the cabin when Cory and Meyers appeared on the river. They were driving the dog team, with Van Bibber on the sled. Van had improved. His seizures had stopped about an hour after Buzby and Harkness had left two days before, but he was very weak.

Because Gillespie was freezing, they had to return to the cabin to find warm clothing for him for the trip back to the airplane. It was growing dark when finally they got Van Bibber to the plane.

Crosson poured the hot oil back into the engine and hurried to start the big radial before it cooled. The Pratt & Whitney Wasp Jr. usually started easily, and Crosson's engine did so this time.

Takeoff had to be downwind, for the hills were too high upstream to chance lifting off in that direction. Crosson's heart must have been in his throat as he poured the coal to the old Wasp and headed her downriver, praying the skis didn't trip on an unseen rock or a chunk of ice, and that he could lift her off and clear the riverbank. The cold, dense air should provide good lift. Would the engine turn up properly in the deep cold?

The Fairchild 71 was a fine performer. The engine, kept warm by Crosson's careful efforts with the plumber's pot, turned full rpms. They leaped off, nicely clearing the high banks of the river. Crosson flew up the Tanana River, then up the Chena River. He arrived over Weeks Field at Fairbanks after dark. A ground crew put railroad flares out to light the runway. Crosson landed safely.

At St. Joseph's hospital, it was discovered that Van Bibber had a strangulated hernia and needed surgery. He recovered, but never hit the trail again.

Buzby traveled the Wood River country for a dozen years after that, but because of rocks, ice, and overflow, never again could a plane have landed where Crosson had.

This rescue illustrates graphically what airplanes did for Alaska. And, it shows that pilots had to know their business. Keeping an airplane flying in the deep cold is tricky and requires a lot of work.

Joe Crosson flew the distance between Wood River and Fairbanks in 25 minutes, the same stretch of icy land that had taken two strong men and a team of 15 dogs more than

30 hours of constant struggle.

Joe Crosson was often called the "mercy pilot" (a sobriquet he disliked) in his early years in Alaska, because of many flights like the one he made for Van Bibber.

I met Joe Crosson in 1941 at Fairbanks. I was talking with Noel Wien one day when Crosson walked into the office. Noel introduced us. I maintained my aplomb with some difficulty, for I realized that I was in rare company—Noel Wien and Joe Crosson. Joe was a northern flyer who was famous in his own right. He too had been one of my boyhood heroes.

Crosson learned to fly in San Diego with his famous older sister, Marvel. In San Diego he and Marvel rebuilt a Curtiss N-9 seaplane, installing an OX-5 engine in it. They apparently also rebuilt the OX-5 JN-4D (Jenny) in which they learned to fly.

The two barnstormed together for several years. In 1926 Joe went to work for the Fairbanks Airplane Company, and their flying partnership ended. Marvel spent the winter of 1927–28 in Fairbanks with Joe. In May 1929 Marvel set a new altitude record, reaching 23,996 feet over Los Angeles in a Ryan Brougham. In August 1929, she was on the second leg of the Women's Air Derby when her plane crashed and she was killed. There were indications that she had become so airsick in turbulent air and desert heat that she had been unable to control the plane. Her body was found with the parachute released but unopened.

Joe did a lot of walking during his first years in Alaska, mostly while returning to Fairbanks to get airplane parts for a plane that he had put down somewhere in the bush. He would land on a river bar with a brakeless airplane, run out of room, and end in the river. Then he'd need repair parts before he could fly again. He would have to walk 80 or 100 miles to reach a road, railroad, or river where he could get a ride.

Often, his Hisso engine quit in flight, and he had to land wherever he could. Sometimes he tried to land a miner or prospector on a field that was too short, and found himself in trouble.

In 1927, Crosson flew an open-cockpit Swallow biplane from Fairbanks to Barrow on a charter trip. A reporter for the Wilkins expedition of that year, A. M. Smith, needed a ride to Barrow because there wasn't room for him in the heavily loaded Wilkins plane. With three hours' notice and only an old ship's compass and a crude map, Crosson flew the Hisso-powered Swallow into the Brooks Range. He followed the Anaktuvuk River to its confluence with the Colville, then headed cross-country over the arctic slope to Barrow. He hit the coast 50 miles east of Barrow, and flying through snow flurries, followed the shoreline to Barrow. When he landed, it was 40 below zero and he had only a few gallons of gas left.

Crosson, his explorer's blood at a boil, decided to return to Fairbanks by another route. A couple of days later, flying alone in the Swallow, he flew south along the Arctic coast where only the dirigible *Norge* had previously flown. For three hours he peered down at pressure ridges, drifted snow, and some of the most barren land in North America. He reached Kotzebue just ahead of a snowstorm. His Swallow was the first airplane ever to reach Kotzebue, and Eskimo residents crowded around, amazed.

A few days later, he headed inland, following the Kobuk River. He landed on rough river ice at the Eskimo village of Noorvik, breaking a landing gear. With local help, he repaired it and flew on to Fairbanks, ending one of the most remarkable flights ever made by any pioneering Alaskan pilot. In winter he had flown a 1,580 mile round trip, much of it over virtually blank areas of the map, in an open-cockpit plane.

In 1928, Hubert Wilkins and Carl Ben Eielson took Crosson with them on their expedition to the Antarctic, in which they accompanied the annual cruise of the Norwegian whaling fleet to Deception Island in the South Shetlands. They had two Lockheed Vegas, including the one that Wilkins and Eielson had flown from Barrow to Spitzbergen the previous year.

When Eielson returned to Alaska in 1929 to form his own company, Crosson was one of his pilots—a year before Crosson and Gillam found Eielson's wrecked airplane.

In 1931, Crosson and Ed Young, another pioneer Alaska pilot, flew two Fairchild 71s on a charter flight for a Fox Movietone News team to determine the precise elevation of Mount McKinley, North America's tallest peak. They flew from Fairbanks on August 29, climbed to 15,000 feet, broke through the clouds and continued up to the actual height of the great mountain—20,320 feet.

In 1935, it was Joe Crosson who flew the bodies of Wiley Post and Will Rogers to the States after their crash near Barrow. A move was made to award him the Congressional Medal of Honor and the Distinguished Flying Cross for that flight, but Joe was a humble man and refused the idea, saying that the medals were unwarranted and not in keeping with what he had done. He and Wiley Post had been friends for many years, and the death of that famous one-eyed pilot was a personal tragedy for Crosson. He had been the person who drove Post and Rogers to the Chena River at Fairbanks for the takeoff of their ill-fated flight.

Pan American Airways formed a subsidiary in Alaska called Pacific Alaska Airways, flying from Fairbanks. Crosson became chief pilot for this company when it was formed about 1930. By 1937, he was manager of Pan American Airways' Alaska Division. In 1941, shortly after I met him at Fairbanks, he was transferred to Seattle. In 1944, Joe left Pan Am to manage his own aircraft and parts business in Seattle, where he remained until his death at the age of 49.

Air Transport Command

MY FLYING for the Northway Project ended in late fall, 1942. I then returned to Fairbanks, where Bessie and I had rented a house. The wartime Air Transport Command (ATC) had been formed, in which most major U.S. airlines contracted with the Army Air Forces to provide pilots to fly military personnel, freight, and mail. Northwest Airlines had contracted to fly the route from Minneapolis, Minnesota, to Alaska. For this, Northwest needed pilots with Alaskan experience.

Northwest Airlines, the first of the big companies to contract with the ATC to provide pilots, had served as far north as Winnipeg, Manitoba, as early as the 1930s. The company's pilots and mechanics were familiar with cold-weather flying. Northwest advised the military in establishing communications and ground services north of Edmonton, Alberta. Also, Northwest pilots ferried military aircraft over this route. Later, Northwest extended its wartime work into Alaska's far-flung Aleutians, flying personnel, freight, and mail for the Alaska Defense Command.

A few days after I had returned to Fairbanks from Nabesna, Captain Benny Christian, a Northwest Airlines pilot I had known in Minnesota, came knocking on my door to ask me to fly for Northwest. I quickly signed up. For years I had wanted to fly for a scheduled airline. I had once applied to Northwest for a job but had been turned down.

Before I could fly with the airline, I had to pass a physical at the famed Mayo Clinic in Minnesota. Then I had to attend instrument flying school in Chicago. The ten hours or so of dual instrument training I had had wasn't sufficient. I flew to Minneapolis from Alaska in an empty C-47, the military version of the DC-3. I spent much of the trip standing behind the pilots in the cockpit. They were on solid instruments, and nothing was visible from the cockpit but white. Zooming along at a cruising speed of 155 miles per hour through clouds made me nervous. "Why don't you drop down and fly under the clouds so you can see where you're going?" I asked.

The pilot laughed. "After you've finished instrument training you'll know better."

Aviation was progressing amazingly fast. Only thirteen years earlier, in 1929, Lieutenant Jimmy Doolittle of the U.S. Army Air Corps had made the first instrument flight. With his cockpit hooded so he could see nothing but his instruments, Doolittle took off from Mitchell Field, on Long Island, New York. After flying for 15 minutes, he landed within a few yards of the spot from which his plane had leaped into the air. That was one of aviation's most significant flights. Within a short time, the precision instruments and radio navigation aids that Doolittle used for his blind flight became standard for long-distance instrument flying. They included a turn-and-bank indicator, the Sperry artificial horizon, the Kollsman precision altimeter, and the Sperry directional gyro. Doolittle's pioneering flight laid the foundation for today's airline travel.

In Chicago, I started my instrument training instruction in a Gullwing Stinson. Bessie and two-year-old Cathy joined me, and we lived in a hotel while I attended school.

Because of our experience in Alaska, fellow student Bob Long (one of my co-workers at Wien Airlines in Nome) and I were treated with respect by the other student pilots. They had seen the newly released film *Bush Pilot*, which glamorized northern bush flying. Of course, the Hollywood idea of bush flying was cockeyed, but these pilots didn't know that.

Herman Lerdahl, one of the pilots with whom I had flown on the Nabesna-Northway job, also went to work for Northwest Airlines. Our paths occasionally crossed over the next few years.

I proved to the other pilots one day that I was really more accustomed to bush strips than city airports. I flew four of these pilots in a company Stinson to Chicago's Midway Airport, where they were to take an examination. I didn't know the airport at all, but when I got near I called in and received clearance to land on a specific runway. I flew a standard left-hand pattern, and saw what I took to be the assigned runway. For some reason I flew on by. There were no more numbers showing on runways below, but there was plenty of concrete, so I landed.

When I taxied to the parking area, a flight controller called, instructing me to report to the tower at once. "Do you realize where you landed?" he asked, severely.

"I guess it was on the runway I was cleared for," I answered weakly.

"You landed on the ramp," he said, looking disgusted. "Where are you from?"

"Nome, Alaska," I answered. "And this ramp is bigger than any field I've landed on for a long time."

"Oh hell, get out of here," the guy said. I took a little kidding over that.

I was transferred to Billings, Montana, where I finished my instrument training. Bessie and Cathy followed me to Billings, and we had some sort of a home life while I trained.

Then I was sent to Alaska as a DC-3 copilot. This lasted but a short time before I was transferred back to Billings to train for my Airline Transport Rating (ATR). I was busily working toward that ATR when, on November 9, 1943, our son, Roy (named for Roy Duggan), was born, at Billings.

I soon earned my ATR. Wartime separated many families for long periods, and Bessie and I were no exception. I knew I would be sent north for my ATC flying, and was unlikely to be based at any one place for long. I hated to leave Bessie alone in Billings with Roy and three-year-old Cathy. We decided it would be best if she returned home to Minnesota for the duration of the war.

For a time she lived in Minneapolis, and then she moved to Roseau so she could be near her relatives and my family. For the next few years I managed to get home to visit my family every four or five weeks, flying on passes or hitching rides on ATC flights.

After my ATC training, Northwest stationed me at Edmonton, Alberta. I flew C-47s hauling military personnel and supplies to Canada's Great Slave Lake, Norman Wells, and Fort Simpson—real northern frontier settlements. Like all ATC pilots, I wore a uniform and was subject to military discipline. I held the rank of captain. Our orders came from the Air Force, our salaries from the airline. An oil pipeline was being built from Norman Wells, in the Northwest Territories, to Whitehorse, Yukon Territory, and we made flights in support of that huge project.

There were many blank areas and dotted lines on the maps we used for flying in northwestern Canada. Mapmakers hadn't gotten around to this vast wilderness. One huge circle of dotted lines was labeled "Trout Lake." We found that Trout Lake didn't form a circle at all; a big peninsula sliced down the middle of the lake. We pilots spent a lot of time drawing in geographic features on maps for our own benefit, and for others who would fly there after us.

In those days there was no way of keeping track of us. Once we took off and flew out of sight of the field, neither dispatchers nor officials at our airports knew precisely where we were. Not infrequently, we made side trips, or diversions, to look over new country and to add to our maps. If we arrived 15 to 30 minutes late, we blamed headwinds.

Once, our route took us close to the South Nahanni River, so we veered over the valley to take a look. I had read tales about the South Nahanni and the Headless Valley. Supposedly, prospectors in 1898 trying to get to the Klondike had disappeared. Many years later their headless bodies were found in the valley of the South Nahanni. Much has been written about this. Author Phillips H. Godsell wrote several magazine articles that retold the story, and Godsell's tales made fascinating mysteries. On the map, the valley was labeled "Verdant," or "Tropical," so I half expected to see palm trees. It was a beautiful river valley, but of course there were no palms or other tropical trees. It looked like any other northern river valley.

One day as we were returning to Whitehorse from Norman Wells, we received a radio call: "Air Force, this is Whitehorse. Your QDM is 270 degrees." I had never heard of a QDM and asked for a repeat. "Your QDM is 270 degrees."

"What does that mean?" I blurted.

"Your heading to Whitehorse is 270 degrees," came the reply. We knew that, of course. But for the first time equipment was available at an airport to confirm an accurate heading to our destination. Because of this early radar installation, they knew exactly where we were. Radar became a valuable navigation aid, but it curtailed some of our little side trips.

For the ATC, we flew hard, day and night. We flew to Fairbanks, to Nome, to Anchorage, and throughout northern Canada. While flying a C-47 between Fairbanks and Edmonton, Gil Enger, a pilot and good friend from Duluth, disappeared. He and his copilot were flying with the ATC on the same routes I was. Enger reported over Northway and was never heard from again. We flew search for days, but never found a trace. To my knowledge, they are still missing. Their airplane is one of the hundreds of planes missing in Alaska, where more planes have disappeared than anywhere else on earth.

Another pilot, Johnny Hart, flying a C-47, radioed in while preparing for an instrument approach from the northwest near Watson Lake, Yukon Territory. Nothing was heard from him again. Within a short time, all of us were alerted. It was the dead of winter and very cold. We searched intensively and found no evidence of his plane, although he had reported from close to the airport. More than a week later, two survivors of the crash arrived at the end of the Watson Lake runway. The airplane had apparently stalled about seven miles from the runway and crashed on its nose in the dense spruce forest.

Johnny Hart and his copilot were both killed in the crash. It was a miracle that the two passengers had survived. One of them could move on hands and knees, the other couldn't move at all. The one who was mobile somehow fashioned a toboggan, put the other survivor on it, then crawled as he pulled the toboggan seven miles to the runway. Temperatures ranged to minus 40 degrees. The whole time, he could hear airplanes landing and taking off.

The ATC planes were painted entirely green at that time. The green of Hart's crashed plane blended with the forest, and it was almost impossible to see even when we knew where it was. Shortly afterward, the tails of ATC planes were painted red.

A third C-47 that disappeared on that run was flown by a very experienced Northwest Airlines pilot named Mensing. He took off from Fort Nelson, British Columbia, bound for Edmonton, but he never arrived. We searched and searched, along with the Air Force rescue planes. Rumors flew that the plane had carried a huge payroll, or a large amount of cash. I don't know whether this was true, but the rumors inspired further searching. That airplane was never found during my time in the North, and to my knowledge is still missing.

In June 1942, after bombing our naval base at Dutch Harbor, the Japanese seized two of the Aleutian Islands, Attu and Kiska, and fortified both islands. Step by step, our Army, Navy, and Air Force moved down the Aleutians, closing in on the occupied islands. In May 1943, in one of the bloodiest battles of the Pacific, Attu was regained by the United States. The Japanese abandoned Kiska, but the American buildup continued in the Aleutians. Staging bases were built for aerial raids on the Japanese-owned Kurile Islands.

To support the military, the ATC flew tons of freight and hundreds of people into the Aleutians. The Aleutian Islands are peaks of submerged volcanic mountains. These pinpoints of land—green in summer, snowy in winter—are like a necklace of tiny jewels stretching in an arc westward from the Alaska Peninsula toward Japan. At the Aleutian chain, the warm Japanese Current of the North Pacific meets cold blasts of air from the Bering Sea. Violent winds and constant storms result, which sweep eastward over Alaska.

The Aleutians are famed as a factory for terrible weather. In the early 1940s, weather prediction had yet to be developed for the remote North Pacific. Visibility there can change from unlimited to none within 30 minutes. Williwaws—bursts of air that surge across the tops of peaks and down steep slopes—can tumble an airplane like a fly in a washing machine. Williwaws can also overturn large boats. Fog seems perpetual among the islands, and during the Aleutian war campaign more airplane losses came from weather than from enemy action.

On my first trip to the Aleutian island of Shemya, I saw a log chain hanging from a pole near the runway. "What's that for?" I bit.

"That's our wind sock," was the answer.

Doctors who gave physicals to ATC pilots planning to fly in the Aleutians predicted they would develop stress ulcers within six months.

I volunteered to fly in the Aleutians because of the challenge of the flying. I was attracted by the beauty of the islands, which form the longest archipelago in the world. Interestingly, Herman Lerdahl, another Minnesotan, flew ATC C-47s in the

Aleutians at about the time I did. Sometimes it seemed that most of Alaska's early pilots hailed from Minnesota. Lerdahl was born (in 1906) in Cyrus. I flew mostly with Dick O'Neil in the Aleutians. O'Neil was a fine pilot. He and I were both captains.

If there is anyplace in this world a pilot must learn to handle winds, the far-flung Aleutian Islands is that place. I became confident of my skill in landing a C-47 in crosswinds—always the bugaboo of pilots. Sometimes we had upper winds blowing 125 miles an hour, and yet the air could be smooth. We determined wind velocity by taking frequent bearings and by using radio navigation. It wasn't unusual for us to fly headings that were 40 or 50 degrees off course to compensate for the wind, and that's a lot of crab in a C-47. In the time I flew there, I became well acquainted with the bases on Attu, Amchitka, Adak, Umnak, Shemya, and other islands. I learned much about flying an airplane in rough air and with poor visibility.

On one of my early trips, I landed my C-47 at King Salmon on the Alaska Peninsula. While our plane was being refueled, the colonel in command of the base called out, "Hi there, Rudy. Good to see you." It was John Cross, the quiet-spoken bush pilot who, at Deering, had advised me to "Give her a little more speed" when I was shooting landings for the first time with a Wien Gullwing Stinson. We had a pleasant visit. His hospitality made our routine stops at King Salmon a pleasure over the next year or so. After the war, John went back to the Arctic to resume bush flying.

One dark winter night as I was flying to Shemya Island, far out in the Aleutians near Attu, I experienced just how quickly the weather could change. Making a letdown from above the clouds, we could clearly see the runway marker lights from about 20 miles. I flew over the runway at 8,000 feet and looked down on those lights, which showed bright and clear the full length of the runway. I made what we called a quick approach to land, not following the complete procedure I would have on instruments. That approach consisted of a few turns as we lost altitude and lined up with the runway. But, when I did line up with the runway for final approach, it wasn't visible. I wondered what I had done wrong. Where was I?

In the few minutes needed to make those turns and descend, fog had moved in. Had it been daylight, we'd probably have seen a layer of fog lying on the edge of the runway, but that night we didn't land at Shemya. I had to decide where I could go from there and how much gas was left. And I had to figure quickly and accurately, because our lives depended on it. We were able to land at Attu, where the weather was marginal, but we squeaked in.

The times when our Aleutian destination field was closed, we knew that we might or might not manage to land at an alternative landing site. We simply didn't know until we reached our destination—or our alternate—whether we were going to be able to land. And because of those quick changes in weather, we constantly watched our fuel supply.

On one flight, we took off from Adak bound for Anchorage. On the way, we were supposed to land on Umnak Island. We found Umnak socked in, making landing impossible. We made one pass at minimum altitude, but we couldn't even see the island.

We flew on toward Anchorage and reached Cold Bay, where the weather was horrible. We found some visibility when we got under the clouds, but the wind was ferocious. I made a pass at the runway, but the wind was so strong we couldn't get the airplane on the ground.

By then we were becoming concerned about our fuel. There was nothing to do but keep going. Flying on the northern, or Bering Sea, side of the Alaska Peninsula, we reached Port Heiden, where we found the same bad weather. Again, landing was impossible.

We were really worried then, so we put the airplane into maximum cruise configuration—throttling the engines back to get maximum distance out of the fuel. We could almost see each turn of the slow-moving propellers as airspeed dropped from 155 to about 125.

Heading for King Salmon, we were estimating our arrival when I received one of the most ridiculous radio calls I can remember: "What will you do if you can't land at King Salmon?" The answer, of course, was that we would fly to the nearest open runway, because by the time we reached King Salmon the engines would be running on fumes.

"We'll try to get to Iliamna," I replied, and let it go at that.

We reached King Salmon. Ceiling and visibility were well above minimums, with a 52-mile-per-hour quartering crosswind on the runway—one stiff crosswind. I remember making the approach knowing we had to land. The prospect of bellying in on the tundra didn't appeal to me.

In a crosswind landing, the pilot must lower one wing and slip the airplane sideways in the air, controlling the movement so the airplane is flying in a straight line along the runway. Such a landing takes a fine balancing of rudder and ailerons. In that strong wind, I put the tilted C-47 down on one wheel, with the upwind wingtip almost scraping the runway. By God, I got her on! To hold the airplane heading straight down the runway, I kept cruise power on one engine, with the other engine idling. I rolled in the ailerons and used all the techniques I had learned for a crosswind landing, keeping about 25 inches of power on one engine. I had trouble stopping because the plane kept pulling to one side. Fortunately, the King Salmon runway is long and wide. We had flown eight and a half hours on what would normally have been eight hours of fuel.

Long hours in the air (it is 1,700 miles from Anchorage to Attu, westernmost of the Aleutian Islands), bad weather, exciting landings, and scenes of great beauty—such as the tops of smoking Aleutian volcanoes sticking above the fog—come to mind when I remember my Aleutian flying.

There was occasional humor, too. Tokyo Rose, who

broadcast Japanese propaganda nightly, warned that all civilians, and women and children (though there were no families on Adak during the war) should leave Adak Island because the Japanese were going to bomb our base there. She named a specific date, and it was just my luck to be on Adak that day. We weren't really concerned, for the Japanese had been driven out of the Aleutians. They hadn't returned, even for bombing raids. Nevertheless, we talked about Tokyo Rose's announcement.

The morning of the supposed raid, I was sitting in an out-house on top of a small knoll near the runway contemplating Tokyo Rose's warning, when, suddenly, there came a terrific explosion. "My God, Tokyo Rose was right," I thought. I bolted out of that outhouse with my pants still at half mast and sprinted down the hill, right in front of the morning crew. It turned out that the Navy had dynamited some nearby rocks. My loose-pants sprint was recounted with humor on Adak and among our flight crews for weeks.

Once, in June 1944, Dick O'Neil and I took off from Umnak, pulled up through the overcast and saw a tremendous explosion ahead. Flames and smoke spewed into the sky. At first we thought it was a torpedoed tanker. We neared the flames and peered down to discover that Mount Cleveland on Chuginadak Island, dormant for a century, was erupting. As we watched, boulders as big as small houses were flung high. The mountain itself looked like a chunk of wood that someone had split with an axe. We flew near, but the sulphur fumes were so strong we feared they might asphyxiate us, so we banked away. Three weather observers who were on Chuginadak Island were never heard from again.

While I flew in the Aleutians, another ATC C-47 was lost, with a pilot and copilot who were my friends. Frank "Bub" Christian (the brother of Benny Christian, who had signed me up with Northwest Airlines) and copilot Ray Dyjak crashed into Cape Adagdak at Adak Island while on instruments.

Contrary to early medical predictions, none of us got ulcers. And finally, the war ended. Northwest Airlines retained those of us who had been hired to fly for ATC, but our seniority was reduced. Most of us became full-time copilots. This demotion was hard to take, for I had flown hundreds of hours as captain.

I was stationed at Minneapolis, and I expected to be a copilot for about 100 years. Admittedly, the steady income was attractive, but the thought of living in Minneapolis for the rest of my life and working a regular schedule was almost unbearable.

When I had a few days off, Bessie and I, with Cathy, who was five now, and Roy, two years old, went to northern Minnesota, where we took a boat ride on Lake of the Woods. A man I had taught to fly in 1937, Fay Young, ran the boat. Mail had not been flown on Lake of the Woods for four years because of the war. Now, Young had a contract for delivering mail, and he needed someone to do the flying.

I quit my job with Northwest Airlines, a job that most pilots would have given their right arm for, and contracted to fly mail into the Lake of the Woods area. This wasn't the last time I was to leave a top-paying, steady job to do something I preferred. I loved wilderness flying.

So I was again in northern Minnesota, flying the area where I had flown for George Arnold in 1935. I owned and flew two Curtiss Robins (one on floats, the other on wheels/skis) and a two-place Taylorcraft. I flew passengers, freight, and mail. The Northwest Angle was still primitive backcountry, and, as was true when I flew for Arnold, my airplane was an important link with civilization for the residents.

My scariest flight at the Angle during my second stint there came when I got word that Mrs. Vickaryous at Oak Island was about to have a baby. Beattie Carlson at Angle Inlet probably had appendicitis. Both needed to be flown to a doctor.

It was a bitter, stormy winter day, with wind blowing high drifts on Lake of the Woods. Fritz Carlson, Beattie's father, was opinionated and determined. "By Gawd, I'm not going to let my daughter go to town alone," he insisted.

"I've got to pick up a pregnant lady, too," I told him. That didn't deter him. He climbed in with his daughter.

"OK," I said. "It'll be a little crowded, but we'll try." I flew to the island where Mrs. Vickaryous waited. She looked as if she could have the baby at any moment.

I don't know who sat where in that narrow, two-person rear seat, but I didn't worry about it. I was determined to get them all to town as fast as I could. I flew straight across 40 miles of The Big Traverse of the Lake of the Woods. Normally, I flew within gliding distance of shore, but I didn't want to waste time on this flight. I didn't want that baby to be born while we were still in the air.

About halfway across the lake, my engine started to miss. The nearest shoreline was Buffalo Point, Canada. I headed that way, but I wasn't high enough to get within 10 miles of it. The engine ran for a few moments, sputtered, and finally quit. I sat her down. The wind had blown for days, and the frozen lake below was rough, with big, hard-packed snowdrifts. If I had been flying anything but that tough old Robin, the landing would have broken something for sure.

There I was on the snow and ice in the middle of huge, frozen Lake of the Woods with a woman about to have a baby, a seriously sick girl, and an anxious old man. The temperature was about 30 degrees below zero. A strong wind was blowing, and my engine was dead. I was sure we would all freeze to death. I knew that if we remained on the ground for 15 minutes, the engine would become too cold to restart. There was no way that the four of us could get to shore. Even if we did, I doubted we could find shelter in the wilderness. I simply had to restart the engine.

I furiously pumped the Lunkenheimer primer. I leaped out and pulled the propeller through, and, thank God, the engine started, although it ran rough. I quickly climbed back in, the engine threatening to quit any moment. There was dead silence from the three frightened passengers in the rear. They knew the danger. I pumped the Lunkenheimer, and the engine picked up a bit. I quit pumping, and it started to miss again. I got the message then. By pumping the Lunkenheimer steadily I could keep the engine running. I opened the throttle and continued to pump frantically with one hand while working the stick with the other. That old Robin rattled and bumped over the big drifts and staggered back into the air. I pumped the Lunkenheimer all the way to Warroad, and the engine didn't miss a beat.

I was exhausted when I landed and the three passengers went on their way. I checked out the engine and discovered that the gasoline intake pipes for the three top cylinders had come loose and air instead of gas was being sucked into the cylinders. Fortunately, the Lunkenheimer primer lines went only to these three top cylinders, so by pumping I had been able to feed them with gas. The other cylinders on the bottom received their normal fuel supply. I tightened the pipes and put safety wire on them to keep them from loosening again.

Within a day or so I learned that Beattie Carlson did not have appendicitis. Also, Mrs. Vickaryous didn't have her baby for two weeks. After that experience, I threatened to refuse to carry pregnant women passengers about to deliver. Twice over the years I came close to having to deliver babies. I asked a doctor for tips on what I should do if I ever had to make a delivery. But luckily, I never had to apply the doctor's advice.

For three years we lived an unpressured life. An August 1947 *National Geographic* article about the Northwest Angle included a full-page photo of Bessie bathing Roy in a galvanized washtub in our cabin. That picture told the story: we lived simply, in a backwoods cabin without plumbing or automatic heat.

But Alaska haunted me. I had seen her great mountains and glaciers, her vast wilderness, her broad rivers. I had known sourdoughs, Eskimos, and Indians. I had flown her length and breadth. Alaska was a challenge, and I dearly loved a challenge. After three years, the mail contract passed to another bidder. It was a good time for us to return North.

Return to Alaska

IT HAPPENED on the Alaska Highway, somewhere in Yukon Territory. The steep hill was slippery with ice and snow, and I nearly reached the top before I spun out. I stomped on the brakes, but the Ford car and trailer slid back. Steering was impossible, and the trailer jackknifed across the road. Then we stopped sliding.

I got out of the car and tried to move the heavily loaded two-wheel box trailer. I pushed by hand, but I couldn't budge it. "Come help me, Bessie," I called. Before Bessie could move, a big truck came barreling over the rise of the hill. Across the front of it was a sign six feet wide—EXPLOSIVES.

Good God, I thought. My trailer was right in the middle of the road and that truck couldn't possibly miss it. A surge of adrenaline hit me and with one frantic toss I threw that trailer off to the side of the road. The explosives rig whizzed by, and the driver's eyes were big and round. He couldn't have stopped.

The postwar exodus of pioneer-minded Americans from

the Lower 48 states to the Territory of Alaska via the Alaska Highway is a little-known emigration. Our reasons for heading up that long road through the wilderness were probably similar to those of other American families making the trek. Excited by the romance and adventure promised by our last frontier, we were looking for a fresh, new life. Because Bessie and I had already tasted life in Alaska, we knew that "the arctic trails have their secret tales," and we wanted to learn more of those tales.

I didn't worry about getting a job in Alaska as a pilot. In my four years of flying about Alaska, I had become acquainted with many key people in Alaska's aviation industry, the airplanes used by Alaskans, and flying conditions in the Territory. And the grapevine had kept me informed of the spectacular growth in aviation in the North during the three years I had been gone.

Before leaving Minnesota on March 15, 1949, I installed a rebuilt V8 engine in my 1935 Ford. I bought a box trailer made from a Model T Ford frame. An old friend, Manfred Holm, put steel wheels on the trailer. We stacked the car high and loaded the trailer until it bulged. Bessie and I rode in the front, and Cathy and Roy were in back with Buster, their collie-shepherd.

After we had driven about 15 miles, Roy piped up, "When are we going to get there?" The children had little understanding of the 3,300-mile journey we were starting.

Although it was spring in the South, the snow berms were so high along the highways in North Dakota and Montana that it was like driving in a ditch. When we reached Edmonton, we learned that no bridge had been built over the Little Smokey River, several hundred miles ahead. Traffic crossed this river on ice in winter and used a ferry in summer.

"That ice can go out any minute," a Canadian mounted policeman warned. If the ice went out, he said, we would have to wait until ferry service started—a long delay. We drove all night to reach the Little Smokey, and found it still frozen. I stopped the car and inspected the ice. Fresh tracks showed that others had recently driven across, so I drove across without concern. We later heard that the ice crossing at Little Smokey had lasted another ten days.

Day by day, we made our way around the curves and up and down the hills on that still-frozen gravel road. Daylight hours were long and temperatures were not extreme. Overnight lodging for travelers was mostly in crude camps that were leftovers from construction of the highway. These buildings provided shelter and adequate food every few hundred miles.

Bessie and I have since driven the Alaska Highway perhaps 26 times. Today, of course, it is a modern highway, mostly paved. Many of the steep sections and sharp turns of the original road have been leveled and straightened. Accommodations are now mostly modern.

Eleven days after leaving Minnesota, I was able to tell Roy, "We'll be there in about an hour."

As we drove the last few miles into Fairbanks, Bessie and I felt as if we were coming home. It was breakup time, and the potholes in Fairbanks' streets were full of water. Collected debris of winter, long hidden beneath the snow, was beginning to appear. But we knew that the streets would dry, grass would replace the mud, and before long flowers would grow in the wonderful perpetual summer daylight. And we looked forward to being with warm-hearted and friendly Fairbanksans again.

We rented a tiny wartime-built house in a residential section of town. We had no sooner moved in than Roy became sick. In the phone directory, we found a doctor's name that was familiar. We called, and Dr. Paul Haggland sloshed through the mud to examine Roy and give him medicine. His house call was the last that any doctor ever made for us. After that, it was up to us to get to a doctor's office. I've always had a warm spot in my heart for Doc Haggland.

I started looking for a job right away. Nonscheduled airlines had started to operate from Alaska. The airplanes, mostly military surplus C-47s, hauled both freight and passengers. I went to visit Tony Johanson, an old friend from Nome, unaware that he owned Sourdough Airways, one of the nonscheds. As we chatted, I learned that he needed a copilot to substitute for a copilot who had asked for a few weeks off. The copilot had bought a Boeing 247 transport plane and was planning to use it in the nonscheduled airline business. He needed the time off to fly the plane back to Alaska.

I was delighted at the opportunity. A few weeks of flying would bring in some money, and it would give me a chance to look around for a flying job I could really enjoy. I agreed to go on a familiarization round trip to Seattle. After that I would replace the copilot for a few weeks. We flew to Seattle without incident. Enroute back to Fairbanks on a dark, cloudy night, we landed to refuel at Annette Island, near Ketchikan, in Southeast Alaska. Tanks full, we took off for Fairbanks.

Once in the air after leaving Annette Island, the copilot called me to the back door, where he wanted to show me something. "It leaks air, and it gets pretty drafty on passengers in the back, but I have a good way of fixing it," he explained. We had a good load of passengers, including two women sitting in the very back seat just ahead of the door. He walked to the rear of the plane and picked up a blanket.

The airplane had a step-door that dropped when opened for entering or leaving the plane. Two handles on the door latched it in place. When they were turned, the door dropped open. The copilot's method of holding a blanket in place in front of the door was to loosen each handle slightly, wedge the blanket behind each handle, and close the handles again.

"Geez, that's not a very good idea," I thought to myself, as he grabbed both handles and tried to open them slightly. One stuck, and unconsciously he reefed on both of them.

His actions alarmed me, and I backed away. I stood with one hand holding the rear seat where the two women were sitting.

"Like this," he explained.

When he put pressure on one handle to get it to move, it gave suddenly. The other handle also turned, apparently accidentally. The door fell open hard and fast, *POW*, with the copilot still clinging to the handles. The copilot was suddenly dangling outside the airplane, upside down, clinging to those two handles. I saw the soles of his shoes for a few seconds, and then they disappeared. He had lost his grip on the handles and was flung by the slipstream into the black night.

One of the ladies in the back seat threw a blanket over her head. She knew something terrible had happened, and she didn't want to look. Had I been standing closer to the door, I'd have fallen out too, pulled by the instant suction.

I rushed to the cockpit to tell Brenner, the captain. He was fussing with the throttles and studying his instruments. "Hey, we have to turn back! That guy just fell out!"

He turned and stared at me. His face turned white. "My God," he said. "I didn't know what had happened. For a minute I thought we had lost an engine."

The open door and hanging steps created a terrific drag, pulling the plane to the left. I went from passenger to passenger, explaining what had happened, and told them we were returning to Annette Island. I examined the door, but there was no way I could close it in flight. The chains that held it in proper open position had broken when it fell open, and the door hung straight down.

We received radio clearance to return to Annette Island. In landing, as the plane slowed, we held the tail up as long as possible by constantly moving the control yoke forward. When the stairway hit the runway, sparks flew and maybe six inches of metal was ground off it. We taxied in and reported the accident.

When the copilot had plunged out that door, we were at 6,000 feet, just north of Annette Island. His body was never found. We never knew whether he fell into the sea, or into the dense rain forest. Strangely, we had aboard an identical replacement door that we were taking to Fairbanks. We installed it and were in the air again within a couple of hours. This horrible accident affected me for a long time.

For a couple of years after that, whenever a pilot opened a cockpit window in flight, for whatever reason, I would be startled. In a DC-3, when a pilot wants to spit, all he has to do is to crack his window a bit and spit into the rush of air and out it goes. It was a common practice. And whenever a window would open, I saw in my mind's eye that poor man flying out the open door and skidding headfirst down the stairs into the darkness.

I completed the few weeks as copilot for Sourdough Airways I had promised Tony Johanson. I could have continued to fly for his small airline, but I wanted to get back to bush flying. An opportunity quickly came my way. One day in Fairbanks I met Wyman R. "Lanky" Rice on the street. When I had last seen him, he had been in charge of aircraft maintenance at Nabesna, during the Northway Operation in 1942. "Heard you were back," he said. "I've been looking all over for you. How'd you like to go to work for us?"

"Us" turned out to be Northern Consolidated Airlines, and Lanky was operations manager. The consolidation included airlines that had operated at Fairbanks, Bristol Bay, and in the Kuskokwim country. Included was a small Bristol Bay airline that had been owned and operated by my old barnstorming friend and prankster John Walatka. Gillam Airways was another. And the small operations of Ray Petersen and Jim Dodson were part of the organization.

Immediately after the war, military surplus C-47s, or DC-3s, were available for as little as $20,000. Bringing them up to the standards required for passenger airlines cost only an additional $5,000 or more. As a result, many small airlines unexpectedly found themselves with one of the finest, safest, and most reliable airline passenger planes in the world.

Four-plus years of war had totally changed aviation in Alaska. After 1945, the Territory found itself with wonderful wartime-built facilities—8,300 miles of navigational airways and 50 first-class airports, 26 of which had control towers. Weather information came from 150 stations and was broadcast to flyers from 49 stations. A total of 54 radio ranges had been installed. Thus, conditions were ideal for the rapid growth of commercial aviation.

Northern Consolidated Airlines (NCA), which I was delighted to join, had two types of runs: bush runs from Fairbanks, flown with mostly Gullwing Stinsons and occasionally a Noorduyn Norseman, serving the Yukon River villages of Circle, Eagle, Beaver, Fort Yukon; and flights with a DC-3 to the coastal town of Bethel, with stops at McGrath, Minchumina, and Aniak. From McGrath, there was feeder-line service to Medfra, Nikolai, Farewell, Takotna, and Ophir. From Bethel, the company serviced a whole passel of tiny Eskimo communities with small planes. Included were Eek, Quinhagak, Platinum, Kwigillingok, Tununak, Mekoryuk, Hooper Bay, Kwithluk, Akiachuk, Akiak, Tuluksak, and Kalskag.

Lanky wanted me to fly the bush runs along the Yukon River. "When do I start?" I said, with a grin. Serving bush people is fun and personally satisfying. The pilot can become acquainted with his passengers and his freight customers. He can operate as an individual and feel like one—he is the guy the bush people wait for, the guy whose help they need.

Alden Williams, a longtime Alaskan pilot, flew me on a familiarization tour, introducing me to the people and places on those wonderful bush runs. I enjoyed the route, liked flying the Gullwing, and was ready to settle down with Northern Consolidated for the long haul. It wasn't long before I had two interesting experiences with the Norseman.

The Noorduyn Norseman, an eight-seat general transport plane built in quantities during World War II, became available as military surplus after the war. Powered with a husky 600-horsepower Pratt & Whitney Hornet radial engine, the Norseman was a tough and reliable bush plane that cruised about 140 miles per hour. Because it gulped 30 or 35 gallons of gasoline an hour, it was an expensive airplane to fly and was used sparingly.

One morning I took off from Fairbanks with a Norseman,

bound for McGrath. It had been cold enough that the oil had been drained for the night, reheated, and poured into the plane's engine just before I left. I landed at Minchumina, a tiny settlement on the shore of nine-mile-long Lake Minchumina, which lies almost in the shadow of Mount McKinley. I taxied off the runway, shut the engine down, and opened the window to talk to one of the men who had come to meet the plane. As we talked, he glanced down. A startled look crossed his face. "There's oil running out of your engine," he said.

A steady stream poured out. I found that the mechanic who had drained the oil from the engine for the night had used a PK screw that was too long to replace the cowling, and he had screwed it right into the oil tank. As long as the screw was tight, there was no leak. But as I flew, engine vibration loosened the screw and oil started to pour out of the hole.

I found another PK screw, put a small rubber gasket on it, and screwed it tightly into the hole in the oil tank. The leak stopped, and I completed my flight. If I hadn't landed at Minchumina and discovered the leak, I would have run out of oil long before I reached McGrath. The engine would have seized, and I would have logged another forced landing.

The other episode was more frightening. I started flying that Norseman shortly after it received a 100-hour inspection. I flew it for most of a month, adding another 100 hours to its flight log, then it was due back in the hangar. When the inspecting mechanic removed fairing strips from the wings, he discovered that the main front spar wing bolt didn't have a nut on it. The bolt had simply been thrust into place, and it could easily have vibrated out. Unknowingly, I had flown the Norseman that way for a month. Why it didn't jiggle out with all of my landings on rough bush runways and my encounters with turbulence that month, I'll never know. If the bolt had slipped out, the wing would have fallen off.

I had just settled down to the pleasant routine of flying to the Yukon River villages when Lanky Rice asked if I would fly as a

DC-3 pilot. From my Northwest Airlines and ATC flying experience, I had about 2,000 hours as captain and as copilot in DC-3s. There weren't many airline transport pilots around, and I was the logical choice. Plus, Consolidated didn't have to train someone from scratch.

With some reluctance, I transferred to their DC-3 runs. The work was less personal than flying small planes to the villages. But the pay was good, and the DC-3 is a wonderful airplane to fly. I flew briefly as copilot, then qualified with Northern Consolidated as captain. (Because one is rated as a captain with one airline doesn't mean he is a captain with another. To move from one airline to another and become a captain requires complete training and familiarization with the new airline, plus seniority.)

I flew NCA's DC-3 mostly from Fairbanks to McGrath and Bethel on the lower Kuskokwim River. In a relatively short time, I was check pilot for Northern Consolidated, which owned two DC-3s—one based in Fairbanks, the other in Anchorage. Three to four DC-3 pilots were based at Fairbanks. Often I was the only captain available.

The years I flew DC-3 aircraft from Fairbanks were among the most memorable and rewarding of my life, and offered some surprising and exciting events.

Bush Flying with the DC-3

THREE AIRPLANES that, in my view, had the most profound impact on aviation, were the Wright Flyer of 1903, Charles Lindbergh's *Spirit of St. Louis*, and the Douglas DC-3. The Wright Flyer showed men how to fly. Lindbergh's feat with the *Spirit of St. Louis* provided excitement that vitalized aviation. And the DC-3 did more than any other airplane to support the widespread existence of reliable airlines. It created a demand for aircraft that could transport big loads, which led to the development of four-engine transports, and, eventually, to jet transports. The DC-3 was the grandfather of modern transport aviation.

American Airlines started flying DC-3s between New York and Chicago in June 1936. By that fall, American was making transcontinental flights with the new Douglas, and it proved so dependable and so comfortable that it was in immediate demand. The Douglas factory hummed with production.

Initially, DC-3s were powered with two 1,000-horsepower

Wright Cyclone engines, but soon the Pratt & Whitney Twin Wasp of 1,200 horsepower became the standard engine.

By 1942, Douglas had built more than 800 DC-3s. During World War II, Douglas plunged into large-scale production of the military versions, mainly the C-47 and C-53. The DC-3 was the air transport backbone for the Western allies, and this great airplane served with distinction in every war zone.

In Europe, the DC-3 is commonly known as the Dakota, a name also used at times in the States. The Soviet Union built an unknown number of DC-3s under license to Douglas. Japan built DC-3s after the war.

Douglas again produced the DC-3 for a time after 1945, but the preference for more modern airplanes soon stopped production. No one knows exactly how many DC-3s in the various modifications were built, but the total was about 11,000—far more than any other type of transport plane. Today, over half a century after the first DC-3 flew, many are still flying for companies, individuals, and small airlines all over the world.

As in the rest of the United States, Alaska's postwar boom in aviation benefited from the easy availability of DC-3s. In 1949, when I began flying the DC-3 for NCA, I enjoyed the instrument flying, but I did miss having my passengers sit within arm's length as they did in a Gullwing Stinson.

Flight schedules for the NCA DC-3s in 1949 had a tendency to get out of hand, and we were late most of the time. The nickname many Alaskans used to refer to the company— "Northern Constipated"—no doubt resulted from our constant lateness. But there was good reason for the persistent lateness. We flew a very personal airline. If a passenger had to run home to change a shirt before he went to town, we waited for him. If a woman had yet to get a baby-sitter before leaving home, we waited for her. It was a family-type, leisurely operation. I remember waiting half a day in a village for one passenger. Also, we catered to important customers; if we hauled a lot of freight for a big mining operation, we didn't object when the owner of the mine asked us to wait for him occasionally. Some major share-holders in the airline lived in some of the villages. They expected us to wait for them. Since we commonly scheduled only one flight a day, so what if we left an hour or so late, or arrived late?

But eventually, Northern Consolidated's management began to feel that our flexible schedule wasn't professional enough, and that flights for our growing company should adhere more closely to posted departure and arrival times. After hearing this a few times, I told Hess Ragins, who was in charge of passengers and cargo, that I believed we could maintain a tight schedule. I had been trained by Northwest Airlines where being late was not tolerated. He promised to buy a treat for my crew for every day we returned to Fairbanks on time.

For eight consecutive days we arrived on time. To accomplish this, I made power settings that compensated for headwinds; safety permitting, I taxied a litte faster on the ground; we worked harder to remain within time limits on instrument letdowns (bringing the plane down through clouds on instruments); I encouraged ground crews to work harder and faster. We didn't wait for late passengers. Hess had to renege—he hadn't expected to have to buy treats for eight days. But being on schedule didn't last long. The old ways were too much a part of the Alaskan way of life.

Flying can be unpredictable. There's an old saying that "flying consists of days of boredom, broken up by moments of sheer terror." I can't say that I was ever bored while flying in Alaska. Inattention might be a better word—inattention is a pilot's undoing. When flying, a pilot must keep his mind on what he is doing. Gravity is the constant enemy when you are high in the sky, and anything mechanical can be flawed. Although we pilots did everything possible to ensure safe, fear-free, gravity-defying flights, I could fly weeks or months of unchangeable routine, then unexpectedly be confronted with a life-threatening emergency. Sometimes these incidents were a real challenge to my judgment and skill.

Once, on a scheduled DC-3 flight, my copilot and I smelled acrid smoke, which we quickly identified as the odor of burning wire insulation. I sent the copilot back to investigate. He dragged burning mail sacks out of the mail compartment, and he put the fire out with an extinguisher. Before the fire was out, he nearly collapsed from smoke inhalation.

We turned back to McGrath, the nearest airport, to determine what caused the fire. The culprit was an irresponsible mechanic who "fixed" an electrical control on a heater. The heater was automatic, set to shut off at a certain temperature. The mechanic (we never learned which one) had replaced a fuse with a bolt, so the heater could not shut off.

Another fire aloft came soon after. A bell in the cockpit of a DC-3 rings if fire breaks out in the wheel well beneath the engine nacelle (the streamlined cowling around the engine, into which the landing gear retracts). On the plane I flew, that damned bell would ring every once in a while. I would make an inspection and find nothing. Sometimes the bell quit ringing on its own, other times it wouldn't. Because it was very loud, sometimes we'd turn it off and then turn it on again when we landed.

I had taken off from Lake Minchumina, headed for McGrath, when the bell started to ring. We peered out the window and saw nothing in the engine nacelle that looked like fire or smoke. "They've got to fix that lousy bell," I said. "We can't have it going off all the time like this." I shut it off.

When we landed at McGrath, I immediately examined both wheel wells. Lo and behold, a junction box with electrical cables had caught fire. The fire had burned deeply into the tire on one of the main landing gear wheels but had gone out—why I'll never know. The tire was so badly damaged that I wouldn't take off with it. The airplane had to remain on the ground at McGrath until another wheel with a tire mounted on it was flown to McGrath and installed.

Much of our flying was on instruments, especially in winter. We DC-3 pilots couldn't allow our thoughts to wander.

Living by checklists, we listened and watched for symptoms of mechanical trouble. Maintaining a more accurate flight schedule was always a concern, and we constantly monitored our instrument letdown and other procedures.

These mental efforts were so routine that there was the lurking inevitability of distraction. Even though most captains, including me, had memorized instrument letdown and emergency pullouts by heart, I never made or allowed the first officers I flew with to make a letdown without an open manual (which specified course and altitude we had to fly in relation to radio signals) in the lap of one of us.

The danger of inattention was brought home to me emphatically one day when I taxied the DC-3 out to leave on the McGrath run. "Consolidated flight one, you are cleared for take-off," came from the tower.

The airplane was at the end of the runway. I had run both engines up to check the magnetos, and we were ready to depart. Instead of opening the throttles and speeding down the runway, I reached up and shut both engines off by pulling both mixture controls back. I instantly realized my mistake, and managed to shove the mixtures back to full rich before the propellers stopped. I don't think the controller in the tower realized what I had done.

But my copilot did, and so did I. My mind had short-circuited. Repeated movements of controls become memorized. This time, instead of using the moves needed to open throttles to start the plane down the runway for takeoff, I had used the almost automatic moves used to shut the engines off at the end of a flight. When such incidents happened, I always remembered something Roy Duggan told me when he was teaching me to fly. "Every few hours, sit down and think, and in your imagination start to fly again like you did the day you soloed. Think of every move you make."

One of the distractions in Alaskan flying was the scenery. I never tired of seeing the beautiful subarctic rolling spruce- and birch-covered landscape as I flew between Fairbanks and

McGrath. During summer especially, I enjoyed studying the geology of the land below. I took some courses in geology at the University of Alaska, which helped me to understand what I saw from high in the sky. That interest in geology led to a strange twist. An unexplained peculiarity of our automatic direction finder (ADF, a radio with a needle that points to a distant transmitter) once caused a uranium stampede.

It happened this way: At a point between Medfra and Von Frank Mountain, 40 miles from McGrath, the ADF needle would swing 180 degrees for a few moments, return to normal (pointing at McGrath), and then swing 180 degrees again for a few moments. It was a consistent anomaly for which we could find no logical explanation. There was no radio transmitter closer than McGrath, but the needle behaved exactly as it did when the airplane passed over a radio transmitter. Going toward a transmitter, the needle pointed ahead. While passing over the transmitter the needle swung 180 degrees to continually point at the transmitter.

I asked University of Alaska scientists about it, but no one could provide a good explanation. I was told that iron and zinc zones are located in many places in the world, and that rain and melted snow sometimes sink into the ground, converting such zones into huge natural storage batteries. In some, the electrical energy is so strong that it's impossible to use electric blasting caps because they detonate unexpectedly.

That explanation sounded as if it might be a clue, so I talked to radio experts. "That's all very interesting," they said, "but that should have no effect on your radio."

While studying this peculiarity, I visited my old friend Roy Duggan, who had moved from Alaska to Oregon. His answer to the puzzle was to take me to the Atomic Energy Commission's lab at Albany, Oregon, where I told the scientists my problem. They couldn't explain it.

My informal inquiry took place when prospectors all over the world were searching for uranium. Jerry Church, one of my copilots, wanted to go to the area and prospect. At the time, I was the only DC-3 captain at Fairbanks, though I had two copilots. There was no way I could get time off to accompany Jerry.

Somehow, word got around. Rumors flew that some pretty hot radioactive minerals were in the area and that Church had inside information. Jerry's telephone started to ring, and people asked him where this place was. He had no intention of telling anyone anything. Soon the phone calls became threatening. Several aggressive men told him that they were going to follow him wherever he went.

Finally, he and his wife, Eris, flew into the area with a scintillator—a highly sensitive Geiger counter. The short landing field in a narrow cut through the willows was big enough for a small, single-engine airplane. On the day that I knew Jerry and his wife had flown there, I flew over in the DC-3 and saw at least 15 airplanes parked around that runway. Most of those had followed Jerry.

With the scintillator, Jerry found radioactivity almost everywhere. Even some of the water was radioactive. He collected samples and had it analyzed. It was uraniforous thoranite, a basic radioactive mineral. However, the mineral was dispersed so thinly that mining was out of the question.

Shortly, I located a brilliant radio engineer. "No radioactive mineral affects a radio direction finder," he said, positively.

"Then what is causing our ADF to react?" I asked.

"I have a theory, and I'll bet on it," he said. "The signals from McGrath are bouncing off Mount McKinley. You're intercepting a cone-shaped signal there." He was right. The mystery was finally solved. But the puzzle was fun for a while. And for a short time a lot of people thought they were going to become rich.

My interest in mineralogy once caused me to pick up two red stones beside the Kuskokwim River at McGrath. I took them home, crushed them with a mortar and pestle, put the powder in an open tube over heat, and watched little balls of mercury pour out.

The Red Devil mercury mine is 100 miles southwest of McGrath. Evidently, somewhere upriver from McGrath, more mercury-yielding cinnabar deposits exist, but to my knowledge no one has ever found them. One old miner, who told me he had once found them, pointed out the spot on a map. I tried to fly in with a small plane, but I couldn't find a landing place within many miles of the spot. And I've never returned.

One of the strangest events that ever happened to me in an airplane was in a DC-3 as I was flying from McGrath to Bethel on a scheduled run. We had passed Aniak, on the lower Kuskokwim River, where the terrain is flat. The allowed altitude for instrument flight is quite low here. We were flying around 2,800 feet, on solid instruments. We saw nothing but the whiteness of clouds. Suddenly, we heard a ripping sound and a severe pounding and beating somewhere on the airplane.

I thought we had lost a main bearing in one of the engines, for the pounding was heavy and loud. Copilot Jerry Church looked back and yelled, "Hey, the radios are jumping around back there." Then, abruptly, the banging stopped. "Go see what the hell's going on," I told Jerry.

He returned in moments, his eyes big. "There's a hole that big in the top of the fuselage," he said, holding his hands about a foot apart. On top of the fuselage of a DC-3 is a large, streamlined post antenna about three feet high. It is mounted on a square where the aircraft's skin is doubled or tripled, with many rivets. No man could possibly tear this extremely stout installation loose with his hands. Somehow, that antenna had been ripped loose, and then, still attached to the wire, it had briefly rapped on the fuselage, before the wire broke and the antenna disappeared in the slipstream.

No one could ever satisfactorily explain how that strong installation was ripped out of the multiple layers of heavily riveted aluminum. If we had hit a goose or other large bird, I think we'd have seen it; and if that's what it was there should have been feathers or blood. There was no such evidence. The antenna was never found, to my knowledge. There was no sound of impact, just a sudden ripping noise and then, briefly, banging. Any object that came from the front and knocked that antenna off had to have passed within two feet of our heads, but we had seen nothing. I finally explained it by saying that I had hit a flying saucer.

The Douglas DC-3 is a well-built, tough, functional airplane. Probably no more reliable engine has ever been built than the Pratt & Whitney 1830 it uses. Nevertheless, I had several engine failures with DC-3s. Once I took off from Fairbanks when the ceiling was 400 feet. We were slightly overloaded. In spite of inspections, we often went out heavy. Our overloads were usually due to extra gasoline because of expected bad weather. Dispatch would tell me I was cleared to McGrath with 500 gallons of gas. I'd tell the gas boy to put in 600 gallons, because I wanted an extra margin of safety.

That day we went on instruments at 400 feet. We were about 20 miles out when one of the engines quit. We feathered the prop and trimmed the flight controls so we didn't have to stand on a rudder pedal. The airplane flew just fine on one engine. I called in and got immediate clearance to return to Fairbanks. We made a normal approach, let down, and landed without difficulty.

One reason I was not reluctant to add that extra gas was that, from my experience with the Air Transport Command, I knew how much the machine was capable of handling. The military allowed us to gross C-47s far heavier than we were allowed by civil aviation regulations. For Northern Consolidated flights, at first we were allowed to load to a gross weight of 24,500 pounds. That soon went to 25,700 or 26,000 pounds.

Flying with ATC, we had commonly flown at 27,500 pounds gross. I remember one pilot who, after a long flight, discovered he had carried a gross weight of more than 29,000 pounds. On a check ride in the Aleutians, I once took off in a C-47 that was grossed to 27,500 pounds. On takeoff, my check pilot reached over and shut off one engine. I flew around the field and landed on the remaining engine. It was a bit of a struggle for the machine, but the C-47 did it. The Air Force wanted us to know what our aircraft could do.

The DC-3 is a tremendously strong airplane, but twice I encountered turbulence so severe that the wing bolts were stretched. On a DC-3 no wing spar runs through the fuselage; the wings are attached with hundreds of small bolts around the perimeter of the wing sections. Heavy, exceedingly strong structural angles are located on both sides of the plane where the wings attach.

One pitch-black night, a DC-3 I was flying on instruments across Turnagain Arm near Anchorage shook like a rag doll in a dog's jaws. A continuous sound of breaking glass filled the cockpit, and I have never understood the source of that sound, for the glass instrument covers remained intact. It was so difficult to fly by instruments that I didn't have time to look for broken glass, or anything else. I was belted in tightly, with my eyes grimly focused on the instruments. I clung to the control wheel with both hands. The phenomenon didn't last long, but after we landed I suggested the wing bolts be checked. The plane was hangared for several days while mechanics replaced the stretched bolts that held the wing on. They also had to replace rivets that had popped here and there on the wings. That was some turbulence.

I found, as many other pilots have, that it is possible to avoid turbulence in Turnagain Arm by detouring a short way out over Cook Inlet. The turbulence results from venturi action—winds speeding up as they flow through a narrow pass.

Another nighttime incident occurred at an airway intersection named Keevee, on the north side of the Alaska Range at the intersection of the Summit Lake and Nenana airway. Again, I was on instruments, flying at 12,000 feet. The turbulence was frightful. Again wing bolts were stretched, and the airplane had to be repaired over a period of several days.

Sometimes minor incidents can precipitate more serious ones. I was once taking off from Bethel in a DC-3 when a main wheel dropped into a pothole on the old runway, built during

World War II. The jolt was so powerful I thought I had hit one of the deep holes caused when the river undermined the runway. I was moving fast, but I knew I should stop if I could. I cut the throttles and stomped on the brakes as hard as I dared. We came to a skidding stop. Then one of the main landing wheel tires blew.

I thought then that a flat or soft tire had caused the bump. But when I walked down the runway, I found the pothole into which the wheel had briefly dropped. Heat from the emergency braking was so intense it had exploded the tire.

The challenge of airline flying in Alaska kept my piloting skills sharp through constant training and repetition. Although no pilot wants life-threatening situations to develop, they do. I developed an ability to meet emergencies in the air.

I got along well with most passengers, pilots, mechanics, and ground crews. But state and federal bureaucrats who loved to flaunt their authority were a reality that gave me trouble. Those types made my blood boil. Twice I had serious tiffs with the CAA.

The first started when I was at McGrath waiting for the connecting DC-3 to return from Bethel. A CAA inspector approached me and said, "Hey, all you guys have until next Wednesday to arrange to have your ATR [Airline Transport Rating] license transferred." At the time, the ATR was printed on a soap-wrapper-like form, big enough to frame and hang on a wall. The CAA had decided to do away with that size license and reissue it on a wallet-sized card.

"OK," I told the inspector, "that's fine. I'll do that."

Well, I forgot about it. Shortly, I received a letter from the CAA in Anchorage telling me that since I hadn't changed my license to the new form, I was now unlicensed—I was no longer a pilot. I ran down to the CAA office at Fairbanks to take care of that right away. When I handed them my ATR license and asked them to issue me the new one, they refused. I had been told to get the transfer by the inspector at McGrath, and I hadn't done it in a timely manner. "You're not licensed to fly anything," the

CAA man told me. "You're not even a student pilot. You can't fly any kind of an airplane."

"You've got to be kidding," I said. "This is a technicality. What the hell difference does it make from one day to the next whether my license is on a soap wrapper or a card? "

"Doesn't make any difference. That's the way it is. You are not a licensed pilot."

At the time, I was the only DC-3 captain Northern Consolidated had at Fairbanks. I called Ray Petersen, president of the company, in Anchorage and told him about it. "I'll take care of it," he promised.

He called the CAA, and in a few minutes he was saying, "No sir, yes sir." They refused to budge. "Billberg cannot fly. He's not a licensed pilot. The only way he can get his license back is to take all the tests again, including the written."

"I'll quit flying first!" I barked, when Petersen called with that news.

"I'll try again," he promised.

This time he got special permission for me to fly Northern Consolidated flights one and two—the DC-3 route from Fairbanks to McGrath and back. I could fly nothing else. Not even a Piper Cub. So I flew back and forth on the limited flights for a while, wondering what would finally happen. I talked to the inspector who had reminded me to get my license changed. "Do you realize this is my livelihood?" I asked.

"Makes no difference," he said.

Then one day when I was about to run out of time for temporary permission to fly the two flights, I received a letter from one of the head guys of the CAA in Washington, D.C. He apologized and asked my forgiveness. "That's the worst bureaucratic boondoggle we've ever heard of," he said. "Your Airline Transport license is hereby reinstated."

But that wasn't quite the end of it. Northern Consolidated Airlines officials and the CAA discovered that about half the pilots in Alaska who held ATRs hadn't changed their licenses. I happened to be just the first guy caught in the squeeze.

The other time I tangled with the federal aviation authorities, it could have reflected on my professionalism and might also have resulted in loss of my licenses. I was alone, flying an Aero Commander from Fairbanks to Nome. It was necessary to radio Fairbanks to get clearance to let down into Nome, so I did that, by the book.

After a bit, I reported at an altitude about halfway down. And a Fairbanks controller barked, "You didn't have clearance to descend."

"Yes, I did," I called back. "I got clearance to descend to such and such an altitude."

"No you didn't," the guy snarled back.

"I did get clearance."

"Control did not clear your flight to descend," he repeated.

Stalemate. It looked like I was in real trouble. Changing altitude without a clearance is a serious offense, potentially life-threatening. Suddenly one of the CAA controllers at Nome interrupted, an older, practical, sensible fellow who had been listening. "Fairbanks, this is Nome CAA. I heard that clearance." That stopped it.

A fun incident I remember from my DC-3 schedule from Fairbanks happened at McGrath. In those days, the pilot had the last word on whether an airplane could land or not, not the weather bureau or the CAA. I arrived at McGrath and circled. Thick fog from the Kuskokwim River covered the roadhouse terminal and one runway. But the other runway was mostly wide open, with perfect visibility. I landed on the end of it, and stopped well before reaching the fog.

I taxied into the fog and had a terrible time finding my way to the roadhouse. I had to stay on the edge of the runway so I could follow runway lights. I taxied very slowly. Passengers waiting in the roadhouse peered into the fog and, like an apparition, my DC-3 appeared. They thought that was some flying.

A week later I was in the office at McGrath and overheard one of the passengers out front talking. I realized he was talking about me. "I saw that guy come in here last week and land the DC-3 and taxi right up to the door when I couldn't even see across the runway. He's one helluva pilot!"

Flying is a serious business, but there was always time for a little fun when we weren't airborne. Blinn Webster, a wonderful pilot with a great sense of humor, thought it would be fun to kid some of the new flight attendants.

Our flight attendants were often college girls who traveled to Alaska to earn money during the summer so they could return to school in the fall. They were always fine young women, and to most of them it was a thrill to be in Alaska. Most of them were cheechakos so it was easy to convince them of some outlandish ideas.

Blinn used brass welding rods to create "gold nuggets." He melted off chunks with a torch and let them drop in the gravel. As they cooled he stepped on them to make it look as if they might have a little sand attached, as a gold nugget often does. He made a pretty good looking collection of "nuggets."

I had a few of these in my pocket, and Fess ("Casey") Stangl, my copilot that day, a practical joker and a great pilot to fly with, was looking at one. He was laughing about it, and commented, "That little point kind of gives it away," he said.

About then the flight attendant came into the cockpit and asked if we wanted coffee. She saw the "nugget" in my hand. "My, what is that, gold?" she asked, excitedly.

"Of course," I answered, straight-faced.

"How can you tell if it's real?" she wanted to know.

I explained it to her carefully. "See the imprint of the sand in it? And that little point, that was the point of last suspension, when it fell off the mother lode." I could see Casey out of the corner of my eye, and he was almost choking to keep from laughing.

The flight attendant ooh'ed and ah'ed, and peered carefully at my "nugget," obviously buying my story completely. Out of generosity, I gave the piece to her. "You'll probably never find another nugget like this one. But I can get all I want, so you can have this one."

Casey and I often laughed about that, wondering if that poor girl had taken her "nugget" to a jeweler to have it mounted on a chain to put around her neck. I never heard another word about it from her all summer, and in the fall she left to go back to school.

Casey Stangl got on my list once. Even today I'd get back at him if I could. But I don't know what happened to Casey. He drifted off, and I never heard from him again. In the early days of flying for Northern Consolidated, we didn't wear uniforms because we not only flew the airplanes, we also handled the freight and baggage. Finally, the airline became a little more sophisticated, and we started to wear uniforms.

The company picked the style, and we were all measured and fitted out. The uniforms looked pretty snazzy, and most of us liked the idea. The one great advantage was that we weren't to touch any freight or carry much baggage because we would get our uniforms dirty.

Casey and I took off from Fairbanks in the DC-3 one day. I had just had my uniform cleaned and pressed, and it looked very sharp. Once we were at cruising altitude, the flight attendant came into the cockpit with two cups of coffee, one in each hand. Stangl was in the copilot's seat, and the hydraulic system started to make a lot of noise. A selector valve was located just back of his seat. Whenever that racket occurred, one of us simply grabbed that lever and moved it through full play and the noise would stop.

With the flight attendant standing behind him, Casey didn't even look back—he grabbed for the handle and his elbow struck a full cup of coffee. It sailed through the air and landed upside down on my newly cleaned uniform cap. Coffee dribbled off all sides of the cap to my shoulders, down my back, and even down my neck. Casey took one look and laughed until I could scarcely get any more use out of him that day.

After a few years, NCA established a new DC-3 schedule. At the same time I would be flying southwest from Fairbanks, a DC-3 would fly northwest from Anchorage, and the two planes would meet at McGrath. I would offload freight and passengers from my plane onto the Anchorage plane, which continued to Bethel. I waited with my DC-3 at McGrath until it returned. On its return, I took from it freight, mail, and passengers bound for Fairbanks.

I spent so much time at McGrath waiting for that airplane to return from Bethel that I felt like a permanent resident. I got to know many McGrath people and learned a lot about the region. This routine continued for several years. I made literally hundreds of trips with the DC-3 from Fairbanks. The main base of DC-3s gradually shifted from Fairbanks to Anchorage, and NCA asked me to transfer to Anchorage.

All of my life I have resisted having someone tell me what to do, so I was not receptive to the idea of moving. Bessie and I had filed on a 160-acre homestead near Fairbanks, and we were living and proving up on the acreage so we would eventually get title. If we left Fairbanks, we would lose the homestead. Also, our son, Roy, was being treated for rheumatic fever, and his doctor suggested that the dry Interior climate of Fairbanks was better for him than the damp coastal climate of Anchorage. We decided to stay at Fairbanks.

Northern Consolidated's operation at Fairbanks was downgraded to smaller planes. The company then bought five war-surplus twin-engine airplanes built by the Cessna Aircraft Company. Those of us who flew this plane usually called it the T-50, or "Twin Cessna." I was to come to know that airplane very well.

Flying the T-50 Cessna

MY MOVE from piloting the DC-3 to the twin-engine T-50 Cessna was a return to real bush flying. I flew alone (no copilot), under visual flight rules (no instrument flying), and all of my passengers were within talking distance. I wasn't just a number that flew by at two o'clock, as I had been when I flew the DC-3 on the same route. My life suited me.

It's considered a compliment to say of a bush pilot, "I'll ride anywhere he'll fly." Sometimes I had a little fun turning that phrase around. On a bad-weather day before takeoff I might turn to a frequent passenger and ask, "Well, shall we try it?"

The invariable answer was, "It's up to you, Rudy."

I would then seriously say, "OK. I'll fly anywhere you'll ride," as I shoved the throttles forward and headed down the runway.

I reassumed the roles of mailman, message-carrier, and purchasing agent for residents of the little bush communities and mining sites that we served. I again started keeping pocket notebooks of errands and shopping lists for my friends in the bush.

Some of my fondest memories are of the coming of spring when I was flying the Fairbanks-McGrath route in the T-50s. Starting in March, as daylight hours lengthened, bringing bright, clear skies and increasing warmth, the wildlife would appear, mostly on the south slopes of the hills and mountains. The first buds gave the land a tinge of green—a feast for the eyes after the bold blacks and whites of the long winter. Moose warmed their bones and fed on the new growth of the sidehills. I commonly flew low enough to be able to see the long tracks that otters left on still-icy lakes, where they had slid on their bellies, hopped a few times, and then slid again. Sometimes their tracks showed where they had climbed to the top of a beaver lodge and slid down the other side. Otters seem to enjoy life.

Does an otter have a compass in its head? Sometimes I thought so, for I often saw where otter families had walked across a lake, their tracks leaving a perfectly straight trail to the distant mouth of a little creek or directly to the only open water. There was no way the animals could have seen their goal: they somehow knew in advance where they were going and set an accurate course.

I saw packs of beautiful wolves bob along in single file, following along a creek or crossing a frozen lake here, a swamp there. Spring is their mating season, and occasionally packs mingled.

Wolverine, the rarest of Alaska's larger fur animals, were visible in spring more often than at any other time. They seemed to be out enjoying the warmth of the sun.

A little later, when the snow had nearly disappeared, out came the bears, often sows with twin cubs at heel. And then the caribou would appear, trekking across the land, heading somewhere that they obviously knew about, leaving spiderweb trails in their wake.

I traveled up there in the sky five days a week, watching

the world come back to life after the long, frozen winter. Life was being renewed and restored, and I sensed a freshness, an excitement, a joy in the wild animals. The experience was uplifting in an indescribable way.

Northern Consolidated Airlines extensively modified the five Twin Cessna airplanes it purchased in 1950–51. The first models that Cessna built of this airplane flew in 1940. Variously called the T-50, the Bobcat, the Crane (by the Royal Canadian Air Force), the AT-17 and the UC-78 (by the U.S. Air Force), and the JRC-1 by the U.S. Navy, the airplane had retractable wheels and could seat the pilot and four passengers. The plane was produced during the war in large numbers as an advanced military trainer. It proved ideal for pilots moving from single-engine airplanes to multi-engine; many World War II bomber pilots were trained in this ship. It was originally powered by two 245-horsepower Jacobs engines.

Alaskans commonly called it the "Bamboo Bomber"—I don't know why, although Alaskans seem to like alliteration. The plane had wood wing spars, and the fuselage was fabric-covered steel tubing. Perhaps the contrast with all-metal transport planes that dominated then provoked the nickname. But most of us in our company circle didn't use the name "Bamboo Bomber" because we felt it a degrading term for what we knew to be an excellent airplane.

Northern Consolidated made a fine bush plane out of the T-50 by replacing the Jacobs engines with 300-horsepower Lycomings, regarded as better engines. A big cargo door was installed, and the floor was modified to handle heavy loads.

The airplane's tremendous boxlike wooden wing spar passed through the fuselage. On those that Consolidated bought, these spars were scraped, checked, and revarnished. During winter, skis were installed (they were not retractable). Later, a few of these airplanes were mounted on floats and renamed the "Bushmaster" by Consolidated.

As rebuilt for bush use, these rugged planes carried a good

load and performed well. If one engine shut down, the T-50's single-engine flight was nothing to shout about, but the airplane's two engines did offer a considerable margin of safety. I didn't feel that I had to zigzag constantly to try to stay within gliding distance of safe landing spots.

Twice, I lost an engine while flying the T-50, but fortunately I was lightly loaded both times. Once I easily flew on one engine for 60 miles to the nearest runway. Had I been heavily loaded, the best I could probably have hoped for would have been to drag around and find an open swamp where I could have put down with the landing gear retracted. It probably wouldn't have been a major disaster.

I flew back and forth between Fairbanks and McGrath in these planes for years: once I calculated that I had made 1,500 flights between the two towns. I often flew just above the treetops when the ceiling was low. If the weather was tough I had to crawl my way around, but flying so often over the same run made me intimately familiar with the route. Many geographical features became clearly fixed in my mind. For example, if I were over a certain point on the Toklat River and couldn't see Roosevelt Hill, I knew that a certain compass heading flown so many minutes and so many seconds would put me at Roosevelt Hill.

I often had to fly from McGrath to small surrounding mining communities. When I started with the T-50s, I had never landed on many of these runways. I went to Tony Schultz, a longtime bush pilot who had flown in the area, and asked what I could expect at each of these locations. What kind of a field is there? What is the air like at these runways? And Tony was very helpful. In the early years, some pilots would lie to their competitors or give them a bad steer. As far as I know, that never happened to me.

The Twin Cessnas had persistent minor mechanical problems, perhaps because of the type of construction, because they were extensively rebuilt, or because they were more than a decade old when we started flying them. I had many interesting adventures, including some close calls, in them.

Once I was flying a T-50 to Anchorage from Fairbanks for a 100-hour check at Consolidated's maintenance shop. Bessie was with me. We were near the treetops, flying through some tough weather. Wind and turbulence were bouncing us around pretty hard when suddenly, "Wham!" I heard an explosive noise behind me and cold air hit the back of my head. I was too busy with the controls to turn around, but Bessie looked back and yelled, "There's a window gone." One of the big cabin windows had blown out. We rode through the turbulent area and flew on to Anchorage without difficulty, despite the sudden addition of air conditioning.

In another Twin Cessna that had just been checked out by mechanics, I landed on the ice of the Yukon River at the village of Ruby. After unloading some mail and a few pieces of freight, I was getting ready to taxi out when one of the ground crew called, "There's a guy here who wants to go to Galena with you."

"Climb in and fasten your seat belt," I called to him. Turning the plane, I taxied to start my takeoff. I gave her full throttle and we sped along the Yukon River ice. The plane was almost airborne when I heard the most horrible crashing and clatter. I immediately chopped the throttles. Something flew into the air and a propeller hit it. The airplane spun around and around and finally lurched to a stop. I peered out to see what in the world had happened.

Within a few seconds, I turned to tell my passenger, who was Indian, "I guess we'll be here for a while." To my amazement there was no one in the airplane. I looked out onto the river and I couldn't see a soul. I don't even know who he was—I didn't have his name on the manifest yet. Somehow he had climbed out, and he must have run for his life, quickly placing as much distance between himself and the airplane as he could.

During the 100-hour inspection, a mechanic had forgotten to put the retaining nut on the end of the axle that held the ski in place. When I started my takeoff the ski had fallen off. It remained fastened to the airplane by a shock cord, which had yanked the ski into the propeller. Damage would have been much greater on a paved runway, but the axle had slid on the ice without harm. When a new propeller and another ski were installed, the plane was ready to fly again.

On another flight, I picked up a plane in Anchorage to fly back to Fairbanks after it had undergone a major annual mechanical check. About three-quarters of the way to Fairbanks, I noticed that the fuel tank I was using was getting low. I turned the selector valve to the second tank, but as I continued to fly the fuel level in the nearly empty tank continued to drop, while the full tank showed no loss of gasoline. I fiddled with the valve, moving it from one tank to the other, again leaving it set so gas should have drained from the full tank.

I had passed Nenana, 50 miles from Fairbanks. I was now watching the fuel gauge on the near-empty tank like a hawk. It continued to go down; the full tank remained full. I followed the Tanana River carefully, without adding distance, remaining within gliding distance of river bars where I might land. It appeared unlikely that I would reach Fairbanks. I ran the engines as lean as possible, and flew at a slow cruising speed to stretch my fuel range.

To my surprise, I made it to Fairbanks with the engines still running. I landed slightly tail high. As the tail came down into the three-point landing position and while I was still rolling down the runway, both engines stopped.

I had come close to having to land on a river bar. The few ounces of gas left in the usable tank had run into the back, where it couldn't feed the engines. A mechanic had installed the new selector valve incorrectly. The cog on the handle didn't properly engage the valve; it was stuck on one tank.

Strangely, another flight of the same kind brought me much closer to death. Again, I had gone to Anchorage to fly a rebuilt Twin Cessna back to Fairbanks. For some reason I was nervous about the flight, although I had no reason to be. Weather was good, the engines ran beautifully, the airplane was light. I carefully checked that airplane over and found nothing wrong. Yet, I continued to be uneasy.

I reached Fairbanks, landed, and taxied to the Northern Consolidated hangar. Mechanic Warren ("Tillie") Tillman came out. "Tillie," I asked, "would you take a really good look at this airplane. For some reason I have a feeling that something is wrong."

He didn't question me. Tillie started working on planes for Alaskan pilots in 1930, and he knew pilots and airplanes. "I'll give her a good look," he promised.

When I arrived at the hangar the next morning, Tillie called me over to that plane. "Look," he said. I peered into the rear of the fuselage where an inspection plate had been removed. There I saw that only two strands of the main elevator cable remained. One jolt of turbulence or a jerk on the controls and I'd have had no elevator—no control for climbing or reducing altitude. Had the cable broken at low altitude, the airplane probably would have crashed before I could do a thing.

I thought about it awhile, then one day I experimented with a T-50 to see if I could have landed the airplane using only the trim tab and no elevator. It could be done, I found, but not if I were flying at 500 or 600 feet. If the cable broke, I would need enough time to analyze the problem and try to solve it with trim control.

There were humorous episodes in those years as well. I grin whenever I think of the time a Fairbanks pilot flew a ski-equipped Stinson Voyager, a four-place, late-1940s plane, from Fairbanks toward Minchumina. Somehow he became lost. He landed in the snow atop a mountain with little or no damage to the plane. He was rescued, and he didn't return for his airplane.

A mechanic for the CAA at Minchumina bought the plane as it was, where it was, and then he had to figure out how to retrieve it. The game warden stationed at McGrath was his buddy. The warden wasn't popular, for he was absolutely merciless in interpreting game regulations. The warden agreed to help the mechanic by flying him to the plane in a government airplane (a no-no, of course). To cover himself, he reported that he was flying a caribou census and taking two observers with him—the mechanic and another friend from Minchumina.

As I flew my route in a T-50 the next day, the CAA at Minchumina called me on the radio and reported that the government Cessna 170 with three people aboard was missing on a caribou count and asked if I would watch for it. "Sure. I'll give a look," I agreed. Such requests are routine, and Alaskan pilots are always alert for downed planes; one never knows when his own turn will come.

I flew lower than normal that day and watched the ground carefully all the way to McGrath. I flew out of my way to check lakes and other places the plane might have landed if engine trouble had forced it down. I reached McGrath without seeing the plane.

On my return flight to Fairbanks, I remembered that the Minchumina mechanic had told me he had bought the airplane perched on the mountain. "I don't know how I'm going to get to the darned thing," he said, after telling me about his purchase. That's it! I realized his warden friend had staged the "caribou count" to fly the mechanic to his airplane.

I had one passenger and explained to him that we might get to Fairbanks a little late, but I thought I knew where I could find the missing plane. "No problem," he said. I deviated from my normal route—just enough to take me to the mountain where the abandoned Stinson sat. Sure enough, I saw fresh airplane ski tracks beside it.

I circled and followed the direction of the ski tracks. They were drifted in a bit, but visible. The tracks ended, then a little farther, tracks appeared again where the plane had touched down as the pilot had tried to take off. Halfway down the side of the mountain, I saw the black and orange government airplane, upside down.

I circled and saw that a door on the plane was open. I thought, "OK. Someone lived. Somebody got out." But there was no sign of anyone near the plane. I continued to circle, searching for tracks, smoke, anyone walking. Then I remembered that the only cabin in the immediate area was at nearby Wien Lake (named for Noel Wien).

I flew the few miles to Wien Lake. Next to the cabin were huge letters stomped in the snow, "HELP. CRASHED PLANE." As I circled over the cabin, three men came out and waved. I was on wheels and couldn't land, so I radioed Lake Minchumina that I had found the missing men, and CAA station manager Dick Collins flew out and picked them up.

I was proud of myself. I had figured the whole deal out, and located the downed plane and missing men all by myself. I thought I'd be some sort of hero. When I arrived at McGrath the following day and taxied to the terminal, about eight trappers and miners stood there. I figured they were anxious to hear the details of how I'd located the missing plane. Maybe they didn't even know I had found it.

I climbed out of the plane and walked over to the gathering. All were friends or acquaintances. "Dammit, Billberg, we hear you found the game warden. Why didn't you leave the SOB there?" one said.

"You should never have told anybody where they were," another said.

"We thought you were our friend," said another, reproachfully.

I was a much-deflated lost-airplane-finder when I departed McGrath for Fairbanks that day. I was consoled knowing my trapper and miner friends would get some satisfaction when the warden's superiors discovered what had really happened on that "caribou count."

Flying a T-50, I once picked up a passenger at McGrath, a stranger. He had a ticket, so I added his name to the manifest and put him in the back seat. He was the only passenger. I was flying along routinely when suddenly there was a big rumpus in the rear. I turned and discovered that my passenger had opened the back door.

Naturally, I had a flashback of the time I saw the copilot fall out of the DC-3, and I nearly panicked. But the guy was just opening the door so he could spit; he was chewing a big wad of snoose. "Knock it off," I yelled. "Don't open that door again!" In another 15 minutes or so he did it again, and I hollered back at him again. He ignored me and continued to open the door to spit.

I was angry, but I couldn't do anything because I couldn't leave the controls. I told myself that when I landed at Minchumina, "I'll straighten this bugger out."

After landing, we both got out of the airplane, and the passenger was walking around spitting snoose. I faced him and said in my most severe voice, "You've got to keep your safety belt on, and don't open that door." I might as well have been talking to a tree for all the response I got. He simply looked at me.

I stalked off, upset, and supervised the loading of the plane. As I got ready to leave, I overheard the man utter a word. I could barely hear him, for he was talking to himself—in Swedish! I had grown up speaking Swedish, and although I had forgotten much of it, I remembered enough to dress the guy down in his own language. That he understood! For the rest of the flight he didn't move an inch and he didn't open the door again.

Another funny episode began one fall day as I was preparing to fly from Fairbanks to McGrath. A bustling, stocky little guy, very self-important, climbed into my airplane and sat in the co-pilot's seat, a practice we allowed with some caution. He had a bunch of suitcases, boxes, and other stuff with him. Once we got off the ground and on our way, I asked, "Where are you going?"

"Nikolai," he answered. He was from New York City, and he had never been to Nikolai, where he had agreed to teach school. The tiny Indian village is about 50 miles east of McGrath on the South Fork of the Kuskokwim River. It was and still is made up of log cabins, a small school, and a Russian Orthodox church.

I landed at Medfra, where he got out. From there, the Indians took him by boat to Nikolai, which at the time didn't have an airplane runway. He was all business as he told the Indians how to handle his baggage.

Two weeks later I landed at Medfra and found the same little guy at the edge of the runway, perched on one of his suitcases, waiting for my flight. I helped him load his bags, and taxied down the runway. "You're not going to teach school at Nikolai?" I asked.

"No."

"What's the matter with Nikolai?"

"Why, there isn't even a theater there!" he exclaimed.

Occasionally our desire to help people out caused us to break even the strictest of regulations. On one flight I was carrying a box of electric dynamite caps from McGrath to the tiny, 35-mile-distant mining community of Ophir. It was illegal to carry passengers when we had dynamite caps aboard. We weren't even supposed to fly within two miles of a radar site with the caps aboard.

As I readied to leave, a woman in absolute despair rushed up to me. "I must get to Ophir," she said.

"Sorry, ma'am, I can't take you. I have very important freight to take, and I'm not allowed to take passengers on this trip."

She looked the empty plane over. "There's nobody going with you. Let me go. I must get home," she insisted. This went on for some time. The woman was persistent.

"OK," I relented. "If you'll sit here and hold this box on your lap and cushion it carefully, and not put it down until you hand it back to me, I'll take you."

She was delighted. She didn't even ask what was in the box, although since she was from the mining community she probably suspected. She sat as still as a mouse and held that box until I landed, took it from her, and handed it to the miner who had ordered it.

I've often thought about that incident with amazement. I believe in safety rules, and I didn't often deliberately break them. If I had been caught, I'd have probably been sorry the damned caps hadn't blown up.

Alaska's Interior is famous for its generally fine weather and low annual precipitation. Nevertheless, I encountered low ceilings and restricted visibility many times as I flew the nearly 300 miles from Fairbanks to McGrath. At times, I almost literally flew from familiar spruce tree to familiar spruce tree.

Terrain and local conditions affect the weather, and after a few hundred trips to McGrath, I began to know what to expect under various weather conditions. The weather might seem to be bad all over, but because of hills, mountains, or other local features, little clear spots might appear here and there, permitting me to leapfrog through.

A phenomenon known as an arctic stationary front sometimes develops along the Fairbanks-McGrath route. It results from the meeting of a high-pressure area to the north that is turning clockwise and a low-pressure area to the south that is turning counter-clockwise. One system is hot and humid and the other is cold, and when they collide, bad weather results, including fog, snow, or rain. Frequently, the front doesn't move except for some undulating. The situation might last for several days.

I often took off from Fairbanks in clear weather and unlimited visibility when Minchumina, halfway to McGrath, was also reporting good visibility. McGrath, my destination, might be reporting a 100-foot ceiling and half-mile visibility, with fog. Before I would get to Minchumina, flight service there would report low visibility, but then McGrath would report clear skies. The front had undulated enough to make these changes.

At other times the front would undulate just enough so that the Kuskokwim Valley down which we flew would be unflyable, leaving no way to reach McGrath on the regular airway route. When this happened, I often flew north to the other side of the Kuskokwim Mountains and found clear weather all the way to McGrath.

Over the years, in bad weather many pilots, unfamiliar with these weather patterns and not acquainted with the terrain and landmarks, tried to follow me to McGrath from Fairbanks. Most failed. Once I heard a radio conversation between a pilot taking off from Fairbanks and the tower: "Consolidated flight one made it through to Minchumina," the tower told him when he asked for pilot reports on the route. He was flying a two-place Taylorcraft, and was probably a private pilot with little experience, but he decided that if Consolidated could make it, so could he. The ceiling was low, and it had been a tough flight for me that day.

Shortly, when I was between Minchumina and McGrath, I heard the pilot call: "I'm on top of the clouds, and I can't see any way down. I need help." During the next hour or so, I listened as the flight controller at Fairbanks did a beautiful job of helping that pilot.

"Can you see anything?" the controller asked.

"Mountaintops to the south," the pilot said.

"That's the Alaska Range. Now you fly [such and such a course] to get back to Fairbanks," the controller instructed. I followed the drama step by step, until the pilot neared Fairbanks and found a hole to get back down through the clouds and land safely.

A bush pilot's familiarity with the landmarks on his route, the places where he could land in an emergency without breaking up the airplane, and the weather patterns—where to expect little pockets of visibility here and there—made the difference. On my days off I often studied my routes by traveling around the country by dogsled, boat, or snow machine. I studied sandbars along rivers to see if they would support an airplane. I learned that the more and larger the rocks along river bars, the more solid the bar was:

Continued on page 223

Sam White and his wife, Mary, about 1930. White, one of
Alaska's earliest pilots, became famous because he was the
world's first flying game warden. *Photo courtesy of the
Pioneers Museum, Fairbanks*

Joe Crosson, around 1926-27, with a Swallow biplane.
Photo courtesy of the Crosson Collection, Alaska Aviation Heritage Museum, Anchorage

This rare photo of Harold Gillam was probably taken at
Teller when Gillam and Joe Crosson were searching for
the lost pilot Carl Ben Eielson in January 1930. *Photo
courtesy of the Alaska Aviation Heritage Museum, Anchorage*

Left: Bessie Billberg gives young Roy a bath in their wilderness log home in the Northwest Angle, Minnesota, in 1946.
Photo by J. Baylor Roberts ©National Geographic Society

Below: Rudy Billberg and his Challenger-powered Curtiss Robin on wheels at Roseau, Minnesota, 1947. Billberg owned the only airplanes in the Northwest Angle at that time (two Curtiss Robins and a Taylorcraft), and flew passengers, freight, and mail.

Billberg's Piper Vagabond on skis is tied down on the ice
of Lake Minchumina, Interior Alaska, in the early 1950s.
Local resident Hazel Menke and her sled dogs are in the
foreground.

In March 1954 at Lake Minchumina, Billberg warms the
engine of his L-5 Stinson. Modified to fit the low engine
of the Stinson, the barrel has a stovepipe that sends the
heat to the opposed engine. *Photo courtesy of Jim Rearden*

A twin-engine T-50 Cessna similar to the one Rudy
Billberg flew for Northern Consolidated Airlines at
Fairbanks in the late 1950s. *Photo courtesy of Jim Rearden*

Flying this twin-engine B–25 Mitchell bomber called
"Antique Five," Rudy Billberg dropped fire retardants on
Alaskan forest fires during the mid-1960s. This World
War II aircraft was refurbished and flown to Australia,
where it is now displayed at a museum.

Above: Rudy Billberg flying a Stinson Voyager through Lake Clark Pass in the Aleutian Range during the winter of 1960. *Photo courtesy of Harold Johnson*

Left: John Walatka as a barnstormer in the 1930s with a Great Lakes biplane. Walatka and Billberg were barnstorming buddies in Minnesota and aviation colleagues in Alaska. *Photo courtesy of Johanna Walatka Bouker*

Rudy Billberg and his mentor and lifelong friend, Roy
Duggan (right) at Vancouver, Washington, in 1985, on
the fiftieth anniversary of Billberg's solo flight.

pure sand might be hard enough to land on, but when a plane stops, its wheels can slowly sink out of sight.

I noted mountain saddles, ridgetops, open swamps with no trees—dozens of places for possible belly landings. A pilot unfamiliar with an area could be fighting bum weather, lose an engine, or have some sort of an emergency within a few hundred yards of a landing spot and not be aware of its existence. Alaskan pilots have to pay attention to such details.

During those years, among the Fairbanks pilots was a flyer who had decided he was going to become the world's best bush pilot. To do this, he flew in any weather, including the toughest, taking terrible chances. He survived for some time despite having several mishaps—a noseover, running out of runway, catching a wing on a willow when he landed. Once he set a Beechcraft Bonanza down in a swamp between Fairbanks and Galena.

He was capable, but he had the wrong attitude for a pilot, for he lacked common sense. His best-known comment was, "When it gets too tough for the Consolidated boys, it's just right for me."

He finally challenged one storm too many. His airplane was never found.

The worst experience I had with a T-50 was at Takotna, a small Kuskokwim River village. Often, with our small planes, we picked up freight left at McGrath by the DC-3s and delivered it to surrounding mining camps and villages. On this day I had a huge load of groceries to fly to the short Takotna airstrip, which lies atop a large hill. The runway ends at a steep, clifflike slope. To help me with the loading and unloading, Consolidated sent Rusty, a good, congenial worker. Sometimes Rusty carried his congeniality too far, and that was the case on this day. He had been drinking fairly heavily, and as he settled into the right-hand seat next to me, his breath was strong in the small confines of the Twin Cessna.

We got into the air, and I noticed that the airplane was loaded tail heavy. I was able to use the trim control to level the plane, and we reached Takotna without any problems. I circled the little runway and carefully studied the wind sock, which indicated a slight wind from the north. Making a long, slow approach, I touched down gently on the end of the runway, and then realized that the plane wasn't slowing as it should. I stomped on the brakes but that didn't slow us at all. The end of the runway was near, and we were still zinging along at a good clip. It was too late to apply power and try to take off and go around.

Events transpired swiftly, as they so often do with an airplane. I decided to try to ground-loop, so I stepped on one brake as hard as I could, to spin us around. I figured I might break the landing gear or something, but at least we wouldn't go over the cliff at the end of the runway. But that didn't help a bit. I tromped on that brake until I feared I would break the pedal, but nothing happened. We were going to go over that cliff, and that was all there was to it.

The airplane ran out of runway and left the ground as it went over the cliff. I think all that saved our lives was the tail-heaviness; the tail started to drop before the front end, contrary to what would normally happen. Little things like tail heaviness can sometimes lead to unexpected results.

The tail hit, then the main landing gear wheels hit, and the airplane kept going. The landing gear was ripped out, and we continued to clatter down the steep mountain. When we finally came to a stop, the plane's right engine was turned around completely, looking at us, so to speak. The belly was torn out, the props were pretzels, fabric was ripped, and tubing was bent and broken.

Neither of us was hurt. "Let's get out quick. There might be a fire," I told Rusty.

He muttered and grumbled, but jumped out. We were standing on the side of the mountain, and I was absolutely dismayed at the airplane—it looked like a trash heap.

"This is a hell of a place to stop. Now we've got to pack

these groceries way back up the mountain!" Rusty complained.

"I hadn't planned on stopping here," I told him, but my irony was lost on him.

Back up on the runway, I noticed that the wind sock was waving and standing out stiffly, indicating a strong wind from the south. The wind had changed 180 degrees, probably about the time I touched down.

Rusty and I didn't have to haul the supplies up the cliff. People arrived shortly to help us. They called McGrath and a plane came for Rusty and me, and a crew arrived to carry the groceries. Another crew pulled the plane back up the side of the mountain and rebuilt it over several weeks so it could be flown out.

A modern pilot who operates solely from paved airports with modern aircraft and dependable engines, and who has the advantage of weather service information, may go through an entire career without damaging an airplane. In the early days in Alaska—when runways were short and unpaved, engines were just beyond the OX-5 stage, no radio navigation aids existed, and virtually no weather forecasts were available—many pilots "broke" airplanes. Often they ran out of runway, or dropped a wheel in an unseen hole, or tripped over a log. I don't think that any of the high-time pilots I knew in Alaska in the early 1940s and even into the 1950s had escaped damaging a plane in some manner. Some bush airline owners, when hiring, preferred a pilot who had dinged a plane or two. "Makes 'em more careful," they claimed.

Whenever you broke an airplane, the CAA required you to complete a long form describing the accident. They asked every conceivable question, it seemed to me, including details of your ancestry, how many toes you had on your left foot, and when you last had a bath and a haircut. One question, "General ability as a pilot?" seemed particularly meaningless to me. What pilot is going to grade himself less than capable?

I'd love to have a collection of the answers that pilots gave to that question. One of the best I've ever heard was attributed to Merle Sasseen, an experienced Alaskan pilot who had suffered several accidents within a relatively short period. His reputed answer: "I used to think I was pretty good, but lately I've started to wonder."

I am reminded of another classic accident report filed by an Alaskan bush pilot. He had started to take off from a small field in a gusty wind, when his plane left the runway and ricocheted off two or three parked airplanes, bounced across a ditch, tore down a fence, "and then," he wrote, "I lost control and the airplane ran into a hangar."

After six years of bush flying five and six days a week, I needed a break. It wasn't practical for Consolidated to let me go for the several months I wanted, but I was determined to go anyway, so I resigned and the four Billbergs went to Florida. By then, Roy was a high-school sophomore and Cathy a senior, and they attended school in Florida for several weeks while we had a change. It was really the only time we uprooted them, except for our move to Alaska in 1949. The kids didn't mind; and they were excited about traveling and going to new schools.

All of us basked in the sun, and I enjoyed the relief from a flying schedule. I thought perhaps I'd get a flying job in Venezuela, but when I applied I suffered quite a jolt: the company wouldn't hire me because they said I was too old. I was in my mid-40s, so I decided that they used that as an excuse. It turned out that I was lucky they hadn't hired me, because there was a revolution going on in Venezuela and planes owned by that company were caught in it.

After Florida, we went to California to explore for several months. Roy and Cathy entered school there and would complete the year with good grades, Cathy graduating.

In the spring, I received a letter from Northern Consolidated Airline's Art Lien. The company needed a station manager for Galena, a large Yukon River village. Was I interested? After six or seven months away from Alaska, with no flying, I was rested and homesick. "I'll take the job if Consolidated will have me," I wired back.

"You're hired," came the reply.

Bessie's mother came to California to stay with the kids until school was over, and Bessie and I headed north to a new challenge.

Galena

I FIRST SAW Galena in October 1941, when Bessie, Cathy, and I were on our way to Nome and Wien pilot Bill Lund landed on a frozen Yukon River bar at the then-tiny Indian village. By February 1958, when Bessie and I moved there to work for Northern Consolidated, World War II and subsequent development had transformed the village. It was now a commercial center and military base with a fine runway. During the war, it was a fueling stop for Russian lend-lease war planes making the flight from Fairbanks to Nome. Later it became a base for interceptor jet fighters that confronted any Russian Bear bombers approaching Alaska over the Bering Sea and Arctic Ocean.

In our roles as station managers, Bessie ran the office, selling tickets, handling radio communications, and doing all the paperwork. The company DC-3s flew mail, freight, and passengers to Galena from Anchorage and Fairbanks. I then flew the goods and passengers brought by the DC-3s to the Yukon River Indian villages of Ruby, Nulato, Kaltag, Kokrines, and Koyukuk, as well as to mining settlements at Poorman, Long Creek, and Greenstone. I occasionally flew north of the Yukon River up the Koyukuk River to the Indian village of Huslia. But most of the Huslia traffic was handled by Wien Airlines, which was entrenched north of the Yukon. Sam White, my longtime friend, flew for Wien Airlines from the Koyukuk River village of Hughes while I worked out of Galena. (The day came when the two airlines combined under the name Wien Consolidated Airlines, but by then we had left Galena.)

Bessie and I were nicely settled in Galena by the time high school was out in California, and Cathy and Roy joined us for the summer. In the fall, Cathy returned to California, where she attended San Jose Business College. Roy went to Fairbanks to attend high school because there was no high school in Galena.

Consolidated's station, a Panabode prefabricated log building, sat beside the runway, with the office in front and our living quarters in the rear. I used a T-50 Cessna for most of the bush flying from Galena. During breakup, when the village runways were soft and muddy, I used a three-place Piper Family Cruiser.

My predecessor warned me about one place on my route. "Watch that Kokrines runway. It's short, and surrounded by rough ice." The schedule called for me to take mail to Kokrines on the second and fourth Fridays of each month. On the Friday just after our arrival, I made my first trip to Kokrines. I loaded the mail and freight in the Cessna, and fought a strong headwind as I flew up the frozen Yukon River. I flew over the village and passed over the doubtful runway, which was on the ice of the Yukon River. It was clearly marked with spruce boughs, but its length was greater than I expected. I made a long, low approach and touched down at the very end of the strip. I used maybe two-thirds of the runway. So much for the short runway: "short" has different meanings to different pilots.

The supposed landing hazard turned out to be nothing

compared with the emotional hazard of the irate missionary who met me. "No, I'm not the schoolteacher," he replied angrily at my question. "I'm the missionary." He then spewed a tirade of abuse about the terrible service provided by Consolidated. He objected to having mail delivered only twice a month, and he demanded, "How am I to get to town in an emergency if the need arises?"

I tried to soothe the man, but failed. I explained that the Postal Service established the frequency of mail service, so Consolidated couldn't be blamed for that. Then I discovered the missionary didn't have a two-way radio, so he couldn't call for help in an emergency, anyway.

I departed, reflecting on his temperament and attitude, wondering what he expected when he moved to an Indian village in the wilderness. It was clear that if it were up to him, no employee of Consolidated would ever enter the Kingdom of Heaven.

Life in an isolated village takes getting used to. Nearest medical facilities were at the Bureau of Indian Affairs hospital at Tanana, 145 miles upriver, and the Air Force Station at Galena had a medic who treated civilians in emergencies. During my years as a pilot in Alaska, I flew many injured or ill people, but it seemed I had an unusually high number of such flights when I lived at Galena.

One of our first such experiences happened soon after our arrival. On March first, we were preparing for the noon arrival of the DC-3 from Fairbanks. Teletype messages and papers were strewn across Bessie's desk. Radio calls came from Anchorage and McGrath about lost baggage, proposed stops for the DC-3, queries as to what time the plane had departed from each stop.

In the midst of this confusion, a local missionary rushed into the office. "Can you fly to the Tanana hospital at once?" he asked. A young woman had given birth two days before, but her baby was dead at birth, strangled by the umbilical cord. The mother had seemingly done well, but now, suddenly, complications had set in.

"Of course. I'll get the airplane ready," I told him, and ran out to ready the T-50 Cessna for the hour-long flight. But shortly the missionary returned. "She's dead. Cancel the flight," he said sadly. We were all upset. Only the previous day I had flown almost to Tanana, and if we had known about the woman I could have taken her on that flight.

Another incident happened in late April, when a little Indian boy at Koyukuk jumped on a tin can and cut his heel almost half off. The FAA (formerly CAA) called at 11:00 P.M. to ask if I could make a flight to pick up the boy; my T-50 Cessna was the only readily available ski-equipped plane. I agreed to try, knowing that it was iffy, because there was a lot of water on the ice of the Yukon River at Koyukuk where we would be landing. It was dark when I left Galena. The cooling night air had helped to set the snow at Galena.

At Koyukuk, villagers had marked the usable runway space on the ice, a short, narrow area between the water and the bank. I circled and set up for landing, coming in low and as slow as I dared. As I touched down, about 10 feet from the wingtip was open water. Just beyond the other wingtip was the riverbank. The Indians were holding lanterns and flashlights to mark the solid ice, and they were so near I feared my wings would knock some of them over, but they must have ducked or gotten out of the way.

The boy, about five years old, was carried to the plane and put aboard with his worried mother. His little foot was wrapped with many layers of bandage, and he made a pitiful sight. I knew the anxiety the mother must have felt as she watched him suffer and wondered whether help would come.

I was grateful that I could fly the boy to medical care. The takeoff went well, and soon we were in Galena. The Air Force medic cleansed the cut and stitched the child's heel back into place. He made a complete recovery.

I wasn't the only Alaskan pilot to find this kind of service rewarding. Bush pilots as a whole have made special efforts to help the sick and injured. The landing I had made on that narrow strip of ice was extremely dangerous, with potential for total disaster, but in an emergency, I felt compelled to at least try. I was moved when I witnessed the struggles of the isolated villagers, and I was especially troubled when children were involved. It was always fulfilling to be able to help.

In mid-May, again at 11:00 P.M., another call came: there were two medical emergencies at Koyukuk. An old man had terrible stomach pains, and a seven-year-old girl was having convulsions. It's a bush pilot adage that folks get sick or hurt mostly at night, when it is stormy, or when a landing field is unusable. In this case the field at Koyukuk had been closed for weeks because it was soggy, but the villagers said there was a strip that would hold a light aircraft and they would mark it off with people and lanterns. Although at that time of year the nights aren't really dark along the middle Yukon, it was dark enough to make it difficult to see for landing.

In ten minutes I was on my way, flying the three-place Piper Cruiser. At Koyukuk the villagers stood with lanterns, marking off the small runway area that was solid enough to land on. I circled and made a long approach, flying so slowly that the wing was practically buffeting on the edge of a stall. I touched down right on the riverbank and stopped about 25 feet short of the last lantern.

I walked over the runway to check it out while the villagers loaded the two patients into the rear of the airplane. The ground was firm where it was marked, but that was about all. I was beginning to doubt whether I could get off with both patients in the airplane; the old man weighed about 180 pounds. However, I didn't want to make two trips and have to land in that tiny dry spot again, so I decided to try. In such a situation, years of experience seem to give one an intuitive answer based on the feel of the ground, the air temperature, the light breeze, the way the plane flew as I came to Koyukuk, the willingness of the engine.

Taking off toward the river seemed ill-advised because if I

didn't make it the airplane would plunge into the water and all three of us would probably die. Going the other way was more sensible because a failure to get off would result only in the airplane ending its flight in the brush. The villagers were pressing me. "You've got to make it. We're pulling for you. These people have to have help. You'll make it," and so on. I didn't like the distraction. I wanted to be able to concentrate.

I taxied back to the riverbank and made sure the airplane was as close to the bank as possible: I needed every inch. I held the brakes and opened the throttle clear to the stop. When the engine was doing its best and the plane was a mass of vibrating parts, I released the brakes and we sped between the lanterns.

It seemed as if we were standing still, that the plane was sluggish, that the soft ground held the tires back. The engine didn't seem to have any power. And yet the lanterns and flashlights were beginning to stream past. Finally, only two lanterns remained, and when they were right in front of the nose I gave a little jerk on the stick, and she came up as though there were never any doubt about it. I was relieved, and those on the ground probably were too. The two patients were so miserable they were unaware of what was going on. I landed at Galena 20 minutes later, and the medical people of the Air Force took over.

That night, I lay awake in bed for some time as the tension slowly drained away. The Cruiser was only tubing and fabric with a fine Lycoming engine attached to it, but it seemed to have a personality, as so many planes do. I appreciated its fine performance that night. A pilot does grow attached to certain airplanes.

We also had some good times with passengers. The next day, as I landed at Nulato, I bounced the plane rather hard. Miss Barnsley, a health department nurse, was there and teased me about it. "Why, I was practically asleep when I made that landing," I told her. I explained about losing sleep the previous night because of the emergency medical flight to Koyukuk.

"You know, Miss Barnsley, I've just had another birthday, and I'm much too old to be out all night like that," I told her.

Then, in mock seriousness I said that kindly people had taken to helping me in and out of the airplane when they saw how I had to struggle.

This joking went on for some time, with several Nulato Indians standing by the plane taking it all in. Finally, one of them said seriously, "Gee, don't let your age get you down like that."

I didn't know what to say, and Barnsley laughed uproariously. I finally told the fellow, "Well, you know, there aren't many guys my age still around." At this he looked blank. I think he was still trying to figure out how old I was when I taxied out for takeoff.

In early July another emergency occurred. At noon, a radio message came from Nulato that a three-year-old boy had fallen on the turning drive shaft of a boat. The universal joint had torn into his side between the ribs and thigh, almost tearing a hole in his abdominal cavity.

I flew the T-50 Cessna in a rush flight to pick up the little boy and his mother. The child was frightened and in much pain, but he was trying not to cry. His nervous mother held him in her arms. Instead of flying directly to the hospital at Tanana, I stopped at Galena to have an Air Force medic look at him to make sure he could make it as far as Tanana. The medic did what he could to stop the bleeding and reduce pain. I then flew on to the Tanana hospital, where the child immediately went into surgery.

When I had a medical emergency aboard and I would call ahead to the FAA at Tanana, the response was always superb. The doctors at the hospital were alerted, and an ambulance and crew, including a doctor, were always waiting when I landed. It was such a relief to taxi my airplane up to an ambulance and have competent medical people take over.

Living at Galena provided us with many fascinating insights into the way of life in the villages along the Yukon. The people survive by trapping and by living from the land. The Yukon supports great runs of salmon, which the residents either net or catch with fishwheels. Fishwheels are mechanized fish-catchers that are giant, handcrafted wood wheels with wire scoops, turned by paddles propelled by the current. Fishermen anchor them in places where the wheels can scoop up salmon migrating upstream.

Informality and the spirt of making-do are basics of life in the bush. Community effort solves many problems that would be beyond the individual. One day, I was to deliver a 575-pound engine for a customer at Koyukuk. With the forklift at Galena, I managed to load the engine into the T-50 Cessna without difficulty, but I wondered how I would unload it at its destination.

When I landed, a bunch of children met the plane. I asked one girl to find four or five men to help unload the engine.

"No mans in town. Only womens," she said.

"How come?" I asked.

"All went trapping."

"OK, get lots of women then," I suggested.

The little girl left, and returned with three men who were in town after all. We managed to get the engine unloaded.

I've always appreciated the way the Yukon Valley Athapaskans express themselves. One day I brought some shotgun shells to one of the Indians. A few days later I asked, "Did you get any ducks or geese with those shells?"

"Yis."

That was all. Not another word. I thought of the cultural contrast between us. If I had asked a non-Native the same question, I'd have heard a detailed account of how he had shot each bird, what difficult shots were made, and so on. Whereas Athapaskans tend to avoid discussing or boasting of their accomplishments.

The Indians' names never ceased to intrigue me. It would have been interesting to know the stories behind the names of some Athapaskans. One day when I landed at a village, I had a package to deliver to a Sebastian McGinty. I looked around for a weather-beaten old Irish prospector, but saw none.

"I guess Sebastian McGinty isn't here," I commented.

Just then, a dark-skinned Indian stepped up.

"Yis, t'ets me."

For some time I had noticed messages written on the fuselage and tail of the T-50 Cessna, always in the same blue color. "Hi Carl. Weather good here. Come see us. Harry," was a typical message. The children in various villages always asked me for my "blue paper," the carbon sheets taken from between forms I had to complete for my shipments. "What do you do with the blue paper?" I finally asked one youngster.

"I write on your airplane," he explained.

Sure enough, that's what was going on. My airplane had become a traveling billboard, carrying messages from village to village. The kids used sticks and the carbon paper to write their messages while I was busy loading and unloading. I started to notice that kids always seemed to meet the plane, and they walked around searching the fuselage for messages addressed to them.

Life in the bush has its humorous side. One incident that tickled us was the story about a trapper and his wife who went far into the headwaters of the Nowitna River for the trapping season. Trapping involves much work, leaving little time for hunting. One of the trapline necessities in the Yukon River Valley is a winter's supply of moose meat. This trapper shot the first moose that strayed near the cabin. Unfortunately, the moose was a cow, which was illegal game.

His wife took the skinned and frozen head inside the cabin, planning to cut the meat from it because it has some of the sweetest found on a moose. The nose is prized as food, as is the tongue. She left the head behind the stove to thaw while she and her husband went out to run their trapline.

Shortly after their departure, a game warden landed his plane near their cabin, and finding no one home, he made himself at home for the night, as is the custom in bush Alaska. He found the cow moose head.

When he flew off the next morning, he took the head with

him as evidence. He flew along the dog team trail of the trapper and his wife. He located the pair, but could find no place to land, so he had to fly on to Fairbanks.

The trapper recognized the game warden's black and orange airplane flying over him and his wife. When the two returned to their cabin and found that the warden had been there and the moose head was missing, the trapper did some creative thinking.

He wrote his version of how the cow moose happened to be killed, and sent it via bush pilot to Fairbanks to a local radio station that aired "Tundra Topics," a nightly program aimed at bush residents. "Tundra Topics" used good bush yarns, and the station eagerly broadcast the trapper's version of how the cow moose came to be killed: "So-and-so, trapping in the Nowitna country, reports that early in the fall his wife went blueberry picking. She carried a rifle and had two dogs with her. During the day the dogs jumped a moose, and the animal charged the dogs. The instinctive reaction of the dogs was to run to their mistress to share their troubles. Thus Mrs. Trapper soon found herself facing an enraged, charging cow moose. She was fortunate she had a rifle. With swift and courageous action she managed to drop the moose only a few feet away."

The story had the desired effect. No jury would convict a woman who alone and unaided had so bravely defended herself from a charging moose. The game warden didn't dare charge the trapper or his wife for illegally killing a cow moose. Nothing was ever said about it.

Galena is a combination of the old and the new. Many residents live in log cabins and burn firewood for heat and cooking. In recent years, modern frame houses have appeared. The nearby Air Force installation is modern. The paved airport runway, shared by military and civilian users, is among the finest in Alaska.

Especially interesting were the two trading posts in Galena. Both were typical outpost stores that sold a wide variety of practical items. Both had frost-heaved floors, and shelves with goods piled high. One had a pool table, which was busy from morning to night.

There is something fascinating about the way goods are offered in a frontier trading post. Nothing is displayed according to the rules of modern merchandising. There are no tables filled with trinkets, no carefully worded signs or price tags. No "on sale" items, or skillfully positioned advertisements to lower a customer's resistence. The odor of most trading posts is a delicious combination of wool, leather, raw fur, kerosene, and wood. Bessie and I found that we could never get out of these stores without buying items we really didn't need. There was something in the homely way everything is informally piled that sent us climbing over stools and boxes to inspect items that caught our eye. I sometimes think wares that are hard to get at tempt a buyer more than those that are carefully displayed.

Dog team racing has long been the major sport of Interior Alaska. The North American Championship race is run at Fairbanks each March, and mushers from the length and breadth of Alaska participate. In recent decades, increasing numbers of participants from other states and countries have competed.

In 1958, soon after we had moved to Galena, Northern Consolidated Airlines sponsored a musher named Raymond Paul, a Native resident of Galena, at the North American. I was to fly Paul and his dog team to Fairbanks, and I used the company Noorduyn Norseman bush plane.

All the seats were removed from the Norseman, making room for the dog team. Paul showed up and I expected him to lead his dogs into the airplane one at a time and tie them in place. To my astonishment, he put a step at the doorway, then calmly drove the team of 14 dogs into the plane, sled and all. Once inside the plane he told them all to lie down and they did.

I climbed in through the pilot's door and got into my seat, wondering what kind of a dog fight might ensue if the animals became upset during the flight. I turned my head and discovered that the nose of the lead dog was right in my ear. The dog was friendly, but his breath was terrible. I couldn't do much about it without throwing the whole team into a tumult.

I taxied down the runway, turned, and lifted the plane into the sky. The dogs were well trained; none moved, no fights broke out, and there were no messes to clean up. The three-hour flight to Fairbanks with that lead dog as "copilot," panting and slobbering on me all the way, was an experience to remember.

My T-50 Cessna developed a mysterious problem in early March. I flew my scheduled deliveries from Galena, as usual, up and down the Yukon River. The early-morning flights followed a zigzag course as I dodged separated layers of fog. The lowest layer was at about 100 feet, yet all layers were interspersed by large patches of blue sky and sunshine. Under the lowest clouds, a light, freezing drizzle was falling, the worst plague of low-level, treetop flying. The drizzle wasn't heavy enough to ice the aircraft dangerously, but it covered the windshield, making visibility difficult.

Within 10 miles of Ruby, I encountered bad icing. Since I could see the town through a small, ice-free strip near the bottom of the windshield, I felt I should go on to Ruby rather than turn around. I managed to land safely despite the icy windshield. The trouble started when I tried to take off.

The airplane was traveling 30 or 40 miles an hour when it veered to the left. Full power on the left engine with none on the right failed to stop the airplane's circular course. I came to a halt and taxied back. Obviously, something was sticking under the left ski. I borrowed a jack and raised the airplane. Indeed, the bottom of the left ski was covered with ice. I thoroughly cleaned it and tried again. Again the airplane pulled to the left despite everything I tried. Again I taxied back, jacked up the airplane, and cleaned ice off the bottom of the left ski. I had plenty of help from the villagers. No one, including me, could figure out why one ski would ice up and not the other.

After fighting the problem for an hour, I chartered a small plane to take my passenger and the mail on to Galena to catch the scheduled DC-3 flight. And then I returned, to resume my struggle to get the reluctant T-50 Cessna to take off from the snowy Yukon River. As I worked, the temperature grew considerably colder. That made the difference. With the left ski bottom cold and clean, I was able to take off and return to Galena.

I decided that the exhaust stack from the left engine, which was pointed at the left ski, must have warmed the ski a few degrees—just enough to cause snow to stick to it.

The problem occurred again the next day, at Galena. As I started to take off down the narrow ski strip beside the paved runway, at about 50 miles an hour the airplane swerved to the left onto the paved and plowed runway, which was used by wheeled planes. Fortunately, there was enough snow on the pavement so that the skis could slide. I taxied back and found that snow was again sticking to the bottom of the left ski. The air temperature was 29 degrees, which made me even more certain that the left engine exhaust was warming the left ski just enough to make snow stick.

Eventually, I added a short length to the exhaust pipe of the left engine, pointing it away from the ski. That solved the problem.

Sticky runways often give bush pilots frustration, and I remember one such story told about Kotzebue pilot Archie Ferguson. One spring he landed on the muddy runway at Koyuk, slid to a stop, and managed to taxi only with great difficulty. An Eskimo resident of the village arrived, and Archie tore into him about the terrible condition of the runway.

The Eskimo said nothing until Archie had finished his tirade, then he said calmly, "Hager land across river." Hager was another Seward Peninsula bush pilot.

To this Archie roared, "Well, why didn't you say so," and jumped into his airplane and struggled off, flew across the river, and landed on the other strip. This landing was really difficult. The plane mired down to its axles, and Archie was fit to be tied.

In the meantime the Eskimo paddled across the river. Archie lit into him again, asking angrily, "Why didn't you tell me this was worse. I'll be stuck here for a week."

To this the Eskimo stolidly answered, "Hager stuck here for week too."

During one night while Bessie and I were asleep, our building started rocking. Chandeliers that normally hung about 18 inches from the center of the ridgepole of the building were slamming against the ceiling on both sides.

We leaped from bed and stood in a doorway, assuming that it was the strongest part of the building. The building didn't collapse, and after a few minutes the world quit rocking.

The earthquake registered 5.7 on the Richter scale, and it was centered northeast of Huslia on the Koyukuk River. Some frame village schoolhouses were slightly damaged, but log houses rode through just fine.

Around the time of the earthquake, a Fairbanks pilot had flown to the village of Huslia but hadn't reported in and was feared lost. The morning after the earthquake the FAA called, asking for all available planes to search for the missing pilot.

I filled the T-50 Cessna with several observers and flew toward Huslia. Once in the air we were amazed at what the earthquake had done. The ice in every lake was broken all around the shoreline, and large cracks stretched from one shore to the other. In places, pressure ridges of broken ice were piled several feet high. In some lakes the ice had been broken into thousands of pieces, and from the air they looked almost like reassembled jigsaw puzzles.

Here and there we saw that where the earth had cracked, mud had been forced to the surface and had flowed across the snow. It was hard to visualize the immense forces necessary to squeeze that mud upward.

At Huslia, I spotted airplane ski tracks on the Koyukuk River, but the ice had sheered under the tracks: the two segments had moved 10 or so feet so the ski tracks were no longer aligned. We didn't find the missing plane and pilot. On our return to Galena, we learned that he had safely reached his destination but couldn't get through on his radio to close his flight plan.

Our lives at Galena revolved around the comings and goings of the DC-3s, and, later, the newer Fairchild F27s. Sometimes tons of mail and freight piled up when the weather was too bad for me to fly to the various villages. Occasionally, lonely Native youngsters, sent home from a hospital or school somewhere, would get stuck at Galena. One of our neighbors, Hazel Strassburg, would usually take them in, and if she wasn't home or had a full house, we would take care of them until I could manage to fly them home.

Hazel is an energetic, motherly woman, who has lived in bush Alaska all her life. She once told us how she and two other women had trapped beaver one season. It was their practice to stay a night or two in each of several line cabins, and from each they tended a number of beaver traps.

One night, the three returned late and tired to one of the cabins. They were in need of a cup of coffee. An old lard pail served as a coffee pot, and one of the women noticed several cups of their brew left from the previous day. Rather than make fresh coffee, she merely reheated the old. Hazel refused the stale coffee, preferring to wait for a fresh cup.

The other two enjoyed their hot drinks, and when the pail was nearly empty, one went outside to dump the grounds, readying to make a fresh batch. Suddenly, a cry and a retching sound came from the woman who had dumped the grounds. Amid the old coffee grounds she had found the bodies of two well-cooked mice.

"See how God punishes lazy people?" Hazel commented.

I wasn't the only Billberg who had to cope with occasional emergencies at Galena. Bessie, as the main radio operator for Northern Consolidated's Galena station, had her share of them. One July evening about seven o'clock, I found Bessie in the office, her ears tuned to the radio. She motioned me to be quiet. She was receiving an emergency call from Selby Lake. An oil exploration party was in desperate need of a floatplane. One of their members had built a raft to cross the lake, and the raft later was seen floating about, empty.

Bessie determined the location of the lake (150 miles north of Galena) and told the party to stand by. She then tuned the radio to another frequency and called the Wien Airlines station at Bettles, 55 miles from Selby Lake, which got the Wien network humming. Within 15 minutes, a Wien plane was on its way to help the geologists.

We later learned that the raftsman had allowed his raft to escape, leaving him stranded on the far shore of the lake where his companions couldn't see him.

One flying adventure I had with a T-50 Cessna, I could have done without. I flew a load of mail and freight to the village of Nulato. The runway there slopes steeply. A pilot can take off uphill with a plane that is light, if it performs well. Otherwise, one always takes off downhill.

I was empty and headed down the runway, pointing downhill, almost airborne on takeoff, when suddenly, red flame shot five or six feet above the cowling of the right engine. I immediately slammed the throttles shut and jumped on the brakes, skidding almost to the end of the runway. The fire seemed to have gone out but I sat and looked at the engine very carefully. I taxied all the way back up the hill and stopped the airplane, climbed out, and inspected all around the engine. I could see no reason for the flames. I decided that too much fuel must have reached the carburetor, causing it to overflow, and that the overflow had ignited. I wasn't thinking.

I started up again and poured the coal to her and right away flame shot high out of the right engine, and this time the fire continued burning when I shut the engines down. While the plane was rolling, I turned it sideways on the hilly runway and locked the brakes to keep it in place.

I leaped out with a fire extinguisher, and after dragging the mail sacks out of the airplane and tossing them onto the runway, I squirted inside the cowling. My frantic effort was like spitting on a house afire. Flames kept billowing out. I was truly concerned, because behind the firewall of the T-50 Cessna engine is the fabric-covered wing. I feared the whole plane was going to burn.

When my fire extinguisher was empty, I scooped loose dirt from the runway with my hands and tossed it inside the cowling. Finally, fire stopped coming out of the engine.

I discovered that a gasoline line had sprung a leak near the engine and the leaking gas had caught fire. As long as the engines ran and the fuel pumps were working, the flame was being fed by gasoline. As the blaze grew hotter, more and more wiring and other inflammables around the engine melted and caught fire. The fire was subdued because the gas flow was stopped when I cut the engines, but the pooled gasoline burned for some time after the engines stopped.

I thought it was the dirt that had put the fire out, but I was wrong. The firewall prevented spread of the fire so long as I was stopped and on the ground. If I had taken off with the airplane afire, I would never have been able to turn and land. The fabric of the wing would probably have caught fire because of the slipstream forcing the flames behind the engine. I'd have probably dunked the plane into the mile-wide Yukon River, and I might not have survived.

I left the airplane parked beside the Nulato runway. A friendly oil company helicopter pilot, who saw the smoke from my burning plane when he was 10 miles away, flew me back to Galena. Mechanics had to install a new motor mount, a new engine, and all new wiring in the singed T-50 Cessna.

Bessie and I especially enjoyed knowing some of the older Natives. One, an Indian named Alexander Demoski, knew a soft touch when he saw one. I watched one day as he entered our office carrying a model fish trap that he had made and planned to sell to Bessie. Native crafts always intrigued us, and Bessie was particularly interested. The conversation between salesman and buyer had me convulsed as I eavesdropped:

"Hello daughter. You my friend. See what I have? This you want."

"Oh, that's nice. How much?"

"See daughter, I show you. You like. See?"

By this time, Alexander was standing close to Bessie. He punctuated each word by banging the top of her head with the flat of his hand. Then he sat in front of Bessie, and with every few words he banged her on the knee.

"I sell you. You have. I like you. You my friend. Seven dollar."

By this time Bessie was mesmerized, and her words resembled those of the old man. "I like. I take. Seven dollar." The deal was closed.

We had frequent visits from the old man, and we looked forward to every one of them. He had made some of the objects especially for us, so they took on a greater value in our eyes. I remember buying a bow and arrow, a hand-carved wooden spoon, and other similar pieces.

One day a weary-looking man came into the Galena office and bought a ticket to Fairbanks on the DC-3. He had about an hour to wait.

"I don't feel good," he complained.

"Why don't you lie down on that bench?" I suggested, pointing to a bench in the waiting room.

He did, and seemed to be resting comfortably. The DC-3 arrived, and I got busy unloading the passengers and baggage. When it was time for the DC-3 to leave, the other passengers started out the door, but the man on the bench didn't move.

I went to wake him, touched his arm, and it flopped to the floor. I gently shook the man, but he didn't respond. Another shake and then a check for a pulse, and I discovered that he was dead. He had stretched out on that bench and quietly died.

Bessie and I enjoyed our time at Galena. Being station managers, working together, and providing service gave us both much satisfaction, and I loved the kind of flying I did there.

The lower Yukon was a pleasant region to live in. The people were warm-hearted, friendly, and interesting. The surroundings are filled with beauty. Great spruce forests grow in the valley of the Yukon. There are many moose, bears, and other wildlife. Grayling, a fine sport fish, swim in abundance in the streams. Salmon crowd up the Yukon River in summer.

Life for most Galena residents is generally leisurely, although as station managers we lived by the schedule of airplane flights. We bought a riverboat and on days off, we often went to nearby tributaries of the Yukon. We collected mineral specimens and rocks, and friends gave us many beautiful agates, which, as a hobby, I sawed on my rock saw and polished. We panned for gold, and thoroughly enjoyed exploring.

After we had been there nearly two years, the government, which regulated airlines, took Galena away from Northern Consolidated Airlines and awarded it to Wien Airlines. Wien was a fine airline, and we were pleased when the management asked us to remain at Galena. But we chose to follow new challenges and accepted Consolidated's offer to be station managers at Bethel, in Eskimo country on the lower Kuskokwim River.

Fighting Forest Fires

SMOKE LAY across the spruce timber below as I flew, permeating the air so thickly that the tangy smell was inside the airplane. I circled, trying to locate through the smoke the leaping tongues of flame in the forest fire. When I spotted what I took to be the main fire, I circled, deciding on my approach. Then I slowed the airplane to just above stalling speed, shoved the nose down, and started across the front edge of the fire. I was perhaps 200 feet above the tops of the spruce, ready to drop fire retardant, when suddenly, a photographer who had begged to accompany me on the flight bolted from the Plexiglas nose of the World War II B-25 bomber I was flying. His eyes were huge and his face was white. He had wanted to get good pictures, but from his perspective, the spruce trees were coming too fast and too close. He thought we were about to crash. I didn't blame him. We were awfully low, and at our speed of about 130 miles per hour the spruce trees must have been a green blur.

During the early 1960s, some bright person decided that

airplanes could be useful in fighting forest fires. Various types of World War II medium bombers and other airplanes of that class were modified by installing tanks that held borate, a fire retardant. Fast-dumping gates were installed in the tanks so the load could be dropped in about six seconds. Ground area engulfed by airplane-dropped borate varied with the kind of gate on the plane's tank, altitude and speed of plane at the drop, type of terrain, and even the amount of prevailing wind. In controlling a fire, the borate was dumped along the edge of or in front of a fire. It was remarkably effective.

During summers for several years in the mid-1960s, I flew one of five or six twin-engine Mitchell B-25 medium bombers in Alaska that were under contract to the Bureau of Land Management for forest fire control. Two or three other Mitchells were used for spares and for parts. The B-25 was also used in the Lower 48 for fire control for a time. Someone declared them unsafe and dangerous for fire control, and their use was discontinued, which to me was nonsense.

In Alaska, after the planes had dropped their loads, the fire was often controllable by smoke jumpers. One summer I flew a DC-3 from which I dropped smoke jumpers. It was exciting work.

It was a thrill to fly the B-25. When empty, that airplane performed like no other I've ever flown. The one minor complaint I had was that the controls were a little on the heavy side. Real muscle was needed when I needed to make frequent maneuvers. I generally flew alone, although there were always people around who wanted to ride in the copilot seat.

The first B-25 I flew we called "Antique Five," which was her radio call. It was a very good airplane that belonged to Merrill and Richard Wien, Noel Wien's sons. In the 1980s, 20 years after I flew it, I saw an hour-long documentary on television describing how someone in California had rebuilt that airplane and flown it to Australia. "This airplane once flew in Alaska," said the commentator. I also saw a documentary of the plane when it flew in Australia, and film clips of it at air shows there. I believe the airplane was then placed in a museum.

Borate fire retardant is a sterile, chalky, white colloidal solution that weighs 11 pounds a gallon. That's heavy; water weighs 8 pounds a gallon, and gasoline 6 pounds. The tanks held 1,000 gallons, or 11,000 pounds. This is much heavier than the 3,000-pound bomb load the airplane was designed to carry. On the graphs of the airplane manual, 11,000 pounds was way up in the red. Flying this overload would have been extremely dangerous except for one thing: if an engine failed, even during takeoff, the borate could be dumped in six seconds. Even after three seconds of dumping, the load would be reduced enough to make a big difference in the airplane's performance. To my mind, this made ours a reasonably safe operation.

The first summer I flew a B-25 was rainy, with few fires, and the fires that occurred were mostly small. Whenever I dropped borate, the fires went out almost like magic. With this being the extent of my experience with forest fires, I thought that Alaska would never again have any really serious losses from them.

When I accepted the job as pilot of a B-25, I had never had any experience with the airplane. I studied the manuals thoroughly—its structure, its equipment, engines, flying characteristics, everything. Each airplane has flight characteristics as distinctive as fingerprints, and the way to get top performance from an airplane is to learn its individual peculiarities. Once I knew what I could expect from the B-25, I was then checked out flying it. Flying that hot airplane was not a casual operation; for safety's sake, nothing could be overlooked. The airplane's two 1,700-horsepower engines, gulping 150 gallons of gasoline an hour, could yank that warplane along at almost 300 miles per hour when it was empty. Normal cruise was around 200 miles per hour.

When dumping borate on a forest fire, I had to really be on my toes, for I commonly had to fly as low as 200 feet. The fire was often on a hillside, in a hole, or in a mountain valley. Two possibilities I always had to keep in mind were engine failure and gate failure. If an engine failed, the load would have to be dumped immediately, for the loaded airplane wouldn't have remained in the air long with one engine. If a gate failed so our load couldn't be dumped, we would have really been in trouble, for the load was too heavy for a landing. With the plane loaded, abrupt maneuvers and steep climbs were also ruled out.

Sometimes I circled over a fire for 20 minutes or more, figuring how to get out of a run if an engine or gate failed. It was the kind of flying that took all the forethought and concentration I could muster.

I made some practice drops early in the game, using water. I embarrassed myself on one of these practice drops. The tank was filled with 1,000 gallons of water, as I taxied the airplane down the runway of Fairbanks International. I ran the engines up to check magnetos, checked all the switches and levers, and received permission from the tower to take off. As I sped down the runway and lifted off, I thought that the airplane felt pretty lively—the 8,000 pounds of water seemed like no weight at all. Pilot John McCormick, boss of our operation, was in another airplane to watch my drop.

I got into position, nosed down, eased into my run, and made my drop. But the airplane didn't react by leaping upward, which puzzled me. "Nice run, but you didn't drop your load," radioed the chief.

"I sure did," I radioed back.

"Nothing came out," he replied. I couldn't understand that, but I had to admit that the airplane wasn't acting as it should.

I returned to Fairbanks International, and there on the end of the runway was a huge wet spot. Somehow in checking my switches and levers before takeoff, I had tripped the switch for the dump gate and spilled 1,000 gallons of water on the runway.

It was an embarrassing lesson, and it never happened again. I shudder to think of the mess on the runway if I had dumped 1,000 gallons of borate. The material wasn't toxic, but 1,000 pounds of chalky emulsion on a runway, even after cleanup, would have certainly left a stain. No doubt it would have been called "Billberg's Mark."

What happens when a B-25 in flight suddenly dumps 11,000 pounds of fire suppressant? Early in their use for fire control, pilots of B-25s dropped borate at cruising speed or faster—200 miles per hour or more. At these speeds, the borate left so suddenly that the airplane lurched upward violently, imposing a negative load on the wings. There was also danger from the retardant, which, as it whooshed out of the gate, would sweep up and hit the tail. Some B-25 tails were reportedly knocked off by the heavy, inert stuff. Eventually someone figured out that speed didn't add the usual safety factor in these circumstances and that in fact, just the opposite was the case.

With this knowledge, we slowed to 120 or 130 miles per hour—just above stalling—to make our drops. At such low speeds, there was always an upward surge of the plane when the load left, but it wasn't bad. Retardant wasn't sucked into the tail, and we experienced only minor negative loads on the wing.

My second year of flying fire control was an entirely different experience. It was a dry year and fires were everywhere—so many that we couldn't possibly handle them all. That summer, some of the fires were so big that dumping half a dozen loads of retardant on them did almost nothing. Longtime Fairbanks flyer Dick McIntyre had bought Antique Five, and I flew it for him that season.

Sometimes there was overkill. I remember when five B-25s took off from Fairbanks loaded with borate, headed for a fire reported by a commercial airline pilot in the Twin Lakes area, north of Lake Clark. I was in the lead plane. Darkness was beginning to fall and I worried a bit about that.

Whenever we were sent out on a fire, we were given its latitude and longitude. On this flight, we flew down the west side of the Alaska Range past Farewell, because a straight-line flight would have taken us over the high mountains. When I arrived at the site, all I found was a small fire. I dropped my borate on it—

very carefully, for it was nearly dark, and visibility near the ground was poor. My drop put the fire out, and, because I was low on gas, I headed through Lake Clark Pass for Anchorage. I heard the other four pilots talking to each other. "Where's the fire?" "I don't see any fire or any smoke."

They all dumped their loads so they could land, and followed me to Anchorage. I thought of the cost of putting out that one tiny fire—five B-25s, flying five or six hours each, each dropping 11,000 pounds of borate. The nontoxic sterile material, scattered over hundreds of feet, probably prevented plant growth for a year or two where it fell, but there was no lasting damage.

The behavior of fire is sometimes strange. A 10-degree drop in temperature is about as effective as a light rain in toning down a fire. Apparently, that is what happened on that evening.

Most of the time, smoke jumpers were put on a fire, either before we got there or afterward to mop up, to see that it didn't flare up again. Occasionally a fire would turn on smoke jumpers. When that happened we were sent out immediately. We'd roar down through the smoke, heat, and ashes and drop borate between the jumpers and the fire. Sometimes such a maneuver was pretty scary.

Once, after a crew of smoke jumpers had contained a fire, they set up a small camp and rolled up in their sleeping bags around a campfire. Somehow a borate-loaded B-25 was sent to the fire. The evening light was poor. The pilot of the B-25 circled several times looking for flames, but the only fire visible was the campfire. He didn't know it was a campfire, of course, when he made a run dumping 1,000 gallons of borate on it.

When he started his run, the smoke jumpers woke up, realized what was happening, got out of their sleeping bags fast, and scattered. The long, slow approach of the B-25 gave them plenty of time to scurry away. The force of 1,000 gallons coming down in one huge glob can lift a person up and bash him into a tree hard enough to kill him.

The jumpers were well scattered when the borate banged

down dead center on their fire, their sleeping bags, and their camp gear. That pilot wouldn't have won a popularity contest with those smoke jumpers.

It was fun flying the DC-3 filled with smoke jumpers. Weather was usually good, and I would circle and decide with the jumpmaster where the equipment and smoke jumpers should be placed. Then I'd make my run at 1,100 feet altitude. When I figured I was over the proper spot, I'd push the button on my control column that rang a bell, and the jumpers would leap out two at a time. Usually I made several passes to drop the 17 jumpers. Then we'd make several passes to drop their parachute-equipped gear.

Once I was sent out with a load of smoke jumpers to a fire near Huslia. It was mostly brushy country, with a few spruce trees. I could see the ground fairly well as I lined the airplane up and made the several passes needed to drop the jumpers and their equipment.

As the last group tumbled out, I noticed that one man must have jumped a few seconds late because he dropped a good 100 yards or more from the others. I banked and came back, checking, and I saw this loner standing on the ground waving his parachute at a black bear a few feet away. The bear was stalking back and forth in a half-circle, clearly threatening. Later, I learned that while floating down, this jumper saw that he was going to land near the bear. "Hey bear, beat it. Scram!" he yelled as he was descending, doing everything he could think of to frighten the bear off.

Puzzled at the strange sounds, the bear looked everywhere but up. Then *wham!* the jumper thudded to the ground beside him. The startled animal ran a few feet, then turned back and started pacing back and forth threateningly. Blackie may have resented this unusual surprise from the sky. I called the lead jumper, who had a walkie-talkie. "You'd better get over to that guy who landed a little apart from you. He's having trouble with a bear," I warned.

Next time I circled, all the jumpers were running toward their endangered fellow. At their noisy approach, the bear ran off at high speed. I continued to circle. I was low, and the roaring of my airplane scared up another bear. It ran top speed directly toward the jumpers. "The bear that was bothering you is gone," I told the lead jumper by radio, "but hang on. There's another one on its way. He'll be there in about 10 seconds!"

Sure enough, the second bear ran right into the gathered jumpers. He skidded to a stop, did a doubletake, ricocheted into the brush, and frantically legged it out of the area.

After I had worked a season or two, the borate was discontinued and replaced with a red-colored retardant called Phoscheck, which was two pounds lighter per gallon than borate. A thousand gallons weighed only 9,000 pounds, and that 2,000 pounds less made the airplane feel and fly much differently. Instead of being sterile, as was the borate, Phoscheck contained some fertilizer so it didn't leave barren streaks on the ground for several years as borate did.

I especially recall one experience with Phoscheck. All the other Fairbanks B-25 drop planes were in the McGrath area on a fire. I had returned to Galena with mine, when suddenly a fire in heavy spruce timber was reported along the Yukon River near Galena, and the report said that the raging flames had crowned— that is, they were burning through the tops of the trees.

I loaded up and flew from Galena to the area and quickly found the blaze. The consuming progress of the fire was frightening to watch. It was traveling so fast I actually had to aim the plane well ahead of the fire—leading it as one would a flying duck with a shotgun. But by the time I reached my aiming point, the fire had reached it. It was really moving. Heat waves bounced my airplane, and, though I was at 200 feet, the flames seemed to lick at my wings. I dropped the entire load in one pass, and the chemical spread over about a quarter of a mile through the treetops (a load of the lighter-weight Phoscheck spread farther than the borate).

No more drops were made on that fire, for more serious ones had started elsewhere. About a year later, as I was flying over the area, I found the place where I had dropped the Phoscheck in that crown fire. The retardant had helped stop the fire. I could see where my drop had started and ended, for it was an island of green living trees surrounded by a blackened and dead forest. The crown fire had gone around both ends, and had continued to burn until there were no more trees a mile or so away.

If all six of our planes had dropped on that fire, we might have stopped it entirely. But that area was wild land, with no people, while other fires at the time were threatening human habitations and were a higher priority for control.

In my last year of flying fire control with B-25s, while on a mission from Tanacross, something minor went wrong with Antique Three, the plane I flew. When I landed, our chief pilot, Paul Hanson (who, with Grenold Collins, owned the two B-25s I flew that season, Antique Two and Antique Three), both a mechanic and a pilot, traded planes with me. I flew his aircraft (Antique Two) to make several drops one day. After he had repaired my airplane, Hanson told me he was going to fly it out and dump its load on the fire we were working on.

During takeoff, he forgot to lock the nosewheel. That's serious with a B-25, because during takeoff an unlocked nosewheel will shimmy, especially with a heavy load when the wheel is on the ground for a long time. I suppose he had reached 40 or 50 miles an hour when that wheel started to shimmy. Once a shimmy starts, it is absolutely uncontrollable, and the nose shook so hard that instrument glass in the cockpit broke. Some of the light lines that carried fluid, such as to the oil pressure gauges, split. That whole airplane shook violently. Paul aborted the takeoff, stopping as fast as he could.

Then he had to work over the airplane, repairing the damage. Finally, he decided it was all right and we traded planes again.

Soon we were called to a fire near McGrath. I flew the

plane there and found the fire on a flat area that was easy to drop on. I lined up with the fire and came roaring down toward the flames. As I pushed the button to release the 9,000 pounds of retardant, the B-25, as is normal, started to rise as the heavy liquid left. Then, to my astonishment, Antique Three started a slow roll.

There was no logical reason for the plane to roll. I had done nothing to initiate it. For an instant I thought a wing was coming off. I quickly countered with opposite aileron, maneuvering back to level flight, and then I immediately climbed. If that plane was going to do acrobatic maneuvers, I wanted lots of room beneath me! When a B-25 starts to roll on its own and you're at 200 feet, the adrenaline pumps and the heart races.

I returned to McGrath, landed, and told Paul Hanson that I didn't dare fly any more loads in that machine. Then I borrowed a ladder and some tools and inspected the airplane from one end to the other. I found that the tail assembly was slightly looser than on the other B-25s, but nothing was broken, nothing had fallen off. I couldn't establish why that airplane started to roll, but I refused to gamble with it. "I'll fly it to Fairbanks," I told Hanson, "but I won't haul any more loads with it until it can be thoroughly checked by mechanics." He agreed.

Before flying to Fairbanks, I went to flight service at McGrath and looked at the weather map. Never before or since have I seen such an extreme weather system. Since I had, of course, flown the McGrath-Fairbanks route hundreds of times, and the weather was all right for a visual-flight-rules (VFR) flight, I took off and slow-flew that airplane all the way, loafing along about 50 miles an hour slower than the normal cruise of 200 miles per hour.

After I landed at Fairbanks, mechanics started going through the plane. While they worked and I waited, rain began to fall, and it rained as it seldom has in Interior Alaska. Within a couple of days, Fairbanks was under water: it was 1967, the year of the historic Fairbanks flood.

Mechanics found that the airplane was loose all over. The

nosewheel shimmy had loosened rivets and probably bent a few parts. There were minor wrinkles in the fuselage skin. If we had continued flying overloads with that plane, something would probably have broken. As fire season was nearly ended, the airplane was parked. I don't think it ever flew again.

Years later, I was driving around the Fairbanks airport when I came to the boneyard where old airplanes are dumped. There stood Antique Three. She was ragged, the metal skin was ripped and hanging loose, control cables drooped, one engine was gone, glass was broken. She looked terrible. Tears came to my eyes when I saw her. I loved that old airplane.

I snapped out of it and looked at Bessie. "I wonder if I don't look a little like that old airplane?" She didn't say much, so I went straight home, combed my hair, shaved, and put on a clean shirt.

As far as I know, that old B-25 is still sitting there.

Return to Nome

BESSIE AND I moved back to Nome in March 1965, nearly 23 years after we had left that city, concerned about attack from the Japanese. This time I flew for Munz Northern Airline. Started by Bill Munz, a real bush pilot and a true eagle, this small local company had been purchased by Dick Galleher. Munz turned to working a jade mine on Alaska's Kobuk River during the summer and an Arizona mine in the winter.

Munz was once a strong competitor of Wien Airlines at Nome. Bill was tough, hard-driving, some say even ruthless. He had a reputation for his bad-weather flying ability. When I first flew at Nome in the 1940s, we used to say, "Munz flies so low in bad weather that he has to climb to get over a herd of reindeer."

He knew all the passes on the Seward Peninsula by heart, and if Bill Munz couldn't get through, no one could. I remember a Wien pilot commenting that "the biggest hazard in flying through Seward Peninsula passes in bad weather is meeting Bill

Munz coming the other way."

In the two-plus decades since I had left Nome, aviation had made tremendous technological advances. The airplane I now was to fly for Munz Northern Airline most of the time was a sleek, streamlined, twin-engine Aero Commander, an airplane first built in 1952, with retractable landing gear. The Commander was fully instrumented, cruised at close to 200 miles per hour, climbed at nearly 1,700 feet a minute, and carried five passengers in warm cabin comfort. It could easily fly above the clouds, nonstop, from Nome to Anchorage or Fairbanks. It was light years ahead of the 1930s Gullwing Stinsons and the Cessna Airmaster that I had flown out of Nome for Sig Wien.

I too had progressed. I now had 30 years of professional flying experience, most of it in Alaska. I had years of flying in and around mountains. I had flown in tough weather, including extreme cold. I had spent years landing on short, rough runways. I had learned over and over again how a few moments of inattention, a too-bold decision, a little carelessness can kill a pilot. I had become as wary as a wolf and checked and double-checked the airplanes I flew, studied the weather, memorized instrument flying techniques, and carried with me—in a battered old briefcase full of charts—backup information on the airplane's performance, lists of radio frequencies, and other important data.

Despite the great changes, I had to laugh at how history repeats itself. As the saying goes, it was déjà vu all over again.

One of my first flights from Nome after my return was eerily reminiscent of my first commercial flight in Alaska in 1941, when I flew three passengers from Deering to Nome and each, trying to help a new pilot to the Seward Peninsula, told me I should fly a different direction to reach our destination.

This time I had one passenger on a flight from Nome to Candle. He had fortified himself for the trip at a local bar. The alcohol made him garrulous and, in his mind, infallible. As we took off in the Aero Commander, the weather at Nome was bad. There was no way to make an instrument let-down through clouds at Candle (because there were no navigation radio facilities at Candle), so I had to fly below the clouds and get there by visual flight rules (VFR). I flew up the coast very low, and as we got closer to Candle, the lower the clouds were and the closer the ground was. My passenger, who occupied the copilot's seat, became extremely nervous. "You're not going the right way. Candle is over there," he said, pointing toward Siberia.

I frequently circled low clouds, zigzagged to dodge the highest hills, and skirted heavy rain showers. And my passenger kept up a steady chatter. "I think Candle's that way," he repeatedly said, pointing in almost every direction except toward Candle.

Because of the bad weather, I couldn't reach Candle and had to return to Nome. I decided to return on instruments rather than battle the low ceiling all the way back. I called Nome on the radio, got permission to enter the airway at a certain place, and climbed through the clouds until we were on top. I then flew directly to Nome, taking about half the time on the return that I had going out.

"I think Candle is over there," my passenger continued to proclaim every few minutes, pointing.

At Nome, on instruments, I let down through the clouds. My passenger, obviously bewildered, and still befuddled with drink, still thought I was trying to find Candle.

As we descended from about 7,000 feet my ears began to plug, so I yawned several times to clear them. After about the third yawn my passenger commented, "You poor guy, you must be tired. That's why you can't find Candle. Now just follow the directions I give you and we'll be there before you know it."

About then we broke out of the clouds. When the guy saw Nome below us his jaw dropped and he stopped talking. I never saw him again.

Nome still had its troubled side. One morning on the way to work I walked in front of a bar and saw so much frozen blood on the walk that it looked like a moose had been slaughtered there. A man had been knifed the previous evening, but one of the local policemen told me, "He's OK. Just a minor wound."

A few days later another pilot and I saw a drunk man marching his wife down the middle of a street with a .30-30 rifle in her back. The police came and quickly straightened the situation out. Neither event made the weekly *Nome Nugget* newspaper.

History also repeated the weather: wind, snow, rain, fog, and sleet still blew across the Seward Peninsula from the Bering Sea in a dazzling array, as it had in 1941–42.

I was delighted to find that Munz Airline owned, in addition to two Aero Commanders, two 1930s Gullwing Stinsons, the same sturdy model that I had flown from Nome for Wien Airlines more than two decades earlier. I hadn't flown a Gullwing for more than 15 years. I appreciated the newer, more reliable airplanes, and I liked the safety of two engines on a plane. I had advanced with the more modern planes and was accustomed to all their benefits. Yet, it seemed like the old days when I again took to the air in a Gullwing Stinson. I suppose it was nostalgia, appreciation of things past, but that old radial engine's growl was music to my ears.

I had been flying late-model Cessnas, Pipers, and other airplanes with mostly opposed engines. These newer airplanes seemed flimsy compared to those old beefy 1930s birds. In some of the Stinsons and others of the era, the windows were real glass, and they cranked up and down like those of an automobile. The pre-flight checklist was quite short and simple, although it had once seemed long and complicated to me. Starting a radial engine is more fun than starting an opposed engine—the radial comes to life gradually, one cylinder at a time, like a groggy bear awakening after winter, especially if the engine has nine or more cylinders.

On takeoff, the radial-powered planes have a little more propeller effect because most of them have longer propellers than the opposed-engine planes do. The pilot must use more right rudder to counteract the tendency to pull out of line until flight speed is reached. Many of the older planes had locking tail wheels (the wheel was kept rigid—not free to swivel as in a turn) to give better directional control on takeoff. Of course, the old radial-engine planes take off more slowly, and the pilot usually sits much higher off the ground, which made them seem slower.

Landing a radial-engine plane is different from modern-day ships: that big round nose is hard to see over. The closer to touch-down, the less the pilot can see. Because of the poor visibility ahead in three-point position (two main wheels and tail wheel on the ground), main-wheel landings were more common with these old planes. When the main wheels touched down the tail was still high, and a little forward stick glued them there. The pilot's experience and skill, as well as the speed of the plane, determined when the stick was to be pulled back into the belly to force the tail wheel down to the ground for positive steering.

During the Depression, when money was scarce, manufacturers began to build light planes. The main builders were Piper, Taylorcraft, Aeronca, and Cessna. With smaller, opposed engines, the airplanes these companies built were economical to fly and less expensive to buy than the earlier radial-engine stalwarts built by Stinson, Beech, Travel Air, Bellanca, Howard, and others. For example, at one time the famous J-3 Taylor Cub could be purchased for $995.

These light planes accelerated training of new pilots in the United States. They were dependable and easy to learn to fly, and until World War II military training virtually exploded the aviation industry, they more or less displaced the heavier radial-engine airplanes. Both private and commercial pilots started using the smaller, lighter, less expensive planes.

While it was fun to return to flying the Gullwing Stinson at Nome, there were some flights for which I wouldn't even consider using that old single-engine plane. One example was a late-winter trip when I flew 200 miles directly across the Bering Sea from Cape Romanzof to St. Lawrence Island. I had two passengers in the Aero Commander, both carpenters. Each had two or three tremendous chests of tools, so heavy that the three of us could hardly lift them into the airplane. There was no way of weighing them, but I'm sure the aircraft was carrying its maximum legal gross weight or more.

The flight was going well when all at once, near the halfway point, my left engine began to shake. I adjusted the fuel mixture. No change. I reduced throttle. No change. I increased throttle. No change. I used carburetor heat. No change. Nothing helped. The shaking increased. It seemed as if the engine was going to leap from its mounts. Then, abruptly, it stopped running. I feathered the propeller and increased power to the other engine. Much to my relief, I found the airplane easily maintained altitude on one engine.

I looked down at the sea, and in every direction all I could see was a violent, turbulent ocean, choked with broken ice. It was not a comforting sight. A high wind drove huge, cresting waves. The sea's surface was so rough that all the ice pans had been smashed into small pieces. (Often, in winter, large, flat ice pans, some big enough to land an airplane on, float about in the Bering Sea. Not this day.)

The right engine continued to run well throughout what seemed to be one of my longest flights ever. With relief I landed without difficulty at the Air Force base at Northeast Cape on St. Lawrence Island. Once safely on the ground, I searched for the trouble and quickly discovered that the engine breather had frozen. This resulted in a buildup of so much pressure in the engine that oil had been forced into the combustion chambers. It fouled the plugs, and the engine quit running.

I was pleased to figure out the problem, but it disturbed me no end. The two engines were identical, with identical breather systems. If one froze, why didn't the other?

While I had been looking in the engine, I overheard one of my passengers telling someone who had met the plane, "Man, I was scared. That engine began to shake just a little, then it shook so bad that the pilot had to shut it off and feather the prop. I wondered what was going on. When I looked down there was the ocean—nowhere to land. Then I really got scared. But I looked at the pilot and he didn't seem bothered, so I figured there was nothing to worry about." A good thing he didn't know my true state of mind.

Had I been able to figure out the problem in flight, I probably could have gotten rid of the ice on the breather by throttling back and slow flying in a nose-up, semi-stall attitude. This might have allowed engine heat to melt the ice.

On another occasion with an Aero Commander, I flew from Nome to St. Michael, a tiny village on the south shore of Norton Sound. I carried two businessmen, who sat across the aisle from each other directly behind the pilot and copilot seats. When the two men left the plane at St. Michael, a woman boarded. She chose a seat far to the rear. Someone was watching over her that day.

I started my takeoff. The airstrip, although rather short for the Aero Commander, was adequate. Because of the short strip, I used maximum allowable takeoff power. The plane surged forward, accelerating rapidly, eating up the short runway. About halfway down the field, when the plane was ready to leap into the air, a sharp explosion jarred the ship. I automatically cut both throttles and jumped on the brakes, skidding to a stop about 50 feet from the runway's end.

I turned around to discover that the entire inside of the cabin was white, as if it had been snowing. The white stuff was all over me, the seats, the floor. Then I saw that a window had been smashed. The white stuff was pulverized safety glass.

My passenger's face was pale, her eyes big.

A chunk about six inches long had broken from the end of the left propeller. It had punched like a bullet into the cabin. After passing through the cabin wall it went through one of the seats, bounced off the floor, and shattered a window on the opposite side. The propeller tip missed my head by about six inches.

I needed to move the airplane off the runway, so I tried to start the left engine. It wouldn't start. I tried the right engine. It wouldn't start. Then I discovered that in the moment of crisis I had cut all the switches and turned off the gas. My instant action was a result of constant training, training so pervasive that my movements were automatic.

I taxied back to the trading post, where I told the two businessmen what had happened. Their faces blanched. If they had still been in the seats they had vacated, one of them would likely have had his head chopped off, and the other might have lost his legs, if not his life.

Dick Galleher flew the other Aero Commander out with a spare propeller. I continued my trip with the plane he brought, while he and a mechanic replaced the propeller and patched the window of the damaged plane so it could be flown back to Nome for permanent repair. Later study with a magnifying glass revealed that a small triangular stone bruise on the leading edge of the propeller had developed a crack. In flight, a modern propeller flexes an amazing amount. The tiny crack had spread as the propeller flexed.

We doubled inspection of our propellers. After that, to prevent formation of cracks, I always carried small files with which to smooth away rock-caused nicks on my propellers while away from the mechanics at Nome.

Flying passengers and freight from Nome to surrounding villages was interesting more often than not. Too frequently we encountered dangerous weather, and we always had to take care during both landing and taking off from the often short, frequently rough or soft—sometimes dangerous—runways at the small villages. For the benefit of my family, I kept a diary during my several years' flying for Munz. This took the place of individual letters to everyone, and the diaries were passed around and eventually returned to me. A few of my entries follow.

March 19, 1965. Otis Hammonds [another Munz pilot] was to take me with him to Little Diomede Island. Since I didn't get to Diomede in 1941, I was glad for the opportunity. We left Nome in one of the old Gullwing Stinsons and flew up the coast, passing Teller, Tin City, and Wales, and then headed across the Bering Strait. Beneath us the restless waters moved slowly, grinding chunks of ice. We noted large ice pans spaced here and there as possible emergency landing places. I was edgy during that short portion of the flight.

The two Diomede islands, Russian and American, lie in the Bering Strait about two miles apart. The International Date Line lies between them. Sheer cliffs rise 1,000 feet or more from the shores of both islands. The only flat field of ice we could find for landing was between the islands. We circled over the Date Line as we approached Little Diomede to land. While waiting for the Eskimos to come for the mail and freight, I looked with fascination at the looming Soviet island. On a high point, there was an installation of sorts. We were told that this is a lookout where the Russians watch the straits and our American island. It wasn't hard to imagine Soviet eyes following our every move as we transacted our business.

The village of Diomede on Little Diomede Island clings to the side of a cliff, with houses propped up by poles. Overlooking the Russian island, the village looks as if the people had been driven from the sea and in their flight grabbed the first place to which they could cling. The island appears barren, wild, inhospitable.

April 1, 1965. Today began as all other days, with doubtful weather covering the Bering Sea Coast. There was little promise of improvement, but by noon conditions had improved. I flew a load to Moses Point with an Aero Commander. The Swedish Covenant Church was to hold a convention at Elim. Since the Elim field had more snow than a wheelplane could handle, we unloaded the people at Moses Point, and from there they traveled by dog team the 10 miles to Elim.

Then there was a trip to Tin City. Weather was a thin obscurement with two-and-a-half-miles visibility and wind from the north at 34 knots, with gusts to 48 knots. The south end of the runway at Tin City is a cliff, so we experienced a terrific downdraft as we approached the end. Dick Galleher went along, for he wanted to show me how to handle the situation. We approached the runway 800 feet high, or roughly 600 feet higher than the end. As we neared, we suddenly came into a sinker, then with the engines wide open we went down like an elevator. Even with the high-approach altitude I carried, I landed at the very end of the runway. When the plane touched down, we were in drifting snow so thick we couldn't see 100 feet ahead of the plane.

After taxiing to the truck that met us, we stopped one engine and unloaded four passengers and the mail. One mail bag blew away, and the truck raced down the runway to retrieve it. On leaving, we taxied to the yellow line in the center of the runway, and I took off by watching that line, which was visible probably for 100 to 150 feet. It was an instrument takeoff if I ever made one.

We returned to Nome to learn that a party of five polar bear hunters wanted a charter flight to Anchorage. At 5:30 P.M. we left for Anchorage, trying to connect with the Seattle-bound Northwest Airlines flight. High winds and turbulence plagued us most of the way. Nevertheless, we arrived with 20 minutes to spare.

We left for home shortly after midnight. Although we still had rough air and high winds, we made it back in 2 hours, 42 minutes, as opposed to 3 hours, 20 minutes on the way out. We arrived home at 3:30 A.M. My total flying time for the day was 9 hours, 1 minute. I was tired.

April 3, 1965. Today was busy. First I made a flight to Bethel (600 miles round trip). On my return, six passengers were waiting to fly to Cape Romanzof—a 380-mile round trip. Weather was good and the landing at Romanzof was easy. Three passengers boarded, and off we went across 140 miles of the Bering

Sea. I arrived at St. Lawrence at sundown. All seats were filled for the flight to Nome, although I waited about 30 minutes for my last passenger to come to the airport from the village by dog team.

When he arrived and we began to load, I found a drunk man sitting in the plane. He was going to Nome, he said. "No," I told him. "I have no room for you. You will have to get out."

He had other plans and got nasty. After verbally struggling with him for 10 minutes, I left to call the Military Police. An Eskimo man came and told me that after I'd left, he and others had taken the recalcitrant fellow out of the plane. I rushed back to the plane and saw several Eskimos holding the fighting inebriate on his back in the snow. They had to hold him down while we taxied away. All this took 20 minutes. This resulted in my reaching Nome after dark, but weather was good for a change so the flight was easy.

April 6, 1965. A few days ago, I had a sore throat and my ears hurt. A doctor prescribed a delicious, bright-red liquid medicine. I liked the cherry-flavored syrup. In a day or so I seemed much better. I decided I was well enough to fly today.

Weather at Nome was a 900-foot overcast, visibility 10 miles. I took off alone, headed for Cape Romanzof. Up through the overcast I flew, picking up a trace of ice, but I broke into clear sunshine at 2,600 feet. My assigned cruising altitude was 7,000 feet, and I relaxed as I climbed on course. As soon as I leveled off at 7,000 feet, I became aware of a dizziness, which alarmed me. With great effort I tried to collect myself, only to realize I was passing out. I called Nome, reported that I was returning, and requested clearance to let down. As I waited for the clearance, I thought I had regained full control, but when I started to write down the letdown instructions, I realized all was not well. The flight controller's words were meaningless to me.

I asked again and finally understood I was being told to hold for nearly 20 minutes because of other planes in the air. I said

OK and read back the instructions satisfactorily, but then found that I had to concentrate hard to remember which needle to look at and what heading to follow. As I was about to declare an emergency and request an immediate approach, I came out of it.

About 25 minutes later I got permission to let down. Once during the letdown, I began to feel slightly dizzy again, but I willed myself to remember what was going on and managed to land normally.

What had caused my near blackout? Was it lack of oxygen due to my cold? I had flown with much worse colds, so I let that theory go. Was it carbon monoxide? I called mechanics at the hangar and asked them to run a check. Then I remembered the medicine I had taken. Off I rushed to the drugstore and asked the druggist. Sure enough that delicious cherry stuff was full of antihistamines, and pilots are forbidden to fly for 24 hours after using this type of drug.

To be safe, I had the doctor check me over. He pronounced me fit, but said I'd better not fly for another day. He ordered me to take no more medicine.

I can't help but think that I might have passed out completely.

April 19, 1965. When weather allowed us to start flying today about noon, I flew the Aero Commander to Tin City and Teller. Then I made a trip to Brevig Mission, near Teller, with the Cessna 180, and I returned about suppertime. Before I shut down my engine, I was alerted to a medical emergency at Koyuk. Would I go with the Aero Commander? I said OK if the airstrip were all right for wheels. No one seemed to know. Finally the FAA learned from Moses Point that Koyuk had been OK on Friday (this is Monday). Since this information is about as current as any we get, I decided to go.

With a Nome doctor accompanying me, I took off at seven o'clock. Arriving over Koyuk at 7:50, I found a terrific wind quartering the runway. Turbulence was severe on the approach, but because of the emergency, I squeaked a landing out of it with my heart in my mouth.

The doctor had to walk the half-mile to the village. A woman who had been in labor all day was unable to give birth. An hour after the doctor left me, a large group of people trooped back to the field pulling a sled with the unfortunate woman in the basket. The doctor said that a normal birth was impossible and we had to fly her to Nome. Darkness was falling, so we hurried to get her on a stretcher and into the plane. Away we flew. The takeoff was exciting, but not nearly as difficult as the landing had been. Still, I was glad to be away. The baby was safely delivered at Nome, and all was well.

May 3, 1965. Started for Cape Romanzof. Weather was clear when I left, but by the time I arrived, visibility was down to three-fourths of a mile because of a local squall. I held to my course north of the cape for 20 minutes and was then able to sneak in with two miles visibility. Then we were off to St. Marys.

Thirty-five minutes after leaving Romanzof, my eyes were searching for the St. Marys' field. Because snow and wind had moved in before my arrival, I had to circle two or three times before I found the runway. Cursed by a strong crosswind and poor visibility, I landed. I found when I turned around to taxi my passenger to the terminal building that the field had all but disappeared. So thick was the snow that I couldn't see to taxi. My passenger climbed out and walked down the runway while I turned around and slowly felt my way to the end, awaiting a lull, which soon came. I took off for Nome, but before I arrived, weather and winds over much of the region made further trips impractical. I went home and sat down to relax and read.

Near 5:00 P.M., the phone rang. There was an emergency at Savoonga on St. Lawrence Island in the Bering Sea. A little boy had shot himself in the eye with a pellet gun. Fortunately, weather at Savoonga was good so I quickly lifted off. Upon my arrival, the village medical aid person recommended that the boy be flown to Anchorage. The boy's father accompanied the little fellow, who was perhaps four or five years old. Before landing at Nome to refuel, I radioed for a doctor to meet us at the airport to see if everything possible was being done to relieve his pain. The doctor approved what had been done, so I took off for Anchorage carrying the boy and his father.

I took Clifford Weyuawana with me, one of the young Eskimos who works for Munz. He was to help by handing me the various books and maps needed for instrument flying. By the time we passed McGrath, the sky was pitch dark. Over Farewell, we hit heavy turbulence. From there to Skwentna, the ride was rugged. Unable to release the controls for a second, I kept my copilot busy looking up procedures, adding and subtracting headings, identifying stations, and doing other chores. At 12:30 A.M. Anchorage time, we touched down in falling snow and delivered the child to the waiting ambulance.

Both Clifford and I were exhausted. We decided to go to a hotel and sleep for a few hours before returning home, but we couldn't find a room. We were about to return to the field to sleep in the airplane when we finally located a motel room. We left for Nome the next morning at nine o'clock.

Reviewing these diary entries always brings back strong memories, and I wish I had been more faithful in recording my activities.

In the winter of 1967, I left Alaska to take a course in aircraft engines and structures at Tulsa, Oklahoma. As always, Bessie accompanied me. I earned an aircraft and power plant license (A and P), which would be useful for me at Munz Northern because I could work as both a mechanic and a pilot. One of the men in my class, a member of a parachute club at the nearby town of Stroud, arranged for me to join the club and take ground lessons in jumping.

I had worn parachutes many times when flight regulations required it, but I had always managed to bring problem airplanes back to earth safely. I had long entertained the idea of making a jump, but somehow the time had never been right. After my years of flying, I wondered if I would have the nerve to leap out of an airplane.

In the early years of aviation, a quaint and impractical recommendation of some was that every airplane passenger be equipped with a parachute. I can't imagine flying an airliner that was in trouble and turning around and yelling, "Everybody jump!"

At the parachute club I was taught how to make a parachute landing fall (PLF), a special way of allowing your body to collapse as you hit the ground. We practiced by leaping from the back of a pickup truck. My 50 years hadn't done a lot for my joints and nimbleness, so I wasn't a good student. I hit the ground like a tub of lard and fell over and bumped myself as I tried to roll, usually a second or two too late. As I practiced and practiced, my body grew so sore that I bought two big mattresses on which to fall.

Finally my jump day came. I was to return to Alaska within two days; if I didn't jump this day, I never would. First the instructor watched me do a practice PLF. Apparently I did all right, for he said I was OK to jump.

While we stood watching others jump, I caught sight of a guy drifting down with a 35-foot diameter parachute, much larger than the others. "That's for me," I said. "I don't bounce when I hit like you young guys. That one will let me down easy." The owner of the chute, pleased to loan it, packed the chute for me with help from other club members. I was the oldest member of their club to have made his first jump there.

The Parachute Club of America requires that a static line (attached to the airplane) be used for the first five jumps, hence I didn't have to pull my own rip cord. There were plenty of instructions: "Spread your arms and legs so you'll stay level and have the greatest resistance. If you don't you'll probably fall head first. Being upside down will frighten you."

When the Cessna jump plane took off, I had the 35-footer strapped to my back and an emergency chute on my chest. The pilot climbed to 2,700 feet. I backed out of the door and stood on the step, holding the wing strut. I was afraid I would hit the tail when I let go. "Don't worry. You couldn't hit it if you wanted to," my instructor shouted.

With the slipstream battering me, I clung to the strut, beginning to wonder if I had made a mistake involving myself in this risky adventure. "Go," the instructor shouted.

I pushed myself off backward. For the first few seconds I despaired, "What have I done now?" A sensation of helplessness filled me. I forgot my instructions and the elegant pose I was supposed to take. Immediately I fell head first. Instead of feeling fright as my instructor had warned, I rather enjoyed the sensation. I had spent hundreds of hours teaching acrobatics in airplanes, so the head-down attitude was nothing new to me.

The static cord attached to the airplane was supposed to pull my chute open after so many seconds. I forgot to count the seconds. "Holy smokes," I thought, for it seemed to me I had been falling for quite a while and the static cord hadn't pulled. I reached for the rip cord and had my hand on it, when at last the main parachute opened, even though I was upside down. The parachute was sleeved, so it opened gradually, not with a snap. I felt as if some big, powerful guy had picked me up by the neck and slowly turned me right side up.

I was tremendously relieved. High above ground I enjoyed the absolutely marvelous sensation of gently swinging beneath that open canopy. I wished that I could have stayed up all afternoon. I was supposed to make the chute slip and go through a series of somewhat limited maneuvers. But I was enjoying the ride so much I forgot all about the procedures I was supposed to follow.

Far below I saw Bessie, camera in hand. Later I joked with

her, "I saw you running around down there with a camera in one hand and an insurance policy in the other."

A light wind blew me some distance. As I neared the ground, I again forgot my instructions. I had been warned, "Don't look down on landing, you'll get confused. Hold your feet together, and be ready to do a PLF. Don't do this, don't do that."

I watched the ground as I had thousands of times in landing airplanes, and I knew precisely when I was going to touch. Not wanting the chute to drag me backward, I managed to turn it so I had the wind to my back. I touched the earth, did a PLF like a pro, rolled over, and dug in my heels as the parachute tried to drag me. I unhooked one of the risers from my harness, and the chute collapsed.

I had done it! My jump was a wonderful thrill. Although I never had the opportunity to jump again, I think sky diving is a grand sport for young (and even old) people who want a little thrill now and then.

Wherever I worked in Alaska, I was fascinated by the land—its geology, its animals, its scenic grandeur. With Bessie, I explored thousands of square miles of northern wilderness by small plane, boat, snow machine, and on foot. One of the memorable areas we explored was a place a short distance from Nome which we called the Mountains of the Moon. I first saw this unusual area in early winter of 1941, during a commercial flight in a Cessna Airmaster.

Alaska's west coast was being lashed by equinoctial storms. Wind-driven squalls of dense snow dashed across the coastal plain, forcing me to cling tenaciously to the shoreline as I followed the coast. At times the sun was visible, but in the wink of an eye the plane would be engulfed in a swirling mass of white. When the sun disappeared, so did the horizon, and the earth itself was obscured. Only nearby scattered driftwood logs and broken chunks of ice on the beach made contact flight (VFR) possible.

When the snow began to thin, more distant points of contrast appeared deeper in the milky bowl in which I flew. But they appeared in the wrong places. Some seemed higher than my airplane. Almost frantically I looked back to the comforting chunks of jagged ice directly beneath me, and as the whiteness gave way to better visibility, the dark spots of contrast fell into place. I realized I had been a victim of the strange optical illusions that plague a pilot in a whiteout.

From one such squall, I emerged into good visibility and judged it safe to leave the coast and cross a large cape. I leaned back in my seat and relaxed. It was then that I noticed a strange group of mountains directly over the nose of the plane. They were not high, but they were jagged, light colored, and barren, seemingly out of place in this coastal plain. For a moment I had a strange feeling that I might have passed through some barrier of time and space, because these mountains looked like what we then guessed the moon looked like, and what we now know it does look like.

I watched the jagged peaks slice the wind into separate rivers of drifting snow that swirled down the lee side and tumbled toward the valley below. From the valley floor, great areas of snow rose suddenly and swirled skyward so violently that I raced for altitude lest they reach out and tear my plane apart. As quickly as they had appeared, the mountains were gone, and once again I was flying over the flat coastal tundra of rolling hills.

Thirty years went by, and in many places and at many times I thought of the Mountains of the Moon that I had seen so briefly. Then, in early June of 1971, when Bessie and I lived at Nome, we flew our Aeronca Sedan out to these mountains for a better look.

In the midst of the barren and strange-looking mountains, we found a beautiful natural landing place. After checking and rechecking the surface, we put down. Our landing began a season of fascinating exploring, picnicking, and prospecting by us and many of our friends.

On one day that summer I saw a thermometer in the shade of our airplane wing read 70 degrees, an almost unheard of air temperature for an area 35 miles north of Nome. We found hematite nodules that were almost of gem quality. We found evidence that someone else had once been there—empty .44-40 shells, a table knife and fork, left perhaps by a wandering prospector.

On our initial walk from our plane, we found a place where a grizzly bear had fed on a musk-ox, dragged it away, and buried it. We also saw signs of reindeer, and we once saw a red fox that seemed to me about twice as long as any red fox I had ever seen.

Other pilots from Nome started landing there after we told them about the place, for our Mountains of the Moon had a strange attraction. Landing was safe and easy. Once, four planes were parked in this remote area at one time. Walking around there is pleasant, for the ground is smooth and hard, in contrast to the hummocky, rough surrounding area.

We visited the Mountains of the Moon about 10 times one summer. Once, as we started out, another pilot asked my destination. I told him, using my name for the place. He immediately recognized it, although my label was new to him. Now the FAA flight service at Nome recognizes the name when pilots file flight plans for the area.

Never did I go there without thinking of my brief, disturbing and spectacular first glimpse of the Mountains of the Moon through a howling Bering Sea snowstorm on that day in 1941.

Rescue at Cape Romanzof

CAPE ROMANZOF, aloof and alone on Alaska's southwest coast, rises steeply from the seashore to an elevation of 2,342 feet. Rocky and jutting far into the sea, this huge cape is surrounded by the sullen Bering Sea and low, swampy tundra. Atop the cape, keeping a lonely defense vigil, is an installation operated by the U.S. Air Force.

Munz Northern Airline of Nome flew a thrice-weekly schedule between Nome and the cape. At the time of this incident, in September 1965, I had been making most of these flights.

Bessie jarred me awake seemingly in the middle of the night. "What's wrong?" I asked.

"The phone's ringing and it's only 4:00 A.M." she answered.

I rushed to the phone to hear my boss, Dick Galleher, say, "Call the FAA. There's an emergency at Cape Romanzof. One of the workers has had a heart attack." I called the flight station and they relayed Romanzof's message to me. A middle-aged civilian worker had suffered a seizure exhibiting all the symptoms of a serious heart attack. His immediate removal to a hospital seemed essential. An Air Force Search and Rescue plane was en route from Anchorage, but cape weather had forced the large plane to land at Unalakleet, its alternate destination.

"Well, good grief," I grumbled. "If they can't get in, how do you expect me to?"

"You have a smaller plane," came the reply. "And your weather minimums are less. Besides, you are far more current on Romanzof's field and conditions than anyone else."

"OK. What's the cape's current weather?"

"Ceiling is 400 feet. Visibility is six miles, and the wind is from the south at seven knots."

"That's not bad," I said. "Tell them I'll give it a try."

In less than 30 minutes, I was at the Nome field. What I found pleased me beyond expression. My twin-engine Aero Commander 680-E was on the ramp, fueled and checked. Engines were warmed and ground checked. The FAA team on duty had assembled all the weather reports, forecasts, plus winds-aloft data, and promised to stand by for all current information. In a car nearby sat Betty Shamblin and Ellen Green, nurses from the Nome hospital, who despite the stormy weather had volunteered to make the flight.

Within minutes we roared off into a dismal leaden sky. Choosing the lowest legal en route altitude to avoid icing, a very real threat, I headed directly for Romanzof, 190 miles across the sea.

The steadily throbbing engines pulled us rapidly to cruising altitude. Then with all controls set for cruise, pad and pencil in hand, I leaned back to copy the latest weather. Before the regular broadcast came on, I heard Nome radio calling me.

"Aero Commander 14 Alpha Mike, this is Nome radio."

"Nome Radio, this is 14 Alpha Mike. Go ahead."

"Fourteen Alpha Mike, this is Nome radio. I have the latest Romanzof weather. Ceiling is 300 feet, visibility three miles, wind south at six knots."

Since the weather would likely change many times before I arrived, I checked the latest weather at my alternate airport, found it acceptable, and continued on. To keep an accurate account of my position, I shot radio bearings continually and from them was able to calculate accurately the direction and velocity of winds at my cruising altitude. They were stronger than forecast, directly against me, and my ground speed was low.

I reestimated my time over Cape Romanzof and was about to call it in when Nome radio called again. Romanzof now had a lower ceiling of 200 feet and decreased visibility of one and one-half miles. Recomputing my fuel, I found it adequate, and flew on. Nearing Cape Romanzof, I heard their operator calling me. I answered. The voice I heard was slow and deliberate so that I would not misunderstand his warning: Romanzof weather, 100-foot ceiling, visibility one-eighth mile.

Cape Romanzof's runway lies high above the sea and surrounding tundra. Tucked neatly into a narrow valley, its mean elevation is 457 feet. The runway slopes to the southwest at a 2.1 percent grade. A note on our instrument approach chart reads: "Caution: Runway located on side of 2,100-foot mountain. Approach from the southwest, land Runway Two only. High terrain on both sides and on north end of runway. Winds in excess of 20 knots may produce severe turbulence."

All this I knew. On my many trips to Romanzof I had practiced approaches and takeoffs in a great variety of wind conditions. One particularly stormy day, Dick Galleher and I spent an hour in a difficult wind practicing takeoffs and landings, each with a simulated engine failure. I knew exactly what the Aero Commander was capable of and what winds could be handled safely. But there was no way I could land with one-eighth-mile visibility.

Since the airfield elevation was 457 feet and the ceiling above it 100 feet, I proceeded with my letdown, hoping to break out over the sea with a ceiling of roughly 500 feet. Then, if the visibility was sufficient, I could hold in the area and wait for an improvement in weather over the runway.

Conditions were as I had hoped. I broke out under the overcast at 600 feet. The visibility underneath was unlimited. I could indeed hold over the flat tundra as long as my gas permitted. In about 10 minutes, the ceiling appeared to rise closely adjacent to the mountain. I flew over, paralleled the high terrain, and climbed as high as cloud cover permitted, but my best effort still left me 100 feet below the runway level. I turned away from the cape and continued to circle over the flats, wondering why medical emergencies always seemed to call forth bad weather.

Not far away on the water-sogged tundra sat the village of Hooper Bay. The houses were clustered on a knoll, and a small landing field stretched along a level area between the houses and the extensive, beautiful beaches of the sea. By landing there, I could still see Cape Romanzof and watch the weather without wasting gas. Ten minutes later I landed at Hooper Bay.

The nurses walked to the village while I maintained a listening watch on Romanzof's radio frequency. In perhaps 30 minutes, when the nurses were almost back to the plane, Romanzof's weather station called. Weather was improving rapidly and perhaps by the time I got there it would be all right to land. We were off again in minutes, only to be disappointed again; before we got there, in a matter of 10 to 12 minutes, the runway was obscured and the wind was rising.

I held once more over the flats until concern for my fuel supply drove me back to Hooper Bay again. Here I found the surface wind blowing across the runway at about 30 miles per hour. This, coupled with a few soft spots on the runway, made landing a bit disagreeable. Immediately upon landing I searched out the agent of another aircraft operator who generously agreed to sell me some of his cache of aviation gasoline.

The rising wind directly across the narrow strip would soon make takeoff hazardous. So, armed with a relatively good supply of gas, I took off at once from Hooper Bay. The wind continued to increase, and with it came lower clouds from the sea. I was about to give up and go home when the Romanzof operator called excitedly. "Ceiling is now 400 feet with four miles visibility. Wind is 14 knots from the south."

The report indicated I would have a direct tailwind for my landing. I decided it wouldn't be too bad. When I arrived at the mountain, I found the wind rising rapidly. As it struck the peak, the wind rose and swept the clouds up with it. I dared not approach the runway in a normal manner. I needed to feel out the winds and turbulence, because a 180-degree turn from a direct approach was impossible. I approached at an oblique angle, from which I could easily turn out and away from the mountain.

This proved to be a wise move, for as I approached the landing strip, the plane was suddenly hoisted aloft as though on an elevator. I turned sharply and dove to stay beneath the clouds. I would have to try again to determine exactly how to handle it.

The second try was better. However, conditions were changing quickly, and in the time it took for my two passes and the final approach to line up with the runway, I was almost too late. With the ceiling and visibility deteriorating and the rising wind fiercely buffeting the plane, the approach was truly a nightmare. With the nose down sharply and power on both engines to overcome the updraft, I streaked onto the runway like a jet fighter and silently gave thanks for the uphill grade.

At that point, the radio operator at Romanzof called from the weather station situated behind a hill. The voice was urgent. "The wind is now on your tail at 26 knots. You'd better not land!"

Because of my greased-lightning landing, I was too busy to answer. He frantically repeated his message. This time I called back to say I was on the ground and taxiing to the parking area.

From then on, for a time at least, all went well. Under the competent hands of station personnel and the two nurses, the sick man was put in the plane on a stretcher bed. A bottle of oxygen was loaded for his use on the return trip, and we received a gift of a large cake and a big pie to be enjoyed by all our ground crew. Cape Romanzof hospitality was always warm: such gifts were common when I landed there.

The takeoff was relatively easy, downhill and into a strong wind. It seemed only moments until I leveled off at cruising altitude. Because of strong winds and no apparent ice, I chose to cruise at 7,000 feet. My calculations showed winds should push us back to Nome in record time, and Nome weather was still at legal minimums. I leaned back to relax a little for the remainder of the trip. But it was not to be so simple.

I was stunned to hear Betty Shamblin call, "We're out of oxygen. Unless we can go down to a much lower altitude this man's life is in great danger."

"Good God!" I croaked. "They must have given us an empty oxygen bottle. Now what?"

I quickly shot radio bearings on Nome and Moses Point. We were about halfway home. I called Nome for the latest weather and information on any other aircraft in my vicinity. There were none, and weather was still at minimums. I was about to request a change to the minimum en route altitude when suddenly we broke out into a large hole in the clouds. An area perhaps 10 miles wide was clear, and far below I saw the restless waters of the Bering Sea. Canceling my instrument flight plan, I circled down. At 300 feet I was under the surrounding overcast. Visibility was good: except for scattered heavy showers, I could see four or five miles. My chances of going on by VFR were good, and in a pinch I could always climb again.

The ocean raged below. The towering waves, white with foam, reached up as if to snatch us from the sky, but the air was relatively smooth, and visibility continued to be good. Betty Shamblin told me the patient was doing better. Very much relieved, I pushed on, and except for an occasional rainstorm, the flying went smoothly.

Another message came in from Nome. "The search-and-rescue plane is holding at Unalakleet and requests that you fly the patient there." Unalakleet was 125 miles east of my position, and weather there was marginal. If I were unable to land there, I'd be low on gas. I was within 15 minutes of Nome, where there was a good hospital to care for the patient when we landed. I refused the request.

Nome's weather was low. I needed a special clearance to make a legal landing. But it was not difficult, and we soon delivered our patient to the Nome hospital. In less than two hours the search-and-rescue plane came to fly the man to Anchorage. I never knew his name, whether he survived, or anything else about him. He simply dropped from sight.

Our part of the mission was over. I chalked the Cape Romanzof rescue flight off as another lucky one.

Agates of the Nowitna

I FIRST HEARD of the agates of the Nowitna River in central Alaska in the early 1940s. "They lie on the bars like potatoes in a field," several old-timers told me. They had seen them in the early 1900s as they rushed through the area in search of gold. The truth of their story was partially borne out by the small agates we found in the gravel of the Yukon River near the village of Galena, downstream from the Nowitna.

The name "agate" is familiar, but the makeup of this semi-precious stone is not so commonly known. Agates belong to the quartz family, but the conditions of their formation make them different. Under certain circumstances, molten quartz spewing out of the earth cools so rapidly that crystals have no chance to form. The result is a very fine-textured rock of glassy luster which is generally called chalcedony. If during the process the molten rock is infused with impurities such as iron or manganese, the resultant rock is colored, banded, or spotted with mossy inclusions, and is generally called agate. Some of the color varieties are so distinctive that they bear names of their own. Purple amethyst is an example.

Although I first heard of the Nowitna agates during my initial year or so in Alaska, it wasn't until 1958 that I saw one. Given to me by a trapper friend, the amber-colored stone stirred my imagination.

The Nowitna, or Novi, as it is locally called, drains an area roughly the size of Massachusetts. Flowing north, it cuts through sharp mountains, rolling, timbered hills, and flat, hummocky swamps to finally enter the Yukon River about 40 miles above the village of Ruby. Its valley, rarely penetrated by man, is a land of deep wilderness and great beauty, richly rewarding to the seeker of rocks, fossils, and solitude.

In the summer of 1960, my son, Roy, then 16, and I left Fairbanks in our small plane and flew to Galena, 270 miles to the west. From there we took a 20-foot riverboat to explore the Novi. Our trip lasted three weeks.

We stopped at Ruby on our way upstream and left there with 115 gallons of gasoline, feeling certain we had enough to reach the agates of the Novi. We found the Nowitna River pouring into the Yukon through a small vent raggedly cut in the frozen muck. Her inelegant mouth, however, is but a sham that hides the charm and beauty to be found a short distance upstream.

Once in the quiet and winding channel of the Novi, we found time to relax. No amount of wind could dangerously ruffle her waters. No eddies or whirlpools tugged at the boat, and her bars and snags were visible through clear water. Beaver swam in her quiet pools, and bull moose, antlers still in velvet, nibbled at the willows along the banks. Young geese, panicked by their squawking mothers, dived frantically or wobbled uncertainly over the bars. Thus we traveled for 90 miles or more, watching by day the grandeur of the living wilderness and camping by night on soft sand beaches.

Then, almost imperceptibly, the land began to rise. The riverbanks became higher and the waters cleared and flowed more swiftly. The bars that graced the river's sweeping curves became firm and gravel-covered. Tall spruce gave way to smaller, stunted trees, and the tops of jagged mountains appeared on the horizon. Moose, beaver, and geese were less often seen, but in their places came the bears. There were blacks and cinnamons (a color phase of the black) in such numbers as we had never seen. They walked idly on the gravel bars, and on these bars we found our first agates. Small and few at first, the Novi agates varied in color from lemon yellow to deep red, with many shades of brown and varicolored banding. The most common were the reds, known as carnelians.

Progress was slower as we made our way against the current; the crystal water occasionally raced and boiled in minor rapids. At nearly every bend we poled or pulled our boat because the shallow rapids could not accommodate the long-shafted outboard. After each of these ordeals, we relaxed by hunting agates on adjacent bars. They appeared in ever-increasing sizes and numbers, until some as large as our fists lay invitingly before us.

We battled the narrowing river for several days, until at last, our gas supply running low, we camped to explore the valley on foot. In this we were unexpectedly restricted, for the curious bears gave us not a moment of peace. They were not aggressive, but their curiosity was without bounds. We heard them snuffle in the brush as we walked near the banks and found their tracks near the tent upon our return. Because of their ability to destroy a camp, we dared not venture far afield.

Even in this limited search we found many fascinating things. We picked agates more selectively, searching for the unusual. Some were banded and colored throughout, while others had only surface color. Many were beautiful combinations of red and green jasper and carnelian agate, with banding or mossy inclusions. We found one crystal-clear fragment of hyalite opal.

Amazingly, the bones of prehistoric beasts lay on the bars in various stages of disintegration. Those of the mammoth were most common. Large teeth and ball-and-socket joints that crumbled at the touch lay upon the sand. Here and there, a recently uncovered bone remained intact. We collected one small mammoth tooth, and then we found three leg bones and a real treasure—a complete hoof, from a tiny Pleistocene horse. These were solid and we carefully packed them away. Fragments of ivory tusks, like pieces of bleached driftwood, were visible on several bars but thousands of years of erosion had destroyed them.

As our dying campfire lulled us to sleep at night, we dreamed of these extinct creatures and their strange, wild, prehistoric world, only to awaken with a start at the subconscious thought of our present wilderness and the bears that we knew were watching us.

The days passed swiftly until our food ran low, and we reluctantly prepared to leave. In our boat, besides the carefully packed bones, we had about 125 pounds of agates to cut and polish at home. The bars we had searched upon were only the beginning of the agate bars that we knew extended upstream for another hundred miles.

Our interest in agates wasn't commercial, although we sold a few to rock shops for $1 a pound to help pay for the cost of our trip. We gave most away. I sawed many on my rock saw, and polished the pieces. Bessie made bolo ties, brooches, cabochons for rings, and other jewelry. They made fine gifts.

What joy it was to ride back with the rushing waters over the shallows through which we had so laboriously pulled our boat on the upstream trip. In two days we were back to the Yukon, and it was then we learned that the bears, after all, had gotten the best of us.

We had cached three five-gallon tins of gas near the mouth of the Novi, as reserve for our return. We found them battered and scattered, with the smell of raw gasoline rising from the soaked earth. The plastic pouring spouts were bitten off, and the cans punctured by sharp teeth. Only three gallons remained. A quick inventory, and the knowledge that the current was with us, assured us we would get home.

The years passed, and the agates of the Nowitna continually called for us to return. In 1966, while I was flying for Munz Northern Airline at Nome, Bessie and I flew in to the upper Nowitna.

Flying has taken me into and out of a lot of jackpots. It got us into a jackpot on this August flight into the upper Nowitna. Dick Galleher loaned me one of his Gullwing Stinsons to fly to Galena. At Galena our friend Harvey Strassburg loaned us a new 150-horsepower Piper Super Cub. We had been delayed on the trip by bad weather—rain, low clouds, poor visibility—and had to spend a night at Unalakleet and then wait for weather to improve before we could leave Galena in the Cub.

Finally, in midafternoon Bessie and I took off in the Cub, a two-seat (front and back) plane. Because of the delay, we now planned to stay only one night. We reduced our gear to a pup tent, a hand axe, and enough food for perhaps three days. We were to regret cutting our food and equipment so drastically.

I dodged squalls and low clouds as we flew up the valley of the Novi, gaining entrance to the upper valley. Light rain persisted, but I pushed upriver until a heavy rain squall forced me to select a river bar that was adequate for a Cub landing.

"Let me look for agates while you make camp," Bessie said, and she rushed off, peering excitedly at the gravel bar.

I quickly set up camp and tied the plane down for the night. Within an hour Bessie had an impressive pile of agates, some as large as big potatoes. We enthusiastically planned to fly farther upriver the next day. Surely the weather would clear.

The rain continued that night. From our warm sleeping bags we listened to it patter on the tent. The leaves rustled in the wind, and a lone wolf howled dismally in the distance. Warm and content, I recited to myself from Isaiah 55:12, "For ye shall go out with joy, and be led forth with peace: the mountains and the hills shall break forth before you into singing, and all the trees of the field shall clap their hands." With that pleasant thought I went to sleep and was only vaguely aware of the continuing patter of rain on the tent.

The next day was gloomy. Rain continued, and the overcast pressed close to the treetops. It would not be possible to fly. We cheered ourselves with the thought that the sun's heat would soon raise the ceiling. All morning and afternoon we walked about the bar, choosing only the finest agates, meanwhile keeping a constant eye on the weather. Near evening a light spot appeared to the east. Hurriedly we packed and I lifted the eager little Cub into the air. It was a short, nasty flight. I dodged clouds and tried to find an opening somewhere around us, but failed. I banked steeply to keep visual contact with the tops of the wet spruce a few feet below us, and returned to the same river bar and landed.

Once again we made camp. When we are camping, Bessie can usually make a home almost literally under a tree. This night we put the tent under the plane's wing because we had discovered the previous night that our sleeping bags became soaked wherever they touched the tent. Drying was impossible in the rain, so we went to bed somewhat concerned about our comfort.

And there was another concern, a much greater one: the river was rising. That night was wetter than the first. The rain dribbled from the wing of the plane onto our tent in such a way as to thoroughly soak our sleeping bags. We were up at 4:30 A.M., desperately hoping to see a break in the weather. Sky signs seemed slightly better, but our hearts sank when we found that the river now covered more than half of the gravel bar which was both our runway and our campsite.

About nine that morning, weather improved slightly and we again loaded the plane and roared off our shrinking runway. Except for low ceilings and scattered squalls, the flying wasn't bad, but the entrance to the canyon was blocked by clouds. We landed on another bar, one I had used previously. For several hours we walked around looking for agates, anxiously watching the weather. Rain had washed the agates clean and they were easy to find.

Shortly before noon, the clouds lifted again, slightly, and we again took the little Cub into the air. Through the tunnel-like canyon we flew, hoping to make it to the Yukon valley. Again the far end of the canyon was blocked by clouds. I tried desperately to push through, only to be turned back.

Now I was really worried, for landing again might mean a tragic end to our trip. We could easily lose Harvey Strassburg's new airplane, and, possibly, our lives. The river was flooding, covering gravel bar landing sites. We seemed trapped in the valley of the Nowitna.

When I returned upstream, planning to land on our second gravel bar, my heart nearly stopped, for there was a torrential squall squarely across the canyon. All the bars in that canyon were covered with water, and our only chance was to continue farther upstream to the original bar. Into the rain I flew. Water dashed against the airplane in such volume as to make the windshield appear an inch thick.

My first attempt to land failed. So poorly did I see through the rain-splashed windshield that I overshot and had to either give the plane full throttle and go around or roll into the river. We went around, and I think the rain lessened a bit, as my second landing attempt succeeded. Once again we were perched on the rapidly diminishing bar.

We didn't unpack, for we wanted to be ready in case of a break in weather. The weather did not improve, and I began to ponder ways to save our lives. The costly airplane was no longer our greatest concern; now, our lives were threatened. We were trapped on the diminishing gravel bar. I anxiously trotted through the dripping woods to find a way to high ground, but at every turn I was stopped by an oxbow lake or deep slough, also rising in the heavy rain. With this route of escape cut off, should the river continue to rise, which it gave every appearance of doing, I could think of only one thing to do—build a raft. A few dry drift logs lay about, and after hours and hours of effort with a small hatchet I managed to chop my way through enough of them to give myself six 12-foot-long, dry logs.

Now the river was raging. Large chunks of earth fell heavily into the water on the cutbank side, across from us. Huge spruce trees, undercut by the gushing currents, crashed into the river and rushed downstream. Bessie kept constant track of the water level with sticks thrust into the gravel—worry sticks, I called them. We saw clearly that at the rapid rate of rise, our airplane would stand in water too deep for a takeoff within 12 hours.

My alternative was to attempt to clear a runway by cutting out low willows that lay next to the bar. I would have to cut an awful lot of willows, and if the weather didn't clear even that would do no good.

Late in the afternoon I left raft building long enough to walk out onto the bar where Bessie continued to mark the rising water, study the clouds, and occupy her mind between times by selecting agates. I looked both upstream and down at the dismal weather. Then, on the opposite bank, a large timber wolf loped into sight along the river's edge. His water-soaked fur and drooping tail made him look depressed and lonely. Perhaps he was the one who had howled mournfully before. I whistled loudly through cupped hands, and he stopped to look. For a long moment he stared at us, then, as if unimpressed, trotted away. At that moment I spotted an odd-looking stone at my feet.

It was a small carnelian agate with a window, and a sort of an eye. I showed my unique find to Bessie. Despite our predicament she quipped, "Looks like an evil eye to me."

I could only be impressed by her courage and spirit, but I rebutted, "No, it's a good eye, a lucky charm, and I'm going to keep it," putting it in my pocket. Then I went back to raft building. Any raft I could build with what was available on that bar would never stand the turbulent river, so we planned to tie my gathering of logs to a tree in the backwater and hope they wouldn't tear loose. If the water continued to rise, my flimsy raft might be our only island of hope.

"I'm going to sleep sitting in the airplane tonight," Bessie decided. "At least my sleeping bag won't get wetter." That sounded like a good idea.

Shortly, while checking her worry sticks, Bessie called to

tell me she had spotted a light patch in the sky to the north. I didn't think much about this report and didn't even go look; I had had enough disappointments in the previous two days.

About 30 minutes later, after tying the airplane to a half-buried driftwood root, I walked out on the bar and realized I could now see the top of a single mountain to the north. We decided to take off for one last look, although doing so might deplete our gas to the point of no takeoff the next morning—if indeed enough dry ground remained for a takeoff.

Our wheels stood in water as we started our takeoff run, but, despite the shortened bar, the little Cub leaped into the air in plenty of time. My apprehension was indescribable as I nosed the airplane upward toward the mountain. At last we flew over the top, and could see a narrow streak of light far to the north.

"I think we can make it," I called back to Bessie, and with rising tension mixed with hope, we flew across the next valley. Sweat ran uncomfortably down my back. My breathing was labored as I tried desperately to keep the light streak in sight. In a few minutes we would know. Then, we were in the valley of the Yukon! What a tremendous relief.

The rest of the flight was anticlimactic, although we had to dodge low clouds and almost brush the treetops, flying from one squall to another. Darkness came fast and the heavy rain continued. I heaved a great sigh of relief when I caught sight of the Ruby field, and as I looked at the waving birch tops scarcely 100 feet below our wheels, I thought again, ". . . and all the trees of the field shall clap their hands."

Two years later, in August 1968, we arranged for another trip to the Novi. This time we were four—Bessie and I, Roy, then 24, and a family friend from Fairbanks, Dorothy Eberhardt. We flew there in a Super Cub loaned to me by my longtime friend Harold Esmailka of Ruby. This time we landed on a river bar much farther upstream than any of us had ever been. Each trip to the Novi has made us eager to return, for the Novi is an enchanting river. The

1966 venture was a frightening experience, but rainstorms such as we encountered don't occur every year.

On the 1968 trip we camped on a bar near the mouth of the Susulatna River. Because we planned to stay a week, four trips with the borrowed Super Cub were necessary to haul in all the passengers and gear. On the last flight, I brought a foldboat.

That evening we sat on driftwood logs around a pleasant campfire. Darkness came slowly, as is usual in the warm months in Alaska. As the last red glow vanished from the sky the night sounds came, crisp and clear on the cool evening air. An owl hooted nearby, and an answer came drifting from far away. From the river came the soft babbling of a family of ducks. Somewhere far upriver a wolf howled, and we heard its cry echo through the hills. We talked of prospecting, of agates, and of the beautiful wilderness around us.

Agates were our prime interest. We were all familiar with the Novi agates and generally knew what to expect. Because we had learned that we'd find the larger agates farther upriver, we agreed to spend most of our week searching upstream. The chill of night pushed close to our fire and at 11:00 P.M., we went to bed.

Our camp was neatly arranged; Roy had done well setting it up while I was flying in the gear. The tents all stood in line, with mine on the downstream end of the bar. About 30 feet upstream was the largest tent, where Bessie and Dorothy stayed; Roy's little tent was another 30 feet away.

Not until I lay quietly alone with my thoughts did I realize Roy might have been influenced by a couple of self-serving females. Camp was arranged so if an irate bear were to storm up or down the bar he would of necessity arrive first at either Roy's tent or mine. Since we could both pilot the plane, one of us was expendable. The women would be warned of the attack by the noise, and the man at the opposite end would rush out to drive the invader away. Before I fell asleep that night, several times I imagined heavy footsteps in the sand.

Early next morning, before the mists cleared from the river, I confronted Bessie and Dorothy with my suspicions. Amid laughter they replied only that they had thought I wouldn't be smart enough to figure it out.

That day we slowly made our way upriver. Bessie and Dorothy walked back and forth across the river bars, carefully inspecting each agate and placing the best in their rock bags.

Roy paddled or lined (pulled with a rope) the boat to the head of each bar, where he would secure it and hunt agates until we all reached him, then he ferried us across to the next bar. I too picked stones, but I did much more wandering in search of secrets the wilderness might hold. We returned to camp in the afternoon.

That night our fire burned high and in its light we piled our agates. There were nearly 50 pounds, we guessed, and we looked with pleasure upon our discoveries. We studied the shapes in search of a clue to their origin. Many were flat, as if they were part of an opaque window pane. Others were curved like the rind of a grapefruit, while some were solid and round, ranging in size from that of a marble to a softball.

I have heard rumors that a great dike of agate crosses the bed of the Susulatna River not far from its confluence with the Novi. Of this we were never certain, for we didn't ever ascend that far. We did learn, however, that some of the agates did not erode from a dike, for on the third day we found an unbroken nodule. It was shaped somewhat like a football, about eight inches long and four inches thick, and was the biggest unbroken piece we had ever seen. Surely this chunk was never part of a dike.

Most agates on the Novi are badly fractured, and large, unbroken pieces are rare. Because of this, excitement ran high in the camp that night. We wondered if the river would reveal geodes (a nodule of stone having a cavity lined with crystals or mineral matter), and semiprecious stones other than agates. Two days later our hopes were partially realized.

We were exploring about three miles above camp near the mouth of the Susulatna. Dorothy had waded the stream to search for stones near the south bank. Roy was lining the boat through the shallows, while Bessie walked slowly about 50 yards behind me. My main interest at the moment was not agates but the fresh tracks of a timber wolf I was following.

Evidently the wolf had his mind on a place far away, for his evenly spaced tracks led me directly to a point of timber on the north shore. Losing the track, I turned to retrace my steps, when I noticed a strange-looking stone. About the size of an apple, it looked like a geode and I nudged it gently with my foot.

For a moment I didn't believe my eyes, for on the underside a gaping hole revealed a cavity lined with amethyst crystals. The excitement that followed must have resembled a small gold rush. All of us searched the area, and Dorothy found the piece that had broken from the geode, but nothing else turned up. These crystals were not museum pieces, but we did learn there are amethyst crystals on the Novi.

We broke camp early the next morning, packed our gear, and readied the plane. We had 300 pounds of fine agates to take with us.

As much as we have wanted to, we have never managed to return to the Novi.

Wildlife Dramas

FOUR DECADES of flying over Alaska have left me with many memories of wildlife seen from the air. I've seen thousands of walrus resting on ice floes in the Bering Sea, and herds of caribou so large that I couldn't even estimate their number. I've seen golden-horned white Dall sheep high in the mountains, and that other great white-furred mountaineer, the black-horned mountain goat, clinging to dizzyingly high cliffs. From the air I have seen hundreds of wolves and bears, foxes and ptarmigan, gulls and ducks, geese and shorebirds. Occasionally a flash of memory comes and it is like a brilliantly colored slide projected on a screen. . . .

In March 1961, I agreed to teach a friend, Val Blackburn, at Minchumina, how to fly. When we lived in Fairbanks, Bessie and I owned a cabin on the lakeshore. We stayed in that cabin while, with my Piper Vagabond, I taught Val to fly. It was a peaceful and fun time.

Daily, I gave Val flying lessons. We did our air work not far from the big lake. During these flights I enjoyed seeing all the tracks made by moose, caribou, and wolves, and occasionally watching the animals themselves.

One day as we were flying southeast of the lake, I looked down and saw a black bear lumbering across country. I was amazed because in March all black bears should have been in their dens hibernating. The bear was lunging through about three feet of snow.

We circled, curious. Then, perhaps 100 yards behind the bear, we saw a large gray wolf. The wolf wasn't pursuing the bear. He was merely poking along, apparently curious to see where the bear was going or what it was doing. As we continued to circle, nearby we noticed five more wolves sitting in a little clearing in the willows and alders. They ignored the bear and simply sat in a ring like a bunch of big dogs.

I decided Bessie should see this curious tableau, so we returned to our cabin and I flew Bessie back to watch.

Meanwhile, the bear had traveled about a mile. The lone wolf was tagging lazily behind him. The five other wolves continued to sit.

The bear found a snow-covered dead moose. He pawed and scratched the snow away, scattering moose hair in all directions, and then he settled down to feed on the frozen carcass. The five wolves, which I presume had killed the moose, didn't seem to care. The lone wolf sat watching.

Early next morning Bessie and I took to the air to see what had transpired. We found the bear lying motionless on his side—either dead or asleep—amidst a big pile of moose hair, meat, and bone scraps. Within 40 or 50 yards sat the six wolves, seemingly unconcerned. Even when we circled near, the bear didn't move.

I skimmed the top of the alders, probably within 15 feet of the bear. He lazily lifted his head and looked up at the airplane, but he didn't get up. He was sluggish. Full of meat, we assumed.

The six wolves continued to sit and look bored, even when several live moose appeared nearby. They didn't seem to care that the bear was eating their moose. But why weren't they interested in the live moose?

On the third day as we flew overhead, Val and I saw the bear lying on his stomach on the carcass. His head moved, watching as we neared. This day only one wolf seemed interested in the sluggish bear. I circled and watched. The wolf was several hundred yards away, walking toward the bear. As he moved toward the bear, he walked within 50 feet of a live moose that was bedded in the snow. What next, I wondered? This bear-wolf-moose drama wasn't being played out the way I would have expected.

As the wolf walked nearby, the moose calmly looked at him without even getting up. The wolf paused to study the moose for a moment, then moved on toward the bear. For some reason the moose apparently realized the wolf wasn't going to attack.

We were grounded on the fifth day by a snowstorm. Next morning the animals had disappeared. All tracks were obliterated by about a foot of new snow.

A few days later I surprised the six wolves out in the open on glare ice near Lake Minchumina. Flying within a few feet of them, I believe I discovered why the big predators showed no interest in bear or moose: they were all so fat they were almost square! Their long, silky fur waved in the wind as, with claws slipping on the ice, they scrambled away from my low-flying airplane.

In the fall of 1962, I saw another strange predator-prey relationship when I was flying along a braided stream north of the Alaska Range. Forced by low clouds to fly within a few hundred feet of the ground, I came upon a scattered herd of perhaps 1,000 caribou on the move—all were traveling the same direction. A herd of this size was not at all unusual, but then I saw what at first seemed to be a strange-looking caribou in the middle of the herd. I circled for a second look and discovered that the weird caribou was actually a hump-shouldered, hulking grizzly bear.

That big bear was walking along with the caribou surrounding him as though he were a member of the herd. Within
40 or 50 feet of the bear, the caribou were browsing and picking
up a bite here, a bite there, as they walked or trotted along.
Meanwhile the bear was walking stolidly along with big, swagger-
ing strides, ignoring the caribou as they ignored him.

I found this an incredible sight. I continued to circle,
expecting to see the bear attack or the caribou scatter. I circled
perhaps a dozen times. The caribou ignored the airplane, but the
bear became nervous. Finally, he turned and walked at a right
angle to the direction the caribou were traveling, heading toward
the riverbank. Many caribou were in his way, and he actually
dodged around them. Even when he began to gallop, the caribou
showed no fear of him. He zigzagged through the plodding herd
and disappeared into the brush.

Why didn't the caribou show fear of the bear, their natural
enemy? Grizzlies commonly kill and eat caribou. Somehow the
caribou knew the bear wasn't interested in making a kill, for not
one showed any fear of him.

I've seen it the other way, too. I spied a moose cow and calf in a
small pond early in the summer of 1952 while flying a T-50
Cessna between Fairbanks and McGrath. The cow was intently
watching a black bear pace back and forth among the willows and
alders on the pond's shore. Her calf, neck deep in the water,
stayed close to her belly. I had no passengers, so I circled and
watched. The bear walked back and forth, as if he were pacing in a
cage, while the beleaguered cow watched his every move.

The black bear is a great killer of newborn moose calves.
That moose mother knew that she had a good chance against the
bear while she was in the water because she could stand on the
bottom. To reach the calf, the bear would have to swim.

The bear knew this too. He was extremely frustrated, for
he did not dare to venture into the pond to try to attack the calf.
If the cow and her calf moved ashore, the bear would have the

advantage. How long can a moose calf survive in cold water? Surmising that the calf would become chilled, perhaps even unable to walk, I decided to give the moose a little help. I dove on the bear. The bear started running. I made sure he was impressed by roaring close above him a second time. The last I saw of him, he was half a mile from the baby moose and still running. I knew he could feed on grass and roots just as well.

One of our most unforgettable wildlife encounters occurred in the 1960s near Nome. Bessie and I were sightseeing, looking over formations of rock. I was flying a small Piper airplane.

"What's that on the hillside?" Bessie called from the back seat.

"Looks like a big rock."

"No, I don't think it's a rock."

I circled, and when we neared we saw what I had taken for a rock was a great silver-gray grizzly. His color was much lighter than that of any bear we'd ever seen. His silky fur was moving in the wind like a field of wheat. He was absolutely beautiful, perhaps the most beautiful animal I have ever seen.

When we flew over he started to move off. Because he was so beautiful, we wanted to get a better look at him. I circled and flew closer. He decided he had to defend himself from the airplane, and he stood on hind legs, facing us as we flew over.

He suddenly seemed to realize that the bird overhead was a mighty big one, maybe more than he wanted to tackle. Unwilling to turn away from us, he backed up the hill while still on his hind feet. The hill was steep and his movements became clumsy. He almost fell over as we zipped by again.

On our next pass, he decided he was going to have to fight. While standing on hind legs, he extended his front legs and opened his jaws, ready to grapple with the noisy plane. That sight remains crystal clear in my mind—a magnificent, silver-gray animal, silky fur flowing with the wind, standing on hind legs with front legs reaching, jaws open, waiting bravely for us to come close enough for him to grab.

We had no desire to harass him; we simply wanted a good look. I'm glad we have that memory, for it is far more valuable to me than any fur trophy a sportsman might have taken. We flew on, tremendously impressed with the beauty and courage we had seen. In my mind that magnificent creature is still wild, alive, and beautiful.

We told people in Nome about the grizzly, but we refused to tell anyone where we had seen it because we didn't want the animal killed. I have nothing against hunting; but that bear was so beautiful and had provided us with such joy, it was painful to think of him being shot. I learned later that other pilots had seen the same bear, but hunters seldom went into that inaccessible place.

Do animals reason? Do they communicate ideas to each other? I think so.

One late winter in the early 1950s, Bessie and I landed our ski-equipped Piper Vagabond on a snow- and ice-covered lake a few miles north of McKinley National Park (now Denali National Park and Preserve). We spent the night in a tiny trapper's cabin located in dense alders about 50 yards from the lake. Our airplane was tied down at the edge of the lake.

In the morning, when I walked to the airplane, I found tracks of a single wolf in the snow. He had walked to the tail of the plane and stood, apparently smelling. Then the curious animal had walked to the skis and smelled them. This wolf walked entirely around the airplane, probably both looking and smelling.

When the animal's examination of the airplane was finished, he had returned almost by the same route he had come. I followed the tracks. Within about 100 yards I came to where five other wolves—the remainder of the pack—had been sitting.

Tracks showed where the pack had been crossing the lake. They must have seen the airplane. The wolves seemed to have realized that the airplane was a possible threat, or certainly something out of place in the wilderness. There was no activity around the plane, for Bessie and I were in the hidden cabin 50 yards away. The pack apparently decided to send only one of their members to learn what it could of the airplane, while the others sat and waited, out of range of trouble. The scout completed his assignment and returned to the pack. Once he returned, the wolves continued on their way without deviating from their original course.

I believe this showed intelligence and communication. One wonders what the single wolf communicated to the pack upon his return.

One August in the mid-1950s, Bessie and I saw another baffling example of animal behavior. As we walked a wilderness trail near our cabin at Lake Minchumina, we heard the sound of rushing water. We quickened our pace because such a sound was unnatural at that time and place. Soon we stood transfixed at the river's edge. The quiet stream of yesterday had become a rushing torrent. The banks, now full to the brim, could not contain the water which poured over into low spots. There had been no recent rains. Nor had there been a heat wave that might have melted distant glaciers. The only logical explanation was erosion—the stream had somewhere cut into a lake. Now in a rush of wild exuberance the enlarged river carried its great new burden toward the sea.

Then, as if appearing on cue to add to the excitement, a family of five otters swept into view, diving and splashing as they bobbed along on the billowing waters. They were about 75 yards away when they noticed us. Immediately, they began the strangest wildlife exhibition that we have ever seen in our lifetime of animal watching.

As if perfected by long rehearsal, the otters gathered into a circle. Holding their sleek bodies in nearly upright position they faced inward toward the center. Then they began a chirruping chatter that resembled the antics of a group of excited children. By some incredible skill the circle remained stationary; it did not move downstream in the strong current.

Abruptly, one otter left the circle, dived and disappeared.

The others remained and continued to chatter. Several seconds passed, then suddenly the lone otter reared vertically from the water not 10 feet from us. Looking directly at us, it hissed and dived out of sight. By the time we recovered from this startling action, the otter had resumed its place in the circle.

Another otter promptly dived to follow the same procedure. This behavior continued until all five in turn had arrived to hiss their individual regards or contempt for us. To climax the show, all dived simultaneously.

"Bessie!" I said excitedly, "your camera, I'll bet they're all coming."

I was right. All five otters rose vertically right in front of us, with half the length of their bodies out of water. They hissed loudly in chorus, then dived and disappeared.

"Did you get the picture?" I asked.

"I don't know," she gasped. "It happened so fast."

The otters reappeared far upstream playing and diving as if nothing had happened. Some scrambled up the bank to cavort through the grass, then slid back into the water. We stood and watched until they were out of sight.

Duggan and Walatka

MY AVIATION memories include not only my own adventures, but also those of others who have flown the skies as I have.

Flying a 14-passenger Lockheed Lodestar, my first instructor and longtime friend, Roy Duggan, made some of the pioneering flights from Anchorage to Seattle. He was a pilot for the then-new Alaska Airlines. The Lodestar, powered by two 1,200-horsepower Wright Whirlwind engines, first flew as a passenger plane in 1940. More than 600 Lodestars were built, and the knowledge acquired from their use helped designers develop the four-engine Constellation and Super Constellation.

The Lodestar was first flown by Alaska Airlines primarily on the tri-weekly flights from Anchorage to Juneau. Then it was used for flights to Seattle.

Alaska Airlines' new Lodestar arrived at Merrill Field in September 1943. This, the first instrument ship owned by Alaska Airlines (and called "Starliner Anchorage"), flew 2,700 hours within, and to and from, Alaska. Two years after its acquisition, Duggan flew it from Merrill Field to Florida to deliver it to another airline that had purchased it. Alaska Airlines then bought a 21-passenger Douglas DC-3, which was larger and more practical for the flights along the storm-blasted Alaska coast.

Duggan described for me one of the first Lodestar flights he made in 1944 from Anchorage to Seattle. I took notes and now retell his story, because it typifies the challenge that pilots faced in the early years of Alaska's transport flying.

Near evening departure time, Captain Duggan drove thoughtfully along the gravel road from Anchorage to Merrill Field. Light from an occasional streetlight reflected off a low overcast while a steady rain fell.

Early weather reports were not good. Anchorage weather was barely above legal minimum for takeoff. A stop was scheduled for Juneau, but Juneau's airport was closed due to weather. Seattle's weather was marginal, and it was forecast to improve before the expected near-dawn arrival of the Lodestar. Patchy early-morning fog was expected. At Merrill Field, dispatch warned Duggan that he could expect intermittent icing conditions.

He calculated the weight of the fuel, passengers, and baggage, and then computed the weight and balance for the plane. He thought about the feasibility of the flight. Although a landing at Juneau would likely be canceled, all else seemed in place, so he submitted his flight papers and walked out to the plane.

Meanwhile, at Juneau, the station manager made arrangements to haul the Juneau passengers by boat the 50 miles to Gustavus. Gustavus, nearer to the open sea, is less affected than Juneau by the buildup of weather against the coastal mountains. Forecasters expected Gustavus to remain above minimums throughout the flight period.

At Anchorage, passengers walked onto the field and climbed aboard. There was no direct-from-the-terminal boarding equipment in those days. Baggage was loaded, and Duggan warmed the engines. After roaring down rain-soaked Merrill Field on schedule, the Lodestar took flight. The two 1,200-horsepower engines pulled the plane quickly to a cruising altitude for crossing the Chugach Mountains to the east.

The first hint of the weather's fury came only minutes out of Anchorage when, as they flew over Portage Pass, heavy turbulence shook the plane violently. Duggan decreased speed to reduce the strain on the airplane's structure. Once they made it across the short pass, the turbulence swiftly subsided. The Lodestar cruised through smooth air over the Gulf of Alaska.

For three hours the airplane flew without difficulty. Light ice occasionally formed on the windshield, a gentle hint of things to come. First Officer Larry Currie received word on the radio that the Juneau passengers would arrive at Gustavus in time to meet the flight.

When Duggan descended at Gustavus to pick up these passengers, his landing was routine, though the weather was lowering and winds were increasing. Before refueling was completed, the six Juneau passengers arrived. They were pleased and eager to catch the flight. Soon, Duggan guided the twin-rudder ship down the Gustavus runway and into the air. Next stop, Seattle.

On instruments as he climbed into the overcast, Duggan headed south. The plane started taking on ice. First noticed on the windshield, it gathered at an alarming rate. Inspection revealed a rapid buildup on the leading edges of both wings. The engines began to shake as ice formed on the propellers. Duggan ordered Currie to use propeller alcohol. Within seconds, ice began flying from the propeller blades. Some of it slammed into the fuselage. The shattering machine-gun-like sound frightened the passengers, but it was music to Duggan and Currie. As long as the ice continued to fly off, the propellers could keep them in the air.

Next, Duggan called for application of the de-icer boots—fluctuating inflatable rubber strips along the leading edges of the wings. These de-icer strips break the ice, allowing the stripstream to carry it away.

The wing ice cracked, but it didn't come off, and this put

the plane in real danger. Ice built up in all the cracks, creating a rough leading edge and greatly diminishing lift. They shut off the de-icer boots and applied more power to the engines to maintain altitude. "Call Control for permission to climb to a higher altitude," Duggan told Currie.

Although radio signals were weak and distorted because of the storm, they understood the Lodestar was cleared to cruise at an altitude 2,000 feet higher. The sluggish airplane refused to climb, even with maximum power. Radio signals weakened as ice built on the antennas. The antenna wire vibrated with the ice load, and it would break if ice buildup continued.

As they wallowed through the sky, the reassuring sound of propeller ice steadily hitting against the fuselage slowed. Much larger chunks at greater intervals crashed into the plane. They struck with such force that the fuselage would have broken, except for the heavy skin reinforcements made especially for this purpose. The larger chunks of ice unbalanced the propellers, and the engines shook violently.

From the faint radio signals received before the ice-covered antennas failed, Duggan learned of a sharp drop in Gustavus weather. Now they couldn't return to that airfield. Duggan pushed the prop controls into full takeoff pitch, which increased the propeller speed and gave much more centrifugal force. This helped throw ice from the shaking blades, but more continued to build. The overburdened plane began to lose altitude. Below, all too close, were jagged peaks of offshore islands. Decision time.

Duggan turned and flew west toward the open sea. Then, both the primary and the backup airspeed indicator systems froze despite their electrically heated pitot heads. Former barnstormer Duggan found himself in a semi-seat-of-the-pants operation; somehow he had to maintain a speed that would keep the sluggish plane aloft. With heavily iced wings, the stalling speed of the airplane increased dramatically.

At this moment a frantic passenger burst into the cockpit.

Thrusting his head between the pilots he yelled, "Vot's da matta? You is schpeeding up the motors!"

Duggan saw red. He didn't need this. He pushed his hand into the man's face and yelled, "Get the hell out of here!" The passenger disappeared, and Duggan and Currie continued to battle the storm.

Often, a relatively small change in altitude will alter icing conditions, and so it was this time. As the plane slowly lost altitude, the icing diminished. But Duggan kept the propellers at takeoff pitch until he was sure the plane was west of the outer islands.

Finally, when calculations of wind, ground speed, and elapsed time indicated there were no obstructions below, Duggan allowed the plane to descend more rapidly. Soon, ice flew from the propellers and melted from wings, windshield, and shaking antennas. At about 1,000 feet, the plane broke clear of the clouds. Visibility was unlimited! With huge waves cresting and wind-blown spindrift flying, the Pacific raged below.

Duggan and Currie looked at each other and both visibly relaxed. Once freed of the ice, the sleek plane responded to power and controls. Slowly, as they neared Seattle, the clouds cleared to reveal the heavens bright with stars. To the east, rugged coastal mountains stood out in sharp relief. Here and there flickering lights of a village or a passing boat gave a small measure of comfort to both passengers and crew.

A faint pink streak showed in the eastern sky, as First Officer Currie radioed for clearance to enter the Seattle control zone.

Duggan told me that the icing of that night was as bad as he had ever encountered. Never before had he lost both airspeed indicator systems at the same time.

Roy Duggan lives with his wife, Christine, in Minnesota, and we frequently visit.

The vast change in technology in the brief interval

between the Curtiss Robin in which Duggan first started teaching me how to fly in 1934 and the fine instrument-equipped, twin-engine Lockheed Lodestar he flew in 1944—only ten years later—is almost unbelievable.

Another aviation colleague who stands out in my memories is my barnstorming friend John Walatka. John left Minnesota in 1938 to fly as a bush pilot out of Dillingham, Alaska. He was a wonderful pilot with a great personality. Recently, his daughter, Johanna Bouker of Dillingham, loaned me some of her father's aviation memorabilia, including his 1930–33 pilot's logbook. In the front of that log he had written a toast:

> Here's to faith in the Creator
> Here's to trust in the aviator
> Here's to grit and determination
> Here's to it: Aviation

In 1930 John held transport license number 8268. Between 1930 and 1933, he flew mostly from Fairmont, Iowa. Airplanes he flew included the Curtiss Pusher, Curtiss Robin, Karri Keen, Cessna four-place, Monocoupe, Travel Air, American Eagle, Barling, Spartan, Stinson Junior, and Taperwing Waco. Engines those planes were equipped with—some of which have been all but forgotten—included the Lambert, OX-5, Genet, Velie, Warner, Lycoming, Kinner K5, and Wright.

Under "remarks" John wrote, "Flew Coupe upside down." "Won Coupe race." "Won dead-stick race." "First in Coupe Race." "Seven forced landings." "Set down for bad line squall." "Took Raymond Ettlinger to hospital—broken neck. Died 3 days later." "Taxied into hole on field at Comfrey and broke landing gear vee, bent propeller and broke left rear wing spar on Stinson." "Air circus at Austin." "Taper Wing Waco—two forced landings. Nice airplane." "First place free-for-all." "Second in dead-stick contest," "Second in dead stick at air show." "Forced down with wet mag." "First place in bomb drop plus OX-5 race (with a Travel Air)." "First in OX-5 race at Austin."

What memories that logbook brought back! Except for minor details, John's entries could have been from my own log-books of the mid-1930s.

In the three years covered by that logbook, Walatka soloed 26 student pilots, including, in September 1932, the redoubtable Leon "Babe" Alsworth, later a well-known Alaskan bush pilot whose flying base was at Lake Clark.

At Dillingham, a small village on the shores of salmon-rich Bristol Bay, John flew with pilot Bert Ruoff, who owned Bristol Bay Air Service.

In one of his letters home to Iowa, dated September 21, 1938, John wrote: "I had my first real nasty experience with an airplane about two weeks ago and am in town [Anchorage] for repairs now. The motor on the Waco quit and I had to set down on the tundra with pontoons, but was lucky as the devil and didn't get a scratch, and none of the passengers was hurt. I only busted one of the pontoon struts. I called for help on the radio and we got out of there in about six hours, as it was only 25 miles from Anchorage."

More details emerge on this forced landing from a news clipping found among John's papers. It detailed, "Pilot Walatka left Dillingham with U.S. Marshall Bradshaw and an insane person aboard. Oscar Underhill, pilot for the Ray Petersen Flying Service, left Dillingham at the same time, and the two men maintained radio contact until they entered the pass [Lake Clark Pass].

"After arriving here [Anchorage] Pilot Underhill reported he had lost contact with Walatka, and seven planes were sent out to aid in a search for the missing ship.

"Walatka was found by one of Jack Carr's planes. He had been forced down by engine trouble, and none of the ship's occupants was injured."

Within a couple of years, Walatka left Bristol Bay Air

Service and became a wildlife agent for the Alaska Game Commission. Another newspaper clipping, dated January 16, 1942, tells how John landed a crippled Monocoupe patrol plane after the propeller shaft broke, throwing the propeller into the wing, breaking four wing ribs. The plane was about 100 feet in the air just after takeoff when the propeller shaft broke. John and fellow wildlife agent Carlos M. Carson had been inspecting a trap. "Only the experienced handling of the Monocoupe by the ex-commercial pilot [Walatka] brought the two men to a safe landing on a small lake," details the account.

World War II changed John's life as it did mine. He left his Game Commission job in 1942 to fly for the Morrison-Knudsen Construction Company at Nabesna, where I soon joined him. At Nabesna, he pitched a wall tent on a three-foot-high log wall. His wife, Lillian, and two-year-old daughter, Johanna, lived there with him through the summer while he flew a trimotor Stinson, hauling airport materials from Nabesna to Northway. That job ended August 28, and the Walatkas were then flown to Fairbanks by Harold Gillam in his Lockheed Electra.

John then returned to Dillingham and Bristol Bay Air Service. By 1944, he owned four airplanes: the Stinson SM8A with which he had started the business, a new Aeronca on wheels, skis, and floats, a Stinson Voyager, and a Stinson Reliant.

When Northern Consolidated Airlines was formed in 1948 from five small bush operations, including Walatka's, John became a member of the NCA Board of Directors. Later, when that company combined with Wien Airlines, he remained a member of the board. For the balance of his life he was on salary as an official of NCA and Wien Consolidated. Summers, he managed the Katmai Camps on the Alaska Peninsula (now Angler's Paradise lodges)— a top-quality wilderness fishing resort started by Northern Consolidated. He flew guests from the camp to remote fishing areas in and around Katmai National Park and Preserve.

In 1973, the federal Board on Geographic Names approved for federal use the name Walatka Mountains, which were described as follows: "Walatka Mountains: highest elevation 4,625 feet, in the Aleutian Range 35 miles north of Mount Katmai; named for John Walatka, pioneer Alaskan bush pilot, who for many years served the communities of the Alaska Peninsula, Alaska."

John Walatka died of natural causes in 1970 when he was only 62.

Flight Plan Closed

TOWARD THE end of my flying career I tapered off, flying less as I approached retirement age. I flew for Cook Inlet Aviation at Homer, a coastal community at the tip of Alaska's Kenai Peninsula. I also instructed students in Anchorage and Fairbanks, and worked as an aircraft mechanic. I no longer kept complete records of my flying hours; every six months, as I took my physical examination and renewed my commercial license, I estimated my flying time. I flew 1,000 hours in some years, but in others I flew only about 100 hours.

I estimate I flew a career total of 20,000 hours. That's not a lot by today's standards. Many modern pilots can document at least twice that much time in the air.

Nevertheless, flying was my life for 46 years, and it was an exciting, satisfying, and delightful career. I went places and had adventures that I couldn't have considered in any other profession. I knew many great pilots. I especially admired some of the skilled barnstormers—Roy Duggan, John Walatka, Merle Buck—

pilots who taught me tricks of flying that helped keep me alive. I was also privileged to know and learn from some of the great pioneer aviators of Alaska—Noel and Sig Wien, Sam White, Harold Gillam, Gordon McKenzie, Herman Lerdahl, John Cross, and Bill Munz.

Truly, I flew in the shadow of eagles.

✛ Aviation Glossary ✛

A-20 Havoc: a mid-wing monoplane bomber powered by two 1,600-horsepower Pratt & Whitney radial engines that was built by Douglas Aircraft and used in World War II. The British called it the Boston.

acrobatics: (modern term is aerobatics) maneuvers involving abrupt changes in altitude and often resulting in unusual aircraft attitudes not used in normal flight. These may include all manner of stunts.

ADF radio: automatic direction finder.

Aero Commander: one of the first twin-engine aircraft designed specifically for business and corporate use. The Aero Commander is a five- or six-seat transport manufactured by Rockwell International.

aileron: the primary control surface located at the trailing edges of the outer wing panels which, when moved up or down, causes the airplane in flight to bank.

air-speed indicator: an instrument for showing the speed of an aircraft through the air.

American Pilgrim: a 1931 10-seat transport aircraft powered by a 575-horsepower Pratt & Whitney Hornet engine. Later models carried 12 passengers. First flown by American Airlines, a number of Pilgrims were used in Alaska where they were popular as a sturdy, reliable bush plane.

artificial horizon: a gyro instrument showing the attitude of an aircraft with reference to pitch and roll as compared to the horizon.

AT-17: *see* Cessna T-50

AT-6: an advanced trainer, the North American Texan, the standard advanced trainer used by the U.S. Army Air Forces during World War II.

attitude: the position of an aircraft in relation to a given reference, usually the ground, along its longitudinal, lateral, and vertical axis.

B-25 North American Mitchell: a conventional twin-engine medium bomber with a twin-tail and tricycle landing gear used extensively in World War II. Used in the famous Doolittle raid on Tokyo in 1942.

bank: to tilt an airplane by means of the ailerons, causing it to turn while rolling either right or left along its longitudinal axis.

biplane: an airplane with two main wings, placed approximately one above the other.

Bobcat: *see* Cessna T-50

Boeing 80-A trimotor: a big biplane with three rudders, powered by three 525-horsepower Pratt & Whitney Hornet engines. First produced in 1928.

breather: a vent in the crankcase of an engine, which allows gases to escape and keeps crankcase pressure approximately equal to atmospheric.

Bushmaster: *see* Cessna T-50

C-47 Douglas: a military version of the Douglas DC-3 commercial transport.

C-53 Douglas: a military version of the Douglas DC-3 commercial transport.

cantilevered wing: a wing in which no external bracing is used.

Cessna 170: a four-place, single-engine airplane built by Cessna Aircraft Company, Wichita, Kansas, between 1948 and 1957.

Cessna Airmaster: a four-place, 145-horsepower fabric-covered cabin monoplane with a cantilevered wing, first manufactured in 1934 by Cessna Aircraft Company.

Cessna AW: a fabric-covered, four-place, wooden-wing, metal-tubing-fuselage airplane built by Cessna Aircraft Company in 1928. Only 40 of these airplanes were built.

Cessna T-50: a low-wing, twin-engine monoplane that appeared in 1940, and, as a military advanced trainer, was produced throughout World War II. It was known by the Royal Canadian Air Force as the Crane, by the United States Army Air Force as the AT-8 and later as the AT-17. Later yet it was adopted as a light transport as the UC-78. The U.S. Navy designated it as the JRC-1. It was also called the Bobcat. A modified version flown by Northern Consolidated Airlines in Alaska was called the Bushmaster.

Challenger: a 185-horsepower, six-cylinder, air-cooled radial engine manufactured by Curtiss during the 1930s.

chandelle: an abrupt climbing turn which makes use of the momentum of the airplane to gain altitude.

cowling: removal metal covering on the nose of a fuselage, used to house the engine and to reduce its air resistance.

crab: to turn partly into the wind to the right or left of course to compensate for wind drift.

Crane: *see* Cessna T-50

crosswind: wind blowing at any angle across the line of flight and causing the aircraft to drift.

Curtiss Robin: a three-place, high-wing, monoplane built from 1928 through 1930. In 1930 a new Robin sold for $2,495.

Curtiss Thrush: (a larger version of the Curtiss Robin) a six-place, high-wing cabin monoplane that used a Challenger engine boosted to 183 horsepower. Later Thrushes used the more powerful J-6 Wright engine.

dead reckoning: a method of navigation by which course and time of flight between two points is estimated by taking course, speed, and wind components into consideration. "Dead" is a shortened version of deduced.

dead stick: a propeller that has stopped turning during flight. Commonly describes the condition when a propeller may still be turning but no longer providing thrust because of engine trouble.

directional gyro: a flight instrument which, when set to conform with a magnetic compass, indicates the aircraft heading. It tends to develop heading errors due to precession (earth rotation), and must be adjusted intermittently by the pilot.

dope: a glue-like varnish used to fill the weave and produce tautness, as well as weatherproofing, of fabric surfaces of aircraft.

Eaglerock: a two-cockpit biplane first built by Alexander Aircraft in 1928. The front cockpit accommodated two passengers.

Fairchild 24: a high-wing cabin monoplane, first produced as a two-seater in 1933. Later it was built in four-seat form, with both Warner and Ranger engines.

Fairchild 71: a seven-seat, light-transport monoplane using the 420-horsepower Pratt & Whitney Wasp. Popular as a bush plane in Alaska in the 1930s. On the ground, the wings hinged back for easier storage. Built in the United States and Canada in the late 1920s.

Fairchild F-27: a turboprop transport of the 1960s.

figure-eights: a common practice maneuver in which the pilot is expected to fly the airplane in the shape of a figure eight, going over the same area with each pass.

Fleet: a biplane trainer built prior to World War II.

Gnome (engine): a rotary engine of World War II. With a rotary engine, the cylinders rotate around a center shaft.

Golden Eagle monoplane: a radial-engine biplane of the 1920s.

ground loop: a violent uncontrollable turn of an airplane while taxiing or while on takeoff or landing.

Gullwing Stinson: the Stinson Reliant Gullwing (named for its graceful wing) was first produced in 1936. It was a four-place, high-wing monoplane produced until early in World War II.

Hamilton Metalplane (airplane): an eight-passenger, all-metal plane first built in 1926. Various models used both the Pratt & Whitney Wasp of 410 to 450 horsepower, and the Pratt & Whitney Hornet of 500 to 525 horsepower.

Hispano-Suiza (Hisso) engine: an eight-cylinder, vee-type, water-cooled aircraft engine of World War I. It was rated at 150 horsepower at 1,450 rpms.

Hisso: *see* Hispano-Suiza

Hornet: a radial engine of 500 to 525 horsepower first manufactured in the 1920s by Pratt & Whitney.

Howard: a 1930s high-wing, single-engine, radial-engine monoplane of four and five seats.

inertia starter: an engine starter that depends on a hand-cranked flywheel. Once the flywheel is spinning, it is engaged and turns the engine over.

J-3 Piper Cub: a light two-place, fabric-covered, high-wing monoplane. Built 1940 through 1946.

JN4-D (Jenny): a two-place, open tandem-cockpit biplane built by Curtiss, powered by an OX-5 engine, and used for training in World War I.

L-5G Stinson: also known as the Sentinel, a two-seat liaison and observation high-wing monoplane with a 190-horsepower Lycoming engine. Stinson built 1,731 of these for the military during World War II.

Lockheed 10-A: known as the Electra, this 10-passenger, twin-engine, twin-rudder plane was first flown in 1934.

Lockheed Electra: *see* Lockheed 10-A

Lockheed Lodestar: (also referred to as the Lockheed 18) an improved and larger version of the Lockheed 14. First flown in 1939.

Lockheed Vega: the Vega 5-C seven-seat cabin monoplane of the early 1930s, powered with a 450-horsepower Pratt & Whitney Wasp radial engine. An advanced airplane for its time, the Vega cruised at 170 miles per hour and had a maximum speed of 195 miles per hour.

loop: an aerobatic maneuver in which the airplane, without banking, describes a complete vertical circle in the sky.

Lunkenheimer primer: a hand-operated pump, commonly mounted on the instrument panel, with which the pilot primes an engine with fuel before attempting to start it.

Luscombe: an aircraft company founded in the mid-1930s by Don Luscombe. Several types of Luscombe airplanes were built, including both two-place and four-place cabin monoplanes.

magneto: (also called a "mag") a self-contained generator that supplies electrical current to the spark plugs in the ignition system of an aircraft engine.

magneto booster: a magneto, turned by hand, for creating a hotter spark while starting an engine.

Monocoupe: a line of light aircraft first produced in 1927. Most were two place, although a four-place Monocoupe was produced.

Noorduyn Norseman: an eight-seat, high-wing cabin transport that used a 600-horsepower Pratt & Whitney Hornet engine. It was first flown in 1935 and built in quantities during World War II.

opposed engine: an engine with two rows of pistons placed horizontally, with a crankshaft between them.

P-39 Airacobra: a World War II fighter produced by Bell Aircraft. This low-wing, single-place plane used a liquid-cooled engine placed behind the pilot. Russia received about half of the P-39s that were built.

P-40 Warhawk: a World War II fighter plane produced by Curtiss. It was the Army's frontline fighter when World War II came to the United States.

P-47 Thunderbolt: a World War II fighter plane built by Republic Aviation.

P-63 Kingcobra: a fighter plane of World War II manufactured by Bell Aircraft, mostly used by the Soviet air arm.

Pilgrim: *see* American Pilgrim.

Piper Cub: any of the planes available in Piper's Cub line—the first being the J-3 Cub and the currently available one being the Piper Super Cub.

Piper Family Cruiser: designated PA-20, about 2,000 of the Family Cruiser were sold. Built between 1946 and 1948, it came in either four-place or three-place models. The PA-20 was later designated as the Pacer.

Piper Super Cub: designated PA-18, a tandem-seat two-place, 150-horsepower Cub, popular in Alaska and elsewhere as a high-performance light plane.

Piper Tri-Pacer: designated PA-22, a four-place, tricycle-gear, light cabin plane first built in 1951. Nearly 6,000 had been sold when production ended in 1960.

Piper Vagabond: designated PA-17, a variation of the Piper Cub was produced between 1946 and 1948. It was two-place.

pre-flight inspection: a visual inspection of the airplane before flight.

radial engine: an engine in which the cylinders are arranged in a circle around a central crankshaft.

radio range: a low- to medium-frequency radio range, a now largely obsolete aid to navigation.

rudder pedals: the foot-operated pedals of an airplane which provide directional control in the air and on the ground.

Sikorsky S-39-B: a 1930s five-seat amphibian powered by a 300-horsepower Pratt & Whitney Wasp Junior.

slip: (also sideslip) to slide an airplane sideways, in a downward direction, usually for the purpose of losing altitude without gaining forward speed.

snaproll: an aerobatic maneuver in which the nose comes up sharply and the airplane rolls 360 degrees with great suddenness.

Spad: a French-built World War I fighter.

Spartan Executive: an all-metal, four- to five-seat, low-wing monoplane cabin plane with retractable landing gear, first built in 1935.

spin: a maneuver in which an airplane, after stalling, descends nearly vertically, nose low, with the aircraft revolving around the near-vertical axis of descent.

stall: the inability of an airplane to continue flight due to loss of lift on the wings.

Standard: a two-cockpit World War I training biplane, with a maximum speed of 70 miles per hour and a landing speed of 42 miles per hour.

static cord: a parachute rip cord attached to the airplane from which a jumper departs. When the jumper reaches the limit of the static cord, the parachute opens automatically.

Stearman biplane: a line of biplanes first produced in 1927. Stearman biplanes were used to carry mail in the 1930s. Famous as World War II trainers were the PT-13, PT-17, PT-18, and PT-27 versions, all similar except for engines. Stearman biplanes have also been popular with crop dusters.

stick: the vertical lever in the cockpit of a plane with which the pilot operates ailerons and elevators. Also used to refer to the wheel or yoke of planes so-equipped, which perform the same service.

Stinson Junior: a high-wing cabin monoplane first produced in 1928 by Stinson Aircraft Corporation.

Stinson Reliant: a four-place luxuriously finished high-wing monoplane. The Reliant was first built by Stinson in 1933, and production ended in 1943. The Reliant line included the Gullwing.

Stinson A: the Model A eight-passenger, trimotor transport produced by Stinson in the early 1930s.

Stinson trimotor: see Stinson Model A. Also, Stinson produced three trimotor airplanes, the A, the T, and the U.

Stinson Voyager: a four-place cabin monoplane first produced by Stinson in 1939. Production was taken over by Piper Aircraft and continued until 1949.

Swallow biplane: a radial-engine biplane of the 1920s.

T-50: *see* Cessna T-50

tachometer: an instrument that displays engine revolutions per minute (rpm).

Taperwing Waco: a popular biplane of the 1930s.

Taylorcraft: starting in the 1930s, Taylorcraft Aviation Corp. and Taylorcraft, Inc., produced mostly two-place, light-weight, high-wing monoplanes. Commonly referred to as T-Craft. The company was purchased by Piper in the late 1930s.

touch-and-go landing: a landing in which the aircraft does not come to a complete stop before starting another takeoff run.

Travel Air: an airplane manufactured starting in the mid-1920s. Early models were biplanes, later models were high-wing cabin monoplanes.

trim control: adjustment of the pitch attitude of an aircraft without use of the elevator.

turn-and-bank indicator: a flight instrument that displays the rate of turn and shows whether the turn is properly coordinated.

UC-78: *see* Cessna T-50.

wing spar: the principal load-carrying beam or beams running lengthwise in a wing.

wing strut: a rigid brace designed to support the wing.

✝ Index ✝

Note: Italicized page numbers refer to photographs

322 In the Shadow of Eagles

✝ About Rudy Billberg ✝

Lindbergh's flight from New York to Paris in 1927 cemented Rudy Billberg's determination to fly. He learned to fly in a Curtiss Robin in 1934. He then flew as a professional pilot for 46 years.

Born in Roseau, Minnesota, in 1916, Billberg's first plane ride, in 1927, was in an open-cockpit Travel Air biplane powered by a Curtiss OX-5 engine. In Minnesota he flew as a barnstormer and instructed student pilots in a pre-war federal civilian pilot training program. During World War II, he flew C-47s in Alaska and northwestern Canada for the Air Transport Command. Before and after the war, he was an Alaska bush pilot.

An adventurer at heart, Billberg, often with his wife, Bessie, explored wilderness Alaska by riverboat, amphibious plane, and snowmobile. While Rudy flew the bush, the Billbergs lived in Nome, in the Yukon River Indian village of Galena, and in several other Alaskan towns and villages.

Billberg is now retired in his home town of Roseau.

✝ About Jim Rearden ✝

A forty-eight-year resident of Alaska and a private pilot with his own airplane, Jim Rearden has written 14 books and more than 500 magazine articles mostly about Alaska. In addition to *In the Shadow of Eagles,* his books include *Cracking the Zero Mystery,* the story of the first Japanese Zero captured (in Alaska) and flown by the United States during World War II, *Tales of Alaska's Big Bears,* a collection of his bear stories, and a novel, *Castner's Cutthroats: Saga of the Alaska Scouts.*

A veteran of the U.S. Navy during World War II, Rearden studied wildlife management at Oregon State College and the University of Maine. During his years in Alaska he has taught wildlife management at the University of Alaska, Fairbanks, was a fisheries biologist in charge of the Cook Inlet commercial fisheries, served as a federal fishery patrol agent, operated his own commercial fishing boat, was a carpenter, and worked in a trading post.

Jim Rearden was Outdoor Editor for *Alaska* magazine for 20 years, and for more than 20 years he has been a field editor for *Outdoor Life* magazine. He lives at Homer, with his wife, Audrey, in a log house he built himself.